The New
Meritocracy

The New Meritocracy

A History of UK
Independent Schools
1979–2015

MARK PEEL

First published 2015 by
Elliott and Thompson Limited
27 John Street, London WC1N 2BX
www.eandtbooks.com

ISBN: 978-1-78396-175-7

9 8 7 6 5 4 3 2 1

A catalogue record for this book is available from the British Library.

Typesetting: Marie Doherty
Printed in the UK by TJ International Ltd.

CONTENTS

INTRODUCTION

I n January 2011 the political broadcaster Andrew Neil attracted much comment with his television programme *Posh and Posher: Why Public School Boys Run Britain*, examining the rebirth of the English political elite.

Neil, a grammar-school boy made good from Paisley in the west of Scotland, argued that, following a period of meritocracy between 1964 and 1997 when every single prime minister was grammar-school educated, the election of the Old Etonian David Cameron in 2010 and his 'cabinet of millionaires' symbolised the return of a narrow political elite. According to Neil, the primary reason for the decline of social mobility was the demise of the grammar schools:

> Thirty years on from the end of the grammars, it's no coincidence that public school boys have triumphed. Without the grammars, there's simply less competition. And that means politics is missing out on a lot of potential.[1]

While Neil's thesis has a certain validity, it should also be noted that the concept of meritocracy didn't simply disappear – it found a new home in the resurgent independent sector. With nearly half of their intake now comprising first-generation pupils, these schools responded to more competitive times by turning themselves into meritocratic powerhouses, offering a much broader education than they had previously.

Although these schools had educated the social and political elite over the centuries, their eminence rested on narrow foundations. In common with so many institutions they had failed to keep pace with the challenges of a rapidly changing world, so that while the academic and sporting elite were well catered for, the majority were ill-served by the narrow curriculum and a conformist culture that stifled individual flair. The journalist and author Charles Moore recalled:

> When I was at Eton in the 1970s, a very large proportion of the boys came from landed families. Many were not, to put it mildly, ambitious. Some read only the *Sporting Life*, and that with difficulty. Today, their numbers at Eton have dwindled dramatically.[2]

Confronted with the election of a Labour government in 1964 committed to the end of selective education, the independent sector found itself on the defensive for much of the next two decades. Yet, when the axe duly came, it fell on the direct grant schools – high-achieving day schools funded partly by central government – and grammar schools, which, paradoxically, strengthened the independent sector, since the majority of the former opted to go private (see Chapter 1).

With the introduction of the assisted places scheme – tax-funded places at private schools – by the Thatcher government in 1980, and the onset of a low-tax economy that boosted the income of the middle classes, the independent sector flourished. Even the return of Labour in 1997 did little to stir the waters as the Blair government sought partnership not confrontation with its former adversary, not least in its attempt to raise national educational standards.

A more serious challenge arose in the form of market forces (discussed in Chapter 2). The 1980s saw schools expand their facilities, refurbish their boarding accommodation and increase salaries, all of which caused fees to soar following their exorbitant rise in the 1970s. With boarding in decline, a number of schools in remote or less affluent areas were forced to close. Others survived by taking girls (see Chapters 12 and 13), recruiting overseas and raising significant sums from their alumni. For those schools in more prosperous parts and offering a first-rate education, the runes were more favourable. Governing boards became more professional, financial management more efficient and the business expanded, all of which laid the foundations for progress in all walks of school life.

At the heart of the Thatcher revolution lay the principles of competition and choice. Parents now play a central role in their children's education (see

Chapter 3); from being fringe participants, they became ever present and have used their consumer power to good effect by demanding the very best. These expectations have added to the workload of many a head and their staff, but despite the tension caused, accountability to parents has undoubtedly forced schools to raise their standards.

Confronted with parental concerns, as well as those expressed by governors, alumni and inspectors, heads are no longer the powerful autocrats of old. Those who fall short are more vulnerable to dismissal or premature retirement than hitherto, as witness the demise of a number of leading heads in the 1990s (described in Chapter 4). At the same time, those heads with a clear vision, forceful personality and a supportive board of governors can still make a difference, as evident in the fortunes of Radley under Dennis Silk, Eton under Sir Eric Anderson and Wellington under Sir Anthony Seldon.

Essential to the fortunes of any modern school is its record of scholastic achievement, a far cry from the 1970s when the independent sector underperformed in comparison to the grammar schools. Consigned to bleak, draughty classrooms and saddled with many an uninspiring teacher, the will to learn often took second place to playing for the rugby XV or becoming a school prefect. Academic indolence was certainly frowned upon but poor exam results were viewed more as a matter of private grief than public mourning. Better for Harrow to beat Eton at Lord's than win a cluster of scholarships to Balliol.

Although consumer power brought an improvement in the 1980s, it needed the establishment of external inspection and league tables in the 1990s to galvanise schools into action (see Chapters 6 and 7). Heads may have raged against league tables and their inability to discern all-round excellence, but a leap up these tables or a triumph over their chief rivals would be a cause for public celebration, in the same way that a slump in fortune would result in recriminations behind closed doors. While the quality of independent school teachers does continue to vary, the lazy and incompetent are now very much the exception rather than the rule. At the same time, their successors are better trained, more versatile in their teaching methodology and more willing to work with their colleagues for the common good.

Raised in a more egalitarian age, better acquainted with the pupils through extra-curricular activities and more sensitive to their concerns, teachers have stepped down from their pedestals to form more fruitful relationships. Confrontation has given way to collaboration and criticism to encouragement, so that lessons have become a more rewarding experience (see Chapters 6 and 7). While exam pressures have somewhat stifled independent thought, teachers, in contrast to their colleagues in the state sector who are constrained by the prescriptive criteria of government inspectors, still have the opportunity to teach in their own distinctive manner.

With its new-found commitment to academic excellence the independent sector continues to dominate entry to Oxford, Cambridge and other elite universities (see Chapter 8). Under political pressure to widen access to universities following the Laura Spence controversy of 2000 when Gordon Brown, Chancellor of the Exchequer, berated Magdalen College, Oxford, for rejecting a top-flight state-educated candidate, admissions tutors have made every effort to comply without lowering their standards. Believing their charges to be the resultant victims of discrimination, independent heads cried foul. However, any threat to their hegemony only made these schools more determined to pass muster, and so far they have succeeded.

And it wasn't merely academic excellence that these schools now stood for. In comparison to the philistinism of old, spanking new arts centres, the arrival of girls and the spirit of the age saw a flowering of music and drama, so much so that current luminaries of the screen such as Eddie Redmayne, Benedict Cumberbatch and Carey Mulligan honed their craft at independent schools (see Chapter 9).

The cult of athleticism had always been one of the pillars of the old public school and, although it has lost some of its old mystique, the competitive ethos has gained ever more supremacy as schools have hired coaches and brought in players on sports scholarships to achieve success. During a period when the opportunities for sport in the state sector have rapidly declined, the privately educated have dominated England's rugby, cricket and hockey teams, as well as Olympian sports such as rowing, sailing and shooting. Chapters 10 and 11 detail the main sporting triumphs of this era and assess whether the will to win has eroded sporting values traditionally associated with independent schools.

For most of their existence independent schools were defined by a rigid hierarchy and repressive discipline that afforded little protection to the weak and vulnerable. Those who suffered from cruelty and abuse were left to suffer in silence. In a more open and accountable age, however, a number of these abuses have come to light and the perpetrators brought to justice. Chapter 14 recounts the worst of these abuses and explains how the Children Act 1989 and frequent external inspection have transformed the nature of pastoral care, highlighting the more relaxed relationships between the pupils and the greater individual attention paid to each child.

In light of recent surveys conducted by the Sutton Trust, a charity campaigning for greater educational opportunities, and others drawing attention to the increasing concentration of prosperity and power in the hands of the few, independent schools have been encouraged by the political elite to forge closer links with the state sector. By the late 1990s a gradual thawing of relations between the two sectors had begun to take place and productive local partnerships established (see Chapter 16). Less successful have been the attempts by the Blair, Brown and Cameron governments to persuade the independent sector to sponsor academies – state-funded schools that are independently managed – the brainchild of Andrew Adonis, Tony Blair's educational adviser, as part of his mission to transform England's schools. While the majority of independent schools opposed sponsorship on the grounds that they lacked the time, expertise and resources to devote to this new enterprise, others feared that by helping a local academy to succeed they would be endangering their own futures.

Such diffidence not only exasperated Anthony Seldon, master of Wellington and a great exponent of the academy movement, but also Sir Michael Wilshaw, chief inspector of schools, who, in 2013, compared the independent sector to 'an island of privilege that does not reach out to the mainland'.[3] The following year Tristram Hunt, Shadow Education Secretary, threatened that a future Labour government would withdraw business rate relief from independent schools unless they did more to help the state sector.

This, then, is the dynamic that runs through this book. Under pressure from politicians, parents, universities and school inspectors, the independent sector has continued to aspire to excellence, so that whatever the improvements in state education during the last decade, the gap between the two sectors has continued to grow.

As the independent sector has consolidated its hold over public life, so charges of privilege have increasingly been levelled at it by its critics. These charges make heads apoplectic because, whatever steps they have taken to become less exclusive, they have still found it hard to shake off their old image – not helped by the return of an Old Etonian prime minister. Yet boaters, blazers, Boris and the Bullingdon Club aside, the growing political commitment to reforming the state sector is based largely on the independent model, a sector in which hope, encouragement, opportunity and respect have taken on a new meaning, enabling many to attain heights never previously contemplated.

Chapter 1

THE CURSE IS LIFTED

F ew institutions have polarised opinion to the same extent as Britain's independent schools, extolled for their standards of excellence on one hand and reviled for their social exclusiveness on the other.

Although these schools – some 1,257 of them educating more than 500,000 pupils – are united by their independence in terms of finance and governance, they are in other respects surprisingly diverse: day and boarding, single-sex and coeducational, highly selective and all-ability, the majority Anglican foundations but some Roman Catholic, Methodist, Quaker and so on*.

Leading the eight associations representing the independent sector is the Headmasters' and Headmistresses' Conference (HMC) comprising the oldest, richest and most prestigious schools traditionally known as public schools (so-called because they were open to the paying public) but since the 1970s better known as independent schools.

Transformed out of all recognition during the mid-nineteenth century, these schools embraced the new middle class and gave it an elitist education dedicated to making its members statesmen, officers and gentlemen. As discipline, respectability and class solidarity became central to public school life, boys' boarding schools became renowned for their eccentric dress, arcane rituals, spartan dormitories, cultivation of the classics, obsession with games, rigidly defined hierarchies, promotion of religious worship and a chivalric code of behaviour.

---

* The figures given here are those schools affiliated to the Independent Schools Council. Overall, some 615,000 pupils are educated privately.

It was a system that survived for the best part of a century through the high noon of Empire and two world wars when many a public school officer paid the ultimate sacrifice.

With the Second World War ushering in a period of rapid social change, the conventions of this self-contained world were living on borrowed time. In 1944 a proposal by the Fleming Committee to broaden the social composition of the public schools by allocating 25 per cent of their places to state primary pupils was thwarted by the schools themselves and the cash-strapped local authorities.

In contrast, R.A. Butler's Education Act of the same year establishing free secondary education enabled the grammar schools – catering for the intellectual elite – to forge ahead of the public schools, leaving the latter to contemplate an uncertain future.

In comparison with the excellence of the grammar school, some 70 per cent of pupils were consigned to a basic education at the under-resourced technical schools (very few went there) and secondary moderns. Deprived of hope or purpose, most left school at fifteen without either academic qualifications or vocational skills.

By the early 1960s, this segregated educational system, determined by examination at eleven – the notorious eleven-plus – and weighted towards the middle-class child, appeared symbolic of a country caught in a time-warp. The resignation of the aged prime minister, Harold Macmillan, in October 1963, offered the Conservative Party an opportunity to renew itself after twelve years in power, but instead it took a retrograde step by choosing a hereditary peer, Alec, Lord Home, as his successor. In these circumstances Harold Wilson's Labour Party, with its commitment to technological innovation and social reform, seemed a breath of fresh air, and, following its electoral victory in October 1964, it set about its mission to modernise Britain.

With the eleven-plus exam increasingly discredited and the tide flowing in favour of comprehensive schools, Anthony Crosland, Education Secretary between 1965 and 1967, spearheaded a major reorganisation of secondary education. An outstanding student at Highgate School and Trinity College, Oxford, Crosland was passionately committed to social equality and saw education as the means to bring it about. His Circular 10/65 requesting local authorities to reorganise secondary education along comprehensive lines occasioned only spasmodic resistance, so that even when the Conservatives returned to power in 1970, the Education Secretary, Margaret Thatcher, felt compelled to go with the egalitarian flow.

Before Labour left office, the Public Schools Commission, set up in 1965, had issued the Donnison Report advocating the integration of the direct grant grammar schools into the local system, and this now became the party's priority on its return to government in 1974. These selective day schools, funded partly by central government for pupils from lower-income backgrounds, had been the means by which leading politicians such as Barbara Castle, Denis Healey and Enoch Powell had risen to eminence. Now faced with losing their grant, 119 out of these 174 schools opted to go private, providing a welcome fillip to the independent sector both in terms of additional numbers and academic kudos. 'It is a sad irony that in destroying the direct-grant schools on the altar of equal opportunity, the 1974–9 Labour government succeeded only in denying opportunity to many poor children and increasing the number of fee-paying parents,' wrote Andrew Adonis and Stephen Pollard.[1]

The abolition of the direct grant schools and most of the maintained grammar schools (those financed by the local authorities) intensified disillusionment with the state sector as allegations of classroom disorder and declining standards, attributed in part to new-fangled theories about child-centred education, abounded in the media. With right-wing academics and politicians drawing blood with their outspoken attacks on comprehensives, it fell to Prime Minister Jim Callaghan, at Ruskin College, Oxford, in October 1976, to call for a return to more traditional methods of teaching and learning. His concern was genuine enough, but because much of the responsibility for state-run schools rested with the local authorities and teaching unions, progress was, at best, patchy. Not surprisingly in these circumstances some disillusioned parents, especially those with a grammar school pedigree, opted to go private.

For all the hostility that independent schools generated among Labour activists and the teaching unions, they fared rather better than the grammar schools because even Crosland viewed their abolition as a violation of his liberal-democratic principles. John Thorn, then-headmaster of Repton School, recalled being invited by Crosland to dinner with a number of his colleagues to discuss business. After an agreeable evening, the Education

Secretary leant back in his chair and drawled, 'Now – what are we going to do about these damned Public Schools?'[2]

With the support of Wilson, Crosland established the Public Schools Commission under Sir John Newsom, a Cambridge academic, to try to integrate the independent schools into the mainstream. Leaning on the research of Dr Royston Lambert, a young sociologist, its proposal to allot half of all boarding places to assisted pupils was resisted on all sides – the schools because they feared a decline in academic standards and the local authorities because they thought it socially flawed. 'In yoking together two separate ideas, the egalitarian undesirability of private education and a sup-posed pool of disadvantaged children who needed to be sent away to boarding school,' wrote the author and television presenter Jeremy Paxman, 'it was a nonsense which satisfied no-one.'[3] With no political capital to be derived from it, the report was quietly shelved by the cabinet and left to gather dust.

Back in opposition, Roy Hattersley, Shadow Education Secretary, caused a stir in 1973 by calling for the eventual abolition of private education, but with Harold Wilson unenthusiastic about such a move Labour stopped short of anything so dramatic, contenting itself in 1974 with a pledge to end chari-table status and all forms of tax relief. Even this proved unattainable for the 1974–79 government owing to the inability of two committees to unravel the complexities of charity law. Shirley Williams, Education Secretary between 1976 and 1979, did try to chip away at the financial resources of independent schools by ending the subsidy given to military and diplomatic personnel and reducing local authority grants, but on the former she was thwarted by David Owen, Foreign Secretary, and only on the latter did she make some progress.

In light of this political hostility, and with the universities and workplace becoming ever more meritocratic, the need to project a more contemporary image wasn't lost on the independent sector. Academic excellence became its leading priority. While classics continued its inexorable decline, subjects such as maths, science and business studies assumed an ever-greater import-ance as the number of privately educated students reading these disciplines at university grew rapidly.

Adolescent disaffection with the old order also helped usher in moderni-sation. Pupil–staff relations improved, discipline was relaxed and compulsory regimentation gave way to greater individual opportunity across broad swathes of school life. 'When the Conservatives won the 1979 election, the independent schools were stronger, more politically astute and less publicly criticised than at any time since the war,' wrote John Rae, headmaster of Westminster School between 1970 and 1986.[4]

That position was further buttressed by the new Conservative government. The abolition of the direct grant subsidy had helped galvanise the party into a staunch defence of selective education, and, following the persistent lobbying of James Cobban, headmaster of Abingdon School, it embraced the assisted places scheme that provided free or subsidised places for able children whose parents couldn't afford fees. The scheme, incorporated in the 1980 Education Act, conformed to the Conservative ethos of self-improvement, but was deeply resented by the teaching unions and the Labour Party. Not only did they object to taxpayers' money subsidising fee-paying schools when the state sector was suffering retrenchment, they also viewed the transfer of many of the state's brightest children to the independent sector as an act likely to exacerbate social divisions.

It so happened that the new Shadow Education Secretary, Neil Kinnock, an ardent Welsh left-winger, was vehemently opposed to all forms of selective education, as he told the Commons in November 1979:

> My absolute conviction is that public schools have been, are, and, for as long as they exist, will continue to be, an incubus on freedom, opportunity and justice in our society. I shall therefore use, as I have used in the past, all the influence that I can bring to bear on my party to secure a policy position which will bring about the abolition of the private schools and other forms of private education.[5]

As Labour moved sharply to the left following the 1979 election defeat, plans to phase out private education by removing all of its subsidies and placing VAT on fees was one of the many controversial measures passed at its conference in October 1980.

The party's declaration of war on the independent sector provoked a predictably uncompromising response. Rhodes Boyson, a junior education minister, called it an envious assault that could end in a totalitarian society of repression and hatred of learning, culture and individual ability, while headmaster after headmaster took every opportunity to place their parents on a war footing. At Rugby School's speech day in June 1982, headmaster Brian Rees, speaking in the immediate aftermath of the Falklands War, thought it astounding that British servicemen who had fought with such distinction should be denied the opportunity to give their children a boarding education, should Labour have its way:

> We need, for example, to reiterate that opinion polls affirm that the majority of people in this country do wish to see Schools which are part of a national heritage preserved, that freedom is valued by the majority of people above a false equality, that the destruction of a single great school will not spread its benefits equally across the land so that a fraction is enjoyed by all, and that a State monopoly in Education will go the way of all State monopolies which become cumbersome, bureaucratic and appear to seethe with discontent.[6]

A fighting fund was set up to save the schools and two human rights lawyers, Anthony Lester and David Pannick, claimed that abolition would breach Article 2 of the European Convention on Human Rights.

At the 1983 election, even the *Times Educational Supplement*, no lover of the independent sector, commented that destroying it was a desperate distraction for Labour because, libertarian issues aside, it would do little to help the state sector. Tethered to the most extreme manifesto in its history, the party was decimated at the polls, but with Neil Kinnock replacing Michael Foot as its leader, there was no let-up in its hostility toward private education. According to John Rae, Labour had 'no idea how to reconcile popular demand for higher standards, better discipline and more choice with a policy to abolish the very schools that are thought to epitomise these virtues'.[7]

At its 1986 conference, Labour passed a resolution calling for the planned ownership of the private school system, but failed to get the necessary two-thirds majority. Abolition didn't feature in its 1987 manifesto though it remained a long-term objective. It needed another heavy defeat, its third in succession, for the party to gradually moderate its views on independent education, as with so much else.

In contrast to Scotland, Wales and the North of England where deindustrialisation had caused mass unemployment and much poverty, the Conservative-voting South was enjoying something of an economic revival by the mid-1980s. In 1986 growth in Britain was outstripping all of its European competitors and a combination of easy credit, lower taxes and deregulation, not least in the City of London, had helped fuel an economic boom. Whether it was the ambitious young swells of the Bullingdon Club, the notorious Oxford dining club comprised of well-connected Old Etonians, or upwardly mobile City traders quaffing their champagne and driving their BMWs, ostentatious displays of wealth had never been so conspicuous. This affluence not only helped boost the independent sector with burgeoning numbers, not least from first-time buyers, but also with the expansion of its facilities.

The sector also received a significant boost from the assisted places scheme. While some schools refrained from joining, fearing that Labour's threat to scrap it would leave them underwriting the fees of those unable to pay, the number rose steadily from 230 at its inception in 1981 to 355 in 1997. It was particularly popular with the former direct grant schools, situated overwhelmingly in the Midlands and urban North, as they adapted to life in the independent sector.

With many a school benefitting from the scheme academically, and with the public firmly behind it, the Thatcher and Major governments continued to extend it, so that by 1997 some 75,000 pupils had benefitted by it at a cost of just over £800 million. And yet for all its success in promoting greater social mobility – a report commissioned by the Sutton Trust charity in 2013 found that over 40 per cent of these pupils were earning over £90,000 a year – and preserving the rich diversity of many schools, it never managed to convert its detractors, foremost of whom was John Rae at Westminster.

One of the most charismatic and controversial headmasters of his era, Rae was a gifted communicator whose frequent media appearances often upset his colleagues by exposing some uncomfortable truths about the type of education they stood for. A Liberal in his politics, Rae combined a strong commitment to independent education with a deep unease about its divisive tendencies. Convinced that the assisted places scheme rode roughshod over the interest of state schools by removing their more able pupils to independent schools, he spoke out against it. Not surprisingly his stance won him few friends in the independent sector, not least from smaller schools that lacked the resources of Westminster, and at the annual gathering of the HMC in 1979 he was shouted down by some of his colleagues when he gave vent to his feelings.

Although Westminster eventually joined the scheme in 1984, Rae persisted in his opposition. Not only did it prove defective by failing to attract the poor — only 10 per cent were from a genuine working-class background — its methods of means-tested selection based on income and not assets were open to abuse. A number of school bursars squirmed in embarrassment as those parents with creative accountants made income disappear. In the opinion of Dick Davison, deputy director of the Independent Schools Information Service (ISIS), what fatally weakened the scheme was the number of beneficiaries who weren't its original target. Once it was abolished in 1997, few looked to revive it in its previous form.

Although education was an area in which Mrs Thatcher vowed to make a difference, she gave it scant attention during the first half of her premiership when her priorities were elsewhere. After a period of stagnation between 1981 and 1987 best remembered for a debilitating teachers' pay dispute, which achieved little other than to boost the independent sector, the prime minister was determined to act. Convinced that the best way to raise standards was to free schools from local authority control and impose central supervision over what was taught in the classroom, the 1988 Education Reform Act introduced the national curriculum, regular testing, the right of all schools to manage their own budgets and the creation of self-governing grant-maintained schools. Relatively few schools availed themselves of the opportunity to opt out, but it didn't stop the Major government from instigating further reforms. Central to these reforms was the introduction of comparative league tables to expose local authorities and schools with poor academic records, and an independent inspectorate, the Office of Standards in Education (Ofsted), to provide a more speedy and rigorous scrutiny of all schools.

Although these reforms broadly conformed to the values of the independent sector, the self-confessed desire of the Minister of State for Education, Angela Rumbold, to see private schools consigned to history by a flourishing state sector committed to parental choice, caused quite a rumpus. At the HMC's annual gathering in 1988, David Woodhead, director of ISIS, warned his audience not to put their faith in politicians, since the Conservative government had no commitment to protecting the independent sector. Given the growing competition from the state sector, fee-paying schools would be well advised to market themselves more effectively and engage more closely with their local communities.

Two years later, by which time the country was mired in recession with all that that meant to private education, John Rae conveyed a similar message in a lecture in the City of London. The education reforms designed to give parents greater choice and influence presented the independent sector with its greatest challenge in decades. According to Rae, 'When the middle class refugees begin to return to the maintained schools, weaker independent schools will go to the wall.'[8]

Concerned about growing ministerial interference in education, especially with the national curriculum, the independent sector reacted with indignation. At the Girls Schools' Association (GSA) conference in 1992, its president, Elizabeth Diggory, headmistress of St Albans High School for Girls, castigated the government for denigrating the teaching profession, and when the Minister of State for Education, Baroness Blatch, sought to reassure her audience that this wasn't the case she was greeted with hollow laughter.

The following year the independent sector was sympathetic to the boycott of school tests on the grounds that they were too prescriptive. Joan Clanchy, headmistress of the North London Collegiate School (NLCS), resigned from the National Curriculum Council and Robin Wilson, headmaster of Trinity School and chairman of the HMC, used a column in *The Times* to convey a similar message:

> To a degree which does not seem to be appreciated by government, an educational service of real value depends above all on drawing the ablest people in the country into the profession, and then trusting their professional competence. League tables, and promised additional torrents of statistical information, will in the long run do very little to help.[9]

By then the travails of the Major government, especially its bitter divisions over Europe and its engulfment in sleaze, had alienated friend and foe alike. In his highly influential *The State We're In*, a searching analysis of the divisions within British society, the political economist Will Hutton called the dominance of the independent sector a 'long-standing offence to any notion of democracy or meritocracy in our society':

> The wider processes of social exclusion and their dependence on privatisation are laid bare by these schools. It is not only that parental income becomes the

crucial determinant of future status, but that the value system that justi-
fies such inequality is compelled to reject ideas of citizenship, inclusion and
universalism.[10]

His view was broadly supported by George Walden, a former Conservative
higher education minister and maverick MP. In a *Sunday Times* article in
September 1995, he wrote of Britain having two educational cultures:

> one that is highly aspiring and patronised largely by the socially advan-
> taged, and another that is steeped in mediocrity and reserved for the
> remaining 93 per cent. ... No country has a good system of state education
> where the most powerful and influential have no part in it, and neither
> shall we.[11]

Soon it would fall to the new Labour government to try to bridge
the growing divide. Labour had remained hostile to the independent sector throughout the 1980s and its attitude only began to change when Jack
Straw became Shadow Education Secretary. A product of Brentwood, a
direct grant school, Straw became a militant president of the National Union
of Students during the early 1970s and special adviser to the leading left-
winger Barbara Castle, but by the time he joined the Shadow Cabinet in
1987 his radicalism was cooling fast. An experienced lawyer, he fully appreciated that abolishing independent schools ran counter to the principles of
the European Convention on Human Rights, as well as alienating many of
the very voters the party needed to win over to form a government. (Polls
repeatedly showed that up to half of Labour voters were opposed to the
abolition of private education.) Adopting a more pragmatic approach, he
told *The Times*, in September 1991, that Labour wouldn't stand in the way
of parental choice, something as a parent himself he firmly believed in, but
his party planned to make state schools so successful that 'only snobs and
eccentrics will choose to pay'. The assisted places scheme would go and charity law would be reformed so that charitable status would only remain for
those that merited it, although the latter was belatedly excluded from the
party's 1992 manifesto.

This gradual rapprochement between Labour and the independent sector took a further step forward when Tony Blair succeeded John Smith as

leader of the party in July 1994. A product of Fettes College, Blair had fallen foul of its rigid disciplinary regime during the heady days of the late 1960s when youthful idealism was on the march. Yet for all his frustration at the school's stultifying atmosphere, these weren't wasted years. A consummate actor who played Mark Antony in Shakespeare's *Julius Caesar* and Captain Stanhope in R.C. Sherriff's *Journey's End*, Blair honed his skills as a natural communicator well able to relate to his audience.

These attributes he put to good effect on becoming leader of the Opposition. Disillusioned by Labour's long spell in the political wilderness, Blair knew that the world had moved on since 1979 and there was no going back on the Thatcher revolution. Much of what she had accomplished he accepted had been necessary, and Labour would win few converts by continuing to preach the virtues of state control over individual opportunity and egalitarianism in education over excellence. Those who argued that grammar and independent schools were better simply because of their wealth and class, he later wrote in his memoirs, *A Journey*, were mistaken:

> The truth is that both types of school are good for other reasons too. They are independent. They have an acute sense of ethos and identity. They have strong leadership, and are allowed to lead. ... They pursue excellence. And – here is a major factor – they assume excellence is attainable.[12]

It is true that Blair became the first prime minister to educate his children in the state sector, but even then his choice of the London Oratory, a Catholic grant-maintained school that had opted out of Labour authority control, upset large sections of the party. Refusing to bow to their strictures, Blair insisted that the choice of school for his children must rest with his wife and himself, a choice that he did not wish to deny other parents. In January 1996 he proved as good as his word when Harriet Harman, his Shadow Health Secretary, chose to send her son to a selective grammar school in Orpington. The decision provoked outrage in a party that counted many state teachers and school governors among its activists and provided Blair with the greatest challenge to his leadership to date. If Tory education policies were so bad, chortled John Major in the Commons at Prime Minister's Question Time, why were Shadow Cabinet members shifting their children from schools run by Labour authorities to those run by Conservatives? 'The answer is that many middle-class Labour MPs in the South of England do not, in practice, agree with all-out comprehensive education anymore,' wrote the political commentator Iain Macwhirter in the *Observer*. 'They see the battlegrounds that pass for inner-London comprehensives "full of under-achieving [whisper it] black children" and they vote with their offspring.'[13]

Rejecting the attempts of David Blunkett, Shadow Education Secretary, to impose VAT on school fees, and of others to phase out the remaining 165 grammar schools, the most that Blair would agree to was to end the assisted places scheme. His leading priority was improving standards in the state sector by building on the Conservative reforms and fomenting a closer relationship with the independent sector. The fact that Labour was even contemplating this alignment was a measure of how far the party had travelled over the previous decade, a journey rewarded by the unprecedented show of support it now commanded in many independent schools.

On 1 May 1997, all of Tony Blair's efforts to modernise Labour paid off handsomely when the party returned to power with a crushing majority over the divided and demoralised Conservatives. The next day the headmaster of Fettes awarded the school a half-holiday in honour of the school's first prime minister as the independent sector reacted calmly to the change of government, confident that it wouldn't engage in acts of retribution.

The scrapping of the assisted places scheme – phased out over a number of years to enable the schools concerned to adjust – while unpopular, proved the limit of Labour's punitive approach. That autumn Stephen Byers, Schools Standards Minister, became the first Labour minister ever to address the GSA and, declaring an end to dogma and prejudice, he promised £500,000 for pilot initiatives that would open the facilities of independent schools to state pupils. His comments won approbation from Jackie Lang, headmistress of Walthamstow Hall School and president of the GSA. Labour had met the independent sector more than half way by laying out the terms in which the two could work together. She applauded his commitment to excellence and charitable status as it then stood.

The cooperation continued the following year when Estelle Morris, Byers' replacement, addressed the HMC and assured it that there would always be a role for the independent sector under Labour. There was much to admire about it, not least its freedoms and the aspirations it held out for every child, she said, earning herself a standing ovation.

As Blair adhered to his promise of following a moderate course in gov-ernment, he was able to tell the 1999 Labour conference in Bournemouth that the class war was over. He spoke too soon for the next day a musical ensemble from Talbot Heath School was booed at a party function when it was announced that the girls were privately educated. It was a foretaste of a bitter dispute that arose the following summer and which had long-term ramifications for university admissions. At its core was the Chancellor of the Exchequer, Gordon Brown, whose roots within the Labour movement ran much deeper than Blair's. Educated at Kirkcaldy High School and Edinburgh University, where he had become the first-ever student rector, Brown never shared Blair's toleration of the British establishment and was clearly uneasy in its company, a trait illustrated by his refusal, as Chancellor, to wear black tie at the CBI's annual dinner.

At a time when his standing, and that of the government, had tem-porarily slipped in the face of an effective Conservative onslaught over immigration, asylum and pensions, Brown sought to regain the initiative by igniting a row over social elitism. Two days before he was due to address a trade union meeting on equality of opportunity, he was made aware of a story circulating in the *Newcastle Journal* about a local headmaster criticising Oxford University for rejecting his star pupil.

Laura Spence was a brilliant student from a Tyneside comprehensive who failed to win a place to read Medicine at Magdalen College, Oxford, despite gaining ten A* grades at GCSE and being predicted five A grades at A-level. After rejecting offers to read Medicine at Edinburgh, Nottingham and Newcastle Universities, she went to Harvard University to study for a BA in Biochemistry. (Had she applied for this subject at Oxford, she would have been admitted.) Given the apparent discrimination behind this case, Brown, no lover of the Oxbridge ethos and its close links with the independent sec-tor, chose to wade in.

Without checking his facts with Magdalen, Brown, urged on by David Blunkett and Alastair Campbell, the prime minister's director of commu-nications and strategy, launched a bitter attack on Oxford's 'prejudicial' admissions system: 'This is an interview system that is more reminiscent of the old-boy network and the old-school tie than genuine justice in our society.'[14] It was high time that the university opened its doors to women and people from all backgrounds.

As Brown's onslaught reverberated around the country, Oxford closed ranks and came out fighting. Roy Jenkins, its Chancellor, accused Brown of uninformed prejudice and Anthony Smith, president of Magdalen, defended the rigour of its entrance system, insisting that ability not background was the criterion for entry to the college. All twenty-two applicants to read Medicine at Magdalen had gained ten A* grades at GCSE, had excellent A-level predictions and had been interviewed by six eminent professors. Far from being impeded at interview, this was the best part of Laura's four-section assessment procedure; far from discriminating against minorities, three of the successful candidates were women and two were state educated. According to Dr John Adamson, a Fellow of Peterhouse, Cambridge, the idea that Oxbridge selection panels, overwhelmingly grammar school or state educated, should have an inbuilt bias towards the well-heeled was absurd. Many colleges had informal quota systems and there were cases of privately educated students rejected by Oxbridge being accepted by Yale, one of America's elite Ivy League universities.

To the columnist Melanie Phillips, the Laura Spence row was merely the latest example of Oxbridge being relentlessly bullied by Labour class warriors fomenting social resentment to cover their intellectual and social bankruptcy, a view similar to that of William Rees-Mogg, former editor of *The Times*. He thought the real scandal arose from the failure of the state educational system, not from the privileges of the independent sector.

'But the case of Laura Spence has exposed the truth about Oxbridge,' declared the educational journalist Peter Wilby in the *Observer*, 'that at the beginning of the twenty-first century it is still a stronghold of social privilege and exclusivity, as much of an outrage against justice and modernity as the old House of Lords was.'[15] Despite laudable efforts by many colleges to widen access, more needed to be done to redress the balance whereby the private sector still claimed nearly half the places at Oxbridge.

Brown's outburst, whatever it might have owed to political calculation, struck a chord with many in his party who shared his anti-elitist sentiments. A month before a survey by the Sutton Trust showed that many bright students from the state sector with the right grades weren't getting to the top thirteen universities and that a privately educated student was twenty-five times more likely to get to these universities than a poor working-class student.

The following year a Labour-dominated parliamentary select committee proposed that universities should be offered financial incentives to take more students with lower A-level results if they came from disadvantaged backgrounds, a proposal that dismayed the ISC. It accused MPs of undermining academic achievement and diminishing the standard of British universities, a charge that made little impression on the government. In October 2001 the new Education Secretary, Estelle Morris, told a conference of vice chancellors that it was indefensible that middle-class pupils were five times more likely to go to university than working-class ones: 'Universities are not a birthright for the middle classes. Richer kids are not brighter than poorer children.'[16] Ensuring that 50 per cent of the under-thirties entered higher education by 2010 was one of the government's leading priorities.

In response to this pressure to widen access or lose funds, ten universities in 2002 did precisely that. Bristol University's history department was singled out for praise by Margaret Hodge, Minister for Universities, for using criteria other than exam performance in its admissions procedure. 'I think A-levels are incredibly important. But we now have a body of evidence that they are not the most effective predictor of how students will do at university,' she said.[17]

Such statements seemed merely to confirm what the independent sector had long suspected. An extensive HMC-GSA survey of that year's offers and rejections by seventeen elite universities of their pupils showed an apparent bias against them, with Bristol, Edinburgh and the London School of Economics deemed the most culpable. These anxieties were publicly aired by Edward Gould, master of Marlborough College and chairman of the HMC, that October. He accused the government of encouraging universities 'to tamper crudely with admissions procedures to promote inclusion by the back door'.[18] Encouraging untapped potential was admirable but Gould feared that cash-strapped universities could be induced to accept more students from low-performing schools by financial incentives from the government.

With British universities declining in quality compared to their American counterparts and beset by gross underfunding, the call for a rise in fees by vice chancellors grew ever louder. It so happened that the elite universities had recently persuaded Tony Blair of their need to raise more finance through variable tuition fees, first introduced in 1998, in face of opposition from Gordon Brown and many in the Labour Party. Not only did this run counter to a promise in their 2001 manifesto, they feared that it would lead to a two-tier system of universities and deter children from poorer backgrounds from applying.

Following a period of bitter cabinet infighting in which no satisfactory alternative was forthcoming, the prime minister and Charles Clarke, Estelle Morris' successor as Education Secretary, had their way. In January 2003 a government White Paper proposed 'top-up' fees of up to £3,000 a year after the next election and the creation of an access regulator to oversee a wider mix at university.

Attention now switched to Bristol, an institution traditionally seen as a bastion of privilege but one which had increased its intake of state-educated students from 49 per cent in 1998 to 60 per cent in 2003. Because of the intense demand for places — 40,000 for 3,000 — it meant that many top students inevitably missed out on an offer. The fact that two of these students, one from King Edward's School, Birmingham (KESB) and one from Bedford School, went to Cambridge instead fuelled fears of systematic discrimination against the independent sector.

As the right-wing press lambasted the government for placing social engineering above academic merit, both the HMC and GSA accused Bristol of unfairly discriminating against students of good schools whether they be state or independent. Given the apparent arbitrary rejection of well-qualified candidates that year, they urged heads to discourage their pupils from applying to Bristol until it could offer guarantees that its admissions system was fair, objective, transparent and consistent.

While Bristol firmly rebutted allegations of discrimination in its admissions, Charles Clarke was forced to disown comments made by Margaret Hodge that proposed setting targets for the number of working-class students going to university. He did, however, call the boycott, the first of its kind, misguided and urged the HMC to engage in a mature discussion with Bristol. It did, and, after receiving assurances from the university that there was nothing untoward in its admissions procedure, it called off the boycott weeks later. The controversy over university admissions, however, was to resurface on many occasions throughout the next decade once the legislation on 'top-up' fees had passed the Commons by the narrowest of majorities in January 2004.

A greater threat to the independent sector came from Labour's tampering with charitable status and a number of tax and rate exemptions applicable to its schools on the premise that education was a charitable activity. This was universally acceptable in the days when elite schools still adhered to the ideals of their founders and provided free places to the poor, but with those days long gone the anomaly affronted not only left-wing critics of private education, but also the majority of the public and even some within the sector itself. Tim Hands, then-headmaster of Portsmouth Grammar School, called charitable status a product of the nineteenth century and Anthony Seldon, then-headmaster of Brighton College, contended that private schools should be forced to increase their links with state schools or lose their tax concessions.

At the same time, the ISC was quick to remind its critics that its schools were non-profit-making bodies that saved the state over £2 billion a year by educating 7 per cent of the nation's children and gave away nearly £300 million in bursaries, compared to the £100 million they received in tax breaks. What's more, an ISC report in 2003 showed that schools were more involved in the local community than ever before.

Although Labour had toyed with abolishing charitable status since 1974, it had backed off at the last minute before the 1992 election, admitting that it would be a time-consuming and complex business. It didn't feature in the 1997 and 2001 manifestos either, although there was, according to David Blunkett, an informal agreement that independent schools would work in partnership with neighbouring comprehensives, an agreement which Blunkett felt the independents had failed to honour. A review of charitable law after the 2001 election by the Number 10 Policy Unit reached the conclusion that most private schools were business institutions and their charitable status was an anachronism. A bill to this effect, first mooted in the Queen's Speech of 2003, was published in draft form the following May. Charitable status would in future be dependent on schools passing a public benefit test, but the government failed to provide a precise definition of public benefit, knowing full well that such a definition would alienate the independent sector and many of its allies in the press.

This lack of precision irritated Alan Milburn, a former Labour Health Secretary and chairman of the joint parliamentary committee of MPs and peers set up to scrutinise the bill. He accused Home Office Minister Fiona

Mactaggart, responsible for charities, of creating confusion. In a scathing report, his committee denounced the schism between the government and the Charity Commission – the latter had been placed in the ludicrous position of applying the public benefit test without the power necessary to do it – and recommended more radical legislation that stripped private schools of their charitable status but gave them tax breaks if they offered sufficient public benefits.

The bill ran out of time before the 2005 election but was introduced for the third time after Labour's third successive victory and secured royal assent in November 2006. Thrust into the firing line, the Charity Commission, under its privately educated, Labour-supporting chairman, Dame Suzi Leather, was soon at war with independent schools by laying down stringent guidelines. In order to maintain their charitable status they would be expected to share their facilities with local state schools and offer more free school places to those from low-income backgrounds. If that meant higher fees to pay for these bursaries, that was a price worth paying, she argued, an alarming prospect for many schools, especially as recession loomed.

Their skirmish came to a head in July 2009 when two small preparatory schools, S. Anselm's in Derbyshire and Highfield Priory in Lancashire, failed the public benefit test because neither had provided sufficient bursaries. Unless they rectified this deficiency within a year, the charity regulator stipulated, these schools would lose their charitable status. The ruling came the year after four independent schools in Scotland had suffered a similar fate at the hands of a separate regulator there, causing consternation within the sector. The ISC warned that higher fees to pay for these additional bursaries would force many schools to the edge of bankruptcy and make the sector more exclusive. 'Class war is an ugly thing,' wrote the political commentator Simon Heffer in the *Daily Telegraph*, 'but Labour seems determined to have one.'[19] Meanwhile Andrew Grant, headmaster of St Albans School and chairman of the HMC, accused the government of launching a medieval offensive against private schools. When Suzi Leather assured the HMC at its meeting in October that the Charity Commission wasn't fixated on bursaries, she failed to convince her audience. Despite giving schools an additional five years to meet the obligations of the public benefit test, a concession deemed too generous by Fiona Millar, a leading advocate of state education, and a later reprieve for the two preparatory schools following their willingness to offer more bursaries, the ISC remained dissatisfied. It resolved to take the charity regulator to court, accusing it of being unduly prescriptive.

Granted judicial review by the attorney general, Dominic Grieve, in 2010, the ISC argued at the Charity Tribunal that the Charity Commission had placed too much emphasis on bursaries for poor children, an argument that held sway. The tribunal ruled that certain parts of the Charity Commission's guidance were erroneous and should be rewritten. Thus while it confirmed that independent schools must demonstrate more than a token effort towards the poor to remain as charities, it was up to the governors and trustees of these schools to decide how best to meet their obligations beyond the school gate.

The judgement, while disconcerting to those who disapproved of public money subsidising privileged institutions, delighted the independent sector. Cooperation was more likely to flourish in an environment where schools could decide for themselves what was right rather than being told what to do by a quango, remarked Barnaby Lenon, former headmaster of Harrow and chairman of the ISC.

The clash with the Labour government over charitable status had – with a couple of exceptions – united the whole of the independent sector, but cooperation with governments of both hues over the academy programme revealed a number of divisions.

Determined to transform the quality of state education when it took office in 1997, the Blair government poured vast resources into its schools and instituted a rigorously enforced target culture to help drive up standards. The results were – initially – spectacular at primary level and encouraging at secondary, with better GCSE and A-level grades helping more students to enter higher education. Yet despite the growth in educational opportunity, the number still underachieving remained a cause of deep concern.

The academy programme was very much the brainchild of Andrew Adonis, Blair's education adviser, later to become the head of the Number 10 Policy Unit and, finally, from 2005, a junior education minister. The son of a Greek Cypriot immigrant and raised in a north London care home before being sent to a boarding school in the Cotswolds, Adonis won a scholarship to Oxford, the prelude to a distinguished career as an academic, journalist and politician. Convinced that half of all comprehensive schools were failing their pupils, especially those from disadvantaged backgrounds, Adonis looked to city technology schools, new independent state schools financed largely by private capital and established by the Conservatives in the early 1990s, as the way forward. The fact that all fifteen of them were performing to expectation gave him the confidence to announce, with Blair's approval, a modest programme of elite schools free of local authority control, to be known as academies, to take over from failing inner-city comprehensives. The first three were opened in 2002 and, two years later, the government set a target of 200 to be completed by 2010. Reaching that target proved difficult as many in the Labour Party viewed these academies as grammar schools by another name.

As part of his mission to build a more cohesive society and help the independent sector rediscover its charitable roots, Adonis looked to these schools to sponsor an academy by assuming complete responsibility for its governance.

In October 2002 the Schools Standards Minister, David Miliband, another leading Blairite, put this proposition to the HMC at its annual gathering. He accepted that it wouldn't be easy to overcome a history of rivalry, resentment and suspicion. In England the divisions between public and private sectors were deeper than elsewhere, but, according to Miliband,

> ... barracking and finger-wagging are not going to serve our children at all. If we are truly serious about raising standards across all sectors, then we must be prepared to think seriously about how we push the boundaries of reform.[20]

Asked by one headmaster what was in it for them, Miliband replied that they had a vocation to educate children and added: 'It's a challenge and these schools are about challenge. And they might learn something.'

With few schools responding to the government's invitation, partly because of the costs involved, Adonis dropped the stipulation that they contribute £2 million to starting costs. Addressing the HMC in September 2007, he said, 'It is your educational DNA we are seeking, not your fee income or your existing charitable endowments.' His appeal did not, however, impress Bernard Trafford, then-headmaster of Wolverhampton Grammar School and chairman of the HMC. Unhappy that academies, new rules on charitable status and changes in private schools' registration were threatening their independence, he told the government to stop meddling in their affairs.

Relations between Labour and the independent sector remained strained during the former's final years in power, but, overall, the Blair–Brown era had been beneficial for the latter, both in terms of numbers and academic attainment. The same couldn't be said of the state sector, for while £28 billion of investment had yielded an undoubted improvement in exam results, too many pupils from lower socio-economic groups still left school without five GCSEs.

In 2005 the Sutton Trust published a study showing a sharp fall in cross-generational social mobility between those growing up in the 1960s and 1970s compared to those growing up thereafter. In no other advanced country was social mobility more limited, it reported. These findings were broadly confirmed by the 2009 report by the independent Social Mobility and Child Poverty Commission chaired by Alan Milburn. It asserted that opportunity had stalled, the professions had become more socially exclusive and that skills in communication and leadership attained through private education gave its pupils an unfair advantage. The report called on independent schools to share their facilities more and for universities to take account of the social background of applicants when considering exam results.

The formation of the Conservative–Liberal Democrat coalition in May 2010, with the prime minister, David Cameron, educated at Eton and his deputy, Nick Clegg, educated at Westminster, illustrated all too clearly these social divisions, as was evident to journalist Dominic Sandbrook, writing in the *Daily Mail*:

> But look again at the footage of our new masters in the rose garden and you will see not just the virtues of two first-class schools, but a damning indictment of the collapse of opportunity in modern Britain. ... And yet, even a former public schoolboy can see that there is something wrong with a system in which a privileged political class clogs up the corridors of power, especially since research conclusively shows that social mobility has stalled since the Sixties, preventing bright children from getting the opportunities enjoyed by their parents.
>
> In many ways, the collapse in opportunity was one of New Labour's greatest failures.[21]

Even before the Coalition took office much attention had been given to David Cameron's background and that of his coterie of blue-blooded advisers, especially his good friend George Osborne, Shadow Chancellor of the Exchequer. Throughout the years of grammar-school-educated prime ministers the politics of class had begun to fade, but following a near-decade of a privately educated Labour prime minister, the election of a Conservative leader from Eton, the first in forty years, in 2005, attracted much comment.

It wasn't just that Cameron had been to Eton, he looked and sounded like an Etonian with his membership of the exclusive Bullingdon Club at Oxford, his well-connected wife and his love of country pursuits. The election of Boris Johnson, Cameron's senior at Eton and Oxford, as Mayor of London in 2008, the creation of 'a cabinet of millionaires' in 2010 (although fewer of them were privately educated than those in the Thatcher and Major cabinets and, by 2014, 65 per cent were state educated), and the increased percentage of privately educated MPs – twenty of whom went to Eton – only added to the impression that privilege was making a comeback.

Keen to play down his affluent background in face of the all-too-predictable attacks from his opponents, Cameron resorted to a number of populist gestures such as dressing casually, riding a bicycle and implying that his children would be state educated. Later, when discussing education policy at the 2012 Conservative Party conference, he couldn't bring himself to say publicly that he had been to Eton, only that he had been to a great school, a far cry from the days of Harold Macmillan, who rarely appeared in public without wearing an Old Etonian tie.

During the intervening half century or so society had become less deferential and politics much more personal. The fact that Labour prime ministers such as Clement Attlee, Harold Wilson and Jim Callaghan had educated their children privately had attracted little or no comment, but when Tony Blair sent his child to a grant-maintained school he was accused of nauseating hypocrisy. Iain Duncan Smith, leader of the Opposition between 2001 and 2003, was similarly chastised for sending his son to Eton, and when his Shadow Home Secretary, Oliver Letwin, declared that 'he would rather go on the streets and beg' than send his children to his local comprehensive in south London, he was forced to apologise.

Perhaps the greatest vitriol was reserved for Diane Abbott, the left-wing Labour MP who had criticised Blair for sending his children to a state selective school, when she chose to go private with her son, citing the low academic achievement of black boys in Hackney schools. She admitted that her decision was 'indefensible' but, like other politicians faced with this dilemma, she put the interests of her child above political principle.

Intent on purging the Conservatives of their obsolete image that had helped them lose three successive elections, and leading a modern, inclusive party, Cameron upset many of his backbenchers by refusing to create new grammar schools. Instead he placed his faith in the Labour government's programme of academies, a policy which had the full support of his Shadow Education Secretary, Michael Gove.

Adopted at four months old and winning a scholarship to Robert Gordon's College in Aberdeen, where he quickly established himself as one of the school's most precocious students, Gove's ability won him a place at Oxford to read English. A great admirer of the Asian educational system, he resolved to make the improvement of the English state sector his central mission by clamping down on progressive teaching and introducing more traditional syllabuses, better discipline and more rigorous exams. 'If more people left the independent sector for the state sector because our reforms had improved state schools, I would be happy with that,' he told the *Independent* in February 2010.[22]

Once in power, Gove greatly accelerated the academy programme and instituted free schools – schools governed by non-profit-making charitable institutions – hailing them as great engines of social mobility. In September 2011, following Blair's initiative of a few years earlier, a number of leading independent heads were invited to Downing Street and asked by Cameron to sponsor academies in the drive to raise standards. It was a message the prime minister relayed to the Conservative Party conference the following month, telling it that the segregated system between private and state schools 'is one of the biggest wasted opportunities in our country'.

If his intention was to cajole the independent sector into sponsoring academies it appears to have had the opposite effect, with many heads resenting the hectoring tone. Tony Little, headmaster of Eton, disputed Cameron's intention regarding a segregated education system; relations with the state sector had never been better, he asserted. According to Bernard Trafford, 'the Tories no longer feel like friends. They feel like former friends who are starting to disown us. We work like fury to raise funds for bursaries.'[23]

Many schools insisted that their help was best channelled through individual partnerships with local state schools, but none of this impressed Anthony Seldon, appointed by Cameron to help Adonis lead the drive for collaboration between the two sectors. After a year of scant progress, he lashed out at his colleagues in the *Observer* in June 2012 for their lack of moral purpose, and urged them to emerge from their state of isolation to engage with the rest of society.

Seldon's frustration was genuine enough, but in his capacity as master of well-endowed Wellington College he failed to appreciate the restraints under which many of his less fortunate colleagues laboured. Most schools lacked the resources to send staff off to form new schools.

These concerns were articulated at the GSA's annual conference that November by its president Louise Robinson, headmistress of Merchant Taylors' Girls' School, Crosby:

> The current government cannot decide whether they are for or against independent schools: they want our DNA, our sponsorship of academies, but we know academies are not the answer to everyone's prayers.

Many of the schools she represented were quite happy to cooperate on their own terms, but at a time when they were under pressure from the growing weight of regulation imposed on them, and the increasing struggle of parents to pay their fees, she thought it a bit rich to expect them to share aspects of their expertise with local competition:

> And competition it is; why should my school offer its CCF expertise and experience to parents who could have sent their children to my school, but chose not to, or to a Government which criticises my morality?[24]

Part of the independent sector's aversion to sponsoring academies lay in the fact that academies weren't fully independent, especially on the vexed question of selection. Galvanised by the strictures of the Charity Commission regarding wider access, many schools had greatly increased their means-tested bursaries, and, in September 2012, eighty independent day schools, in partnership with the Sutton Trust, supported an open access scheme in which they pledged to match free subsidies from their own bursary funds, if the government agreed to pay part of the fees. Such a scheme, they claimed, would enable them to admit pupils on merit alone, irrespective of whether their parents could afford the fees.

The scheme, published in a letter to *The Times* and signed by forty-four heads, was given short shrift by the Coalition government, especially the Liberal Democrat side, on the premise that it encouraged selection. It was yet one more rift in the chasm that had opened up between the government and the independent sector, much to the disillusion of the latter. 'British public schools are the envy of the educational world even though we are demonised by some here at home,' lamented Christopher Ray, high master of Manchester Grammar School and chairman of the HMC in 2012–13. 'The existence of incredibly successful independent schools is an irritant to many Labour politicians, a puzzle to Liberal Democrats, and, it often seems, an embarrassment to the Prime Minister.'[25] His disillusion was such that in July 2013 he left Manchester Grammar to take up an appointment in the Middle East, one of several leading heads of independent schools to seek refuge abroad, all complaining about antipathy towards the private sector. And yet popular support for independent schooling remained encouraging, numbers steady despite the recession, the worst in memory, and academic results as good as ever. In truth, the schools had become victims of their own success as other sources of social mobility had dried up, a state of affairs that led to further conflict with the Coalition government.

Ever since the Laura Spence affair, access to elite universities had remained very much on the political agenda, and the rise of tuition fees to £3,000 in 2006 was accompanied by an access regulator, which could ban a university from charging full fees if it failed to accept enough students from low-income backgrounds.

Although the Office for Fair Access (OFFA) did not use its powers, the mere threat was enough to persuade universities to intensify their efforts to promote wider access. Students were asked to provide more background data on their application forms and universities increasingly took this information into account.

Despite the 2006 rise in tuition fees, another rise was deemed necessary by the Coalition government to help accommodate the massive growth in higher education since 1997, and legislation passed in December 2010 enabled universities to raise fees to £9,000, subject to them drawing up an access agreement with OFFA. The Act aroused bitter opposition from students, who directed their ire mainly at the Liberal Democrats because of their 2010 election pledge to abolish tuition fees.

One of their MPs who abstained in the vote was Simon Hughes, the deputy leader; he called for a drastic reduction in the intake of privately educated students at university, sentiments previously expressed by Nick Clegg. Fresh data from the Sutton Trust in 2011, which revealed that four independent schools and one selective Cambridge sixth form college sent more candidates to Oxbridge between 2007 and 2009 than 2,000 state schools and colleges, gave added impetus to the case for greater social diversity. In February 2012 Vince Cable, Business Secretary and leading Liberal Democrat, irked Conservative MPs by appointing Professor Les Ebdon, former vice chancellor of the University of Bedfordshire and an uncompromising advocate of positive discrimination towards poorer students, to be the new head of OFFA.

If the independent sector viewed Ebdon's appointment with misgivings, its concerns were given added weight by speeches from two leading cabinet ministers that May. Michael Gove told an educational conference at Brighton College that it was morally unacceptable for the privately educated to so dominate the nation's political, professional and sporting elite; and Nick Clegg, addressing a conference on social mobility, said it was a damning indictment of modern Britain that some people were born with a sense of entitlement while others simply faced exclusion. Claiming that class still played a major part in shaping people's lives, he warned that the growing rift in attainment between private and state schools was having a corrosive impact on society. In order to help solve this problem he supported Universities and Science Minister David Willetts' earlier suggestion that universities should admit state-educated candidates with lower grades.

Clegg's remedy didn't impress Tim Hands, master of Magdalen College School, Oxford, who accused him of 'adopting old style communist tactics'. Only by having a competitive entry system would British universities retain their global renown. Ministers would do better to concentrate on improving state education rather than 'capping the achievements of pupils in independent schools'.[26]

Hands' disillusion with the political class was evident in his presidential address to the HMC in October 2013. In a withering excoriation of successive governments, he noted how excessive political interference had 'emasculated

the education system of the country'. The post-1980s drive to improve academic standards was based on the mistaken belief that one did not need to
make a child happy as one's first priority. 'Indeed it is believed that if you
make a child academically successful then happiness will follow,' he stated.[27]
Hence developed the flawed mechanics of league tables and an increasing
obsession with a prescriptive rather than liberal curriculum.

Castigating the government's construction of academies and free schools
that promised independence as 'an Orwellian trick of language that obscures
the state's grip', he declared that children were too precious to be abandoned
to the anonymous and impersonal guardianship of the state: 'The state is not
currently suitable to direct education unaided or unchallenged because it
does not understand the child.'[28]

'When the headteacher of one of the UK's leading independent schools
delivers a speech that would not be out of place coming from the general
secretary of a teaching union, are we not living in strange times?' wrote
Wendy Berliner in the *Guardian*. She continued:

> And when, the next day, a chief inspector of schools [Sir Michael Wilshaw],
> who is the darling of the Tory political class, lays into independent schools
> for being too independent, have we not reached a deeply weird place in the
> evolution of the relationships between a Conservative-dominated coalition
> government and the fee-paying sector in the UK?[29]

While some heads feel that the independent sector tends to be unduly
sensitive to press criticism – most newspapers, for all their love of a good
scandal, are broadly supportive – the toxic charge of privilege was one they
found difficult to ignore, especially given the failure of the political elite to
reduce the gap between rich and poor.

In an interview with the *Daily Telegraph* in March 2014, Barnaby Lenon
complained that the independent sector was being undermined by senior
politicians peddling ignorant myths about private schools. There were plenty
of well-off families sending children to state schools and many children
from low-income backgrounds on bursaries in independent schools. Oxford
University currently refused to set a state-school target because one-third of
its students receiving bursarial support were former members of independent
schools. To use the term independent school 'as a proxy to privilege' was a

mistake. Nine out of ten of these schools were involved in formal relation-ships with neighbouring schools. Relationships between the two sectors had never been so good.

Days after his interview, Lenon could point to ISC-commissioned research compiled by the global consultancy company Oxford Economics, which estimated that independent schools contributed £9.5 billion in gross value to Britain's GDP, provided 225,000 jobs and generated £3.6 billion of tax revenue.

Two months earlier, in a speech at the London Academy of Excellence, a selective sixth-form college founded in 2012 in collaboration with eight independent schools, Michael Gove called for state schools to be more like private ones. He acknowledged their improvement but said they must set their standards so high that they became indistinguishable from the likes of Eton and Harrow. England's private schools were the best independent schools in the world. Why shouldn't its state schools be the best state schools in the world?

Plaudits such as these were a testament to the great resurgence in inde-pendent education since 1979, but this resurgence had come at a cost, with ever-higher fees – the theme of the next chapter.

Chapter 2

A QUESTION OF
AFFORDABILITY

Although John Rae termed the years 1964–79 a 'public school revolution', the truth was that the ancient regime wasn't yet history. The atmosphere in schools may have relaxed, but facilities often remained Dickensian, the governance was amateurish and the common room still resembled a rarefied gentlemen's club somewhat detached from the real world.

It needed the political hostility of the 1960s and 1970s, coupled with the deteriorating economy, to puncture some of this complacency. A fourfold increase in oil prices, the onset of mass inflation and a steep rise in teachers' pay caused school fees to nearly triple during the 1970s, thereby taxing the resources of middle-class professionals now that many of them were paying out of income rather than capital. At a time when boarding was becoming less fashionable (middle-class families were taking a more prominent role in child-rearing), schools could no longer simply rely on the loyalty of their alumni, especially now that wives had a greater say in deciding where their children should be educated. Exposed to unheated dormitories, compulsory rugby and two weekend leaves a term, the prospect didn't look very enticing and many opted for day schools instead.

With school rolls an ongoing concern, Westminster and Radley College broke new ground in 1979 by cooperating with the BBC in compiling film documentaries about their schools. For John Rae, a polished media performer, the decision to let in the cameras to raise Westminster's profile was a chance not to be missed, even though a number of his governors expressed severe misgivings, especially when it was explained to them that the BBC would retain editorial control over the film. His confidence was amply vindicated when the sixty-five minute documentary, watched by 12 million viewers, was shown in September 1979. Amid the many media plaudits, the *Daily Telegraph* called it the best PR for the independent schools since the Battle of Waterloo, with its focus on inspirational teaching, articulate pupils and a relaxed atmosphere.

The Radley experience was rather different. The warden, Dennis Silk, was in two minds about cooperating and only went along with the idea to dispel various myths about boarding schools. 'Besides what has Radley got to hide?' a friend assured him. Unlike Westminster, the Radley documentary was a laborious operation filmed over two terms and transmitted in ten thirty-minute instalments early in 1980. Such intrusiveness took quite a lot out of the school, but despite Silk's regret that some of the small change of boarding school life was given undue prominence, not least the rather indecorous house disco, the general verdict was positive. *The Times* called it the most intimate, detailed and objective account to date of the independent schools and applications to Radley soared.

The more benign climate of the 1980s, with its lower taxes, higher incomes for middle-class families – many wives were now working – and the assisted places scheme all helped the independent sector, as did the influx of first-generation parents, keen to give their children the best start in life. By 1989 there were record numbers opting for private education – some 7.2 per cent of the population – leading the headmaster of Tonbridge School, Christopher Everett, to confidently predict that that figure could rise to 10 per cent within another decade.

Accepting that much of their accommodation needed modernising and that a broader curriculum required new facilities, schools began vying with each other in the scale of their ambitions. New technology centres, sports halls and theatres became all the rage and staff numbers expanded rapidly to teach an ever-wider number of subjects such as drama, business studies and physical education (PE). The cost, though, had to be borne by higher school fees, which continued to rise way beyond the rate of inflation, a fact that raised siren voices among some. 'We run the greatest danger of pricing ourselves out of existence,' commented John Kendall-Carpenter, headmaster of Wellington School and chairman of the Boarding Schools Association, at their annual conference in May 1982.[1] He alleged that fees were being driven up needlessly because heads were competing with each other to offer vanity projects of dubious economic worth.

His warning was later echoed by Simon Langdale, headmaster of Shrewsbury School between 1980 and 1991, when he analysed the declining roll in boarding:

> Where so much attention is focused on 'market forces', it is strange that Governors of schools experiencing falling numbers have been reluctant to face up to the fundamental cause of this problem: which is that their product has quite simply become too expensive for a significant part of their market.[2]

Independent schools were the only business left in Britain that had not seriously reviewed what were easily their most important costs – staffing – in contrast to banking, farming and the armed forces, all of which were shedding labour. Langdale accepted that boarding schools were labour intensive, but why had staff numbers grown so much? Everyone, he concluded, was 'beguiled by the virtue of choice'. It was now the norm to offer a number of subjects taken by a minority of pupils. 'No-one seems to have faced up to the real costs of implementing this ideal.'[3]

Others to sound the tocsin were the management consultants Deloitte Haskins & Sells. It warned the independent sector in November 1984 that its survival was at stake if it didn't improve its management. Average fees had been rising at 15 per cent over the previous five years when inflation had been at 9 per cent. Operational costs should be kept under control, executive leadership should be based on clear managerial accountability and better links should be established with state schools in order to gain wider acceptance.

In an age of growing efficiency and cost-effectiveness, schools were slow to adapt to new market realities whether those be related to staff themselves or their employers. While some school governing bodies, such as those at Eton, Bedford and Radley, and smaller ones such as Trent College, Strathallan and the Royal School, Bath, demonstrated the height of professionalism, at best it was a very mixed picture. Too many governing bodies were narrow in composition and complacent in their approach. 'The extraordinary bumbling manner in which some independent school governing bodies conduct their affairs would bankrupt an industrial company in months,' John Rae told a gathering of prep school headmasters in September 1989.[4] Now that the management of schools had become increasingly business-focused, it was no longer appropriate to have a board of governors comprised overwhelmingly of old boys, bishops and local worthies detached from everyday life. Too often their selection of a head was a haphazard business and their treatment of staff, intentionally or not, appeared detached at best and condescending at worst.

In 1981 the boarding roll stood at 120,000, but while overall numbers rose by 8 per cent between 1984 and 1990, boarding fell by almost 10 per cent, a decline that ISIS admitted it couldn't explain other than in terms of its failure to counter outdated notions of boarding and a few cases of child abuse, although most of these had yet to come to light. The fact that many columnists and opinion formers in the media were precisely the very types to have suffered from the brutal philistinism of those establishments in times past merely added fuel to the fire; however, not only dissident voices were raised.

In 1983 Daphne Rae, wife of Westminster's headmaster, caused a rumpus with her semi-autobiography *A World Apart*, an irreverent account of life in single-sex schools. 'For those headmasters who ran remote and less fashionable establishments,' John Rae later wrote, 'it was infuriating that the Raes, so comfortably placed at Westminster, should rekindle parents' anxieties about what went on in boarding-schools.'[5]

In 1994 Tim Card's *Eton Renewed* disclosed that one of its former headmasters, Anthony Chenevix-Trench, had had such a predilection for corporal punishment that it contributed to his dismissal, unleashing a media frenzy on this sensitive topic. This was followed almost immediately by Jonathan Dimbleby's biography of Prince Charles and the revelation that he was bullied remorselessly at Gordonstoun, prompting the thought that if he was not safe at school, who was?

In 2000 Nick Duffell, a former privately educated psychotherapist and founder of the support group Boarding School Survivors, wrote *The Making of Them*, detailing the severe emotional damage that could result from boarding at a young age. Starved of parental love and deprived of privacy, children were forced to reinvent themselves to cope with the hardships of this alien world, especially the power of the peer group. This emotional detachment often prevented the formation of close relationships with family, friends and colleagues in later life, and proved a poor preparation for political leadership, the subject of his later book, *Wounded Leaders: British Elitism and the Entitlement Illusion*, in 2014.

Duffell's thesis stirred strong opinions on all sides, but there can be no denying the fact that his voice echoed those of a number of ex-boarders who felt traumatised by their experiences. On reflection the failure to tackle this culture of intimidation and fear must rank as the most shameful legacy of the old public school system.

The plight of the boarding school was exacerbated by the recession of the early 1990s, which, in contrast to the one a decade earlier, affected the prosperous South as small businesses and home owners wilted under high inflation and punitive interest rates. In 1991 the boarding roll suffered a 4 per cent decline from the previous year and in 1992 numbers fell below 100,000. 'Behind the figures, the breeze of competition is blowing harder than it ever did in the 1980s,' wrote Andrew Adonis, education correspondent of the *Financial Times*, 'fanned by the declining numbers of school-age children.'[6] Those particularly at risk were rural boarding schools in low catchment areas. According to John Rae:

> Once the pendulum had swung decisively in favour of academic success the less-academic boarding schools that had traded successfully under the banner of 'public school' were doomed. The snobbery that equated boarding school with public school and public school with good school cuts no ice with today's generation of parents.[7]

A number of these schools were girls' schools with numbers under 300 (and by no means all of them snooty). Ever since the drift to coeducation in the 1970s, they had voiced their disapproval of their pupils being poached, especially when the economic wellbeing of a boys' school was placed above the interests of the girls themselves. Yet, for all their justifiable consternation, it was an undeniable fact that many of these schools paled in comparison with those such as Charterhouse and Marlborough, and given the opportunity to switch for the sixth form, many girls jumped ship leaving their schools to list in recessionary storms.

While blue-blooded establishments such as Cranborne Chase School in Dorset, Oxenfoord Castle School, near Edinburgh, and St Michael's School, Petworth, were forced to close, St Anne's School, Windermere (now Windermere School) escaped the axe. Beset by shabby accommodation, declining numbers and a succession of heads, it was scheduled for closure in 1999, only to be rescued by a parent consortium. Led by a new professional board of governors and an experienced head of marketing, the school embarked on a major refurbishment programme and became coeducational as part of its road to recovery. Later it adopted the International Baccalaureate (IB) to help appeal to its large overseas market.

Another group to suffer was Catholic boarding schools now that their education comprising spartan facilities, wayward discipline and poor exam results no longer commanded the automatic loyalty of traditional Catholic families. With religious tribalism in rapid retreat, many of these families sent their children to Eton, Harrow and Radley, schools that went out of their way to accommodate Catholic worship. In 1991 Ampleforth, the smartest of the Catholic schools, finding itself fifty pupils short of its 620 capacity, made several lay teachers redundant and its abbot, Father Patrick Barry, warned that if present trends continued it could lead to the collapse of Catholic education.

Three years later, Belmont Abbey School, near Hereford, closed after 150 years, and in 1999 Douai School, founded in 1619, became the first HMC member to suffer this fate. Downside School was also in trouble, its roll having fallen from 600 in the 1960s to less than 300 in 1995. 'There was a certain arrogance and complacency among us,' headmaster, Dom Antony Sutch, later recalled. 'We thought Catholic parents would just go on sending their children here as they always had. But they leaked away, our reputation slumped and we were disappearing downhill.'[8]

With closure beckoning and morale at rock bottom, Sutch was amazed to survive his first year, admitting to sometimes needing a tot of whisky to keep going. Assuring everyone that Downside would survive, he nevertheless implemented some far-reaching changes: reducing staff numbers, admitting non-Catholic pupils, improving the facilities and making more lay appointments. By 2014 all the leading Catholic independent schools – Downside, Ampleforth, Stonyhurst, St Benedict's School, Worth and the Oratory – had lay headmasters, admitted girls and, in the case of Worth and the Oratory, Catholic pupils no longer comprised the majority.

With more parents prepared to switch between the two sectors, the 1990s recession forced other schools to take drastic action: Malvern College merged with Ellerslie Girls' High School and Hillstone Preparatory School to become coeducational; Rydal School in North Wales merged with the neighbouring girls' school, Penrhos College, to become Rydal Penrhos; Cheltenham College made staff redundant; Taunton School threatened to send debt collectors to those who defaulted on fees; while many others were amenable to those seeking discounts.

All schools felt compelled to promote themselves more vigorously, splashing out on market research to identify new markets and public relations consultants to raise their profile. Aside from the glossy new prospectuses, open days and organised tours, invariably conducted by the pupils themselves, there were ever-greater efforts to participate, albeit rather casually at first, in annual boarding school exhibitions organised by ISIS. Particularly important were the links with feeder schools, especially as many parents sought their advice regarding which secondary school they should consider for their children. Astute heads courted their prep school counterparts and treated them like royalty when hosting conferences or individual visits. The number of prep school headmasters invited to 'An Evening with Brian Johnston' (the celebrated BBC cricket commentator) at Loretto School in March 1989 was symptomatic of the headmaster Norman Drummond's success in filling his school to capacity.

Heads also took every opportunity to sit on prep school governing bodies and preach at their services. Bob Williams, a Rugby housemaster, recalls that there had been no marketing at the school before the arrival of Michael Mavor as headmaster in 1990. Thereafter Mavor sent his missionaries out to proselytise the prep schools with the message that Rugby had changed.

In October 1993 'One Big Happy Family', the first national report of boarding pupils based on an anonymous questionnaire organised by ISIS, found that 78 per cent of them were happy. Four years later, the Boarding Education Alliance launched the first concerted effort by a large group of boarding schools to change parental and public perceptions of modern boarding through a three-year PR campaign. Central to this campaign was its emphasis on the family atmosphere.

The Children Act 1989 had forced boarding schools to give due attention to improving comfort and privacy, as well as providing suitable adults with whom pupils could discuss their problems. Consequently, smaller, smarter dormitories with adequate space for personal possessions, heated bedsits for the older pupils, self-catering facilities and cheerful common rooms all appeared.

Many boarding schools expanded their day sector, often providing transport to and from neighbouring towns, as well as introducing weekly and flexi-boarding and providing taster weekends for those pupils contemplating boarding. Those schools which presented a friendly image and genuinely addressed the needs of the child were more likely to attract custom, especially as parents increasingly deferred to the wishes of their children in their choice of school.

Another major innovation was the establishment of prep schools, or a junior boarding house, to accommodate pupils from the age of eleven, since this was the age of transfer from primary to secondary level. Although these innovations proved unpopular with local prep schools, it made economic sense for senior schools and gave them greater control over their own destinies.

Despite the transformation of boarding schools throughout the 1990s, overall numbers continued to fall, not helped by cutbacks in the armed services, traditionally the bedrock of many a boarding school. By 1995 they had declined by 25 per cent over the previous five years and were it not for the growing overseas intake, then constituting some 20 per cent of the overall boarding roll, that fall would have been even more precipitous.

Given the falling demand at home, boarding schools increasingly went global in search of custom. The trend had first begun in the 1970s with an influx of students from Hong Kong, and now, with the end of the Cold War, the liberation of Eastern Europe from Soviet control and the gradual opening up of China to the West, potential new suitors were ready to be wooed.

Foremost among them were the new Chinese super-rich who had prospered with the relaxation of state controls and sought an elite British education for their children, as well as the opportunity to learn English, increasingly the language of international commerce. Study at a British boarding school would enhance the likelihood of attending British universities, where there had been a ten-fold increase in Chinese students during the previous decade.

The steady trickle that began in the 1990s became a deluge after 2006, so that by 2013 the number had risen to 4,000 pupils from mainland China. 'A lot of parents have a belief that the Chinese system is failing their children,' says Ian Hunt, managing director of Gabbitas, the education consultancy. 'It is too formalised, too narrow in perspective. The British system offers independent learning and leadership skills, creativity and problem solving, public speaking and debating.'[9] Even the communist elite weren't immune to the allure of a privileged British education, as evidenced by the decision of the disgraced party official Bo Xilai and his wife, Gu Kailai, convicted of murdering English businessman Neil Heywood in 2011, to send their son to Harrow. So desperate have some of the Chinese elite been to get their children into top schools that they have splashed out sums of up to £50,000 to British agencies, some of which have reciprocated with outdated or worthless advice.

For many schools the overseas contingent has become a lifeline. A classic example is Roedean, the exclusive girls' school on the edge of Brighton, where its once-healthy intake of 800 has roughly halved in recent years. Converting necessity into virtue, Frances King, headmistress between 2008 and 2013, flagged up the advantage of a strong international ethos in an increasingly global working environment yet, as she readily conceded, such a radical change in the school's culture disturbed some of her more traditional clientele:

> The danger is, Roedean has this name people think they know – an all-white, jolly hockey-sticks school. And these lovely parents from Wiltshire walk down the corridor and have the shock of their life. My students come from Brighton, from Hong Kong, from Nigeria, France, Wisconsin [in America] and [some parents] can't really cope with the reality of the school. Our intake is around 50 per cent international, 50 per cent British.[10]

Closer to home, the Germans have become attracted to British schools, not least their small classes and broader curriculum, at a time when its own educational system has declined following reunification in 1990. Leading the field were Sevenoaks, Malvern and Oakham, followed by Rossall, Charterhouse, Haileybury, Uppingham, Wellington, Ardingly, Bedford and Stowe, all of whom offer the IB.

Few schools have changed as much as Rossall, a traditional North of England boarding school near Blackpool. From a peak of 559 boys in 1977, numbers dropped quite substantially during the 1980s. In addition to the general decline in boarding and parents opting to educate their children

closer to home, with all that that entailed for schools in the sparsely popu-
lated North-west, Rossall faced fierce competition from many good local day
independent schools. Even the introduction of girls wasn't enough to halt the
exodus. Its salvation lay in overseas students. By 2010 they comprised 35 per
cent of the intake – with Germans, Chinese and Vietnamese each comprising
over thirty pupils each – and two-thirds of its boarding element. 'It is not a
school made up of "people like us",' commented then-headmaster Stephen
Winkley. 'It is very diverse and there's a globalistic outlook among students.
They mix with each other very well.'[11]

Russians have also been drawn here partly as a result of the quality of
education and partly the stability of the environment compared to the dark-
ening horizons back home. Although not all of them adapt to the communal
ethos of a British boarding school and the element of compulsion involved,
numbers have grown from 800 in 2007 to 2,150 in 2013.

Other nationalities include French, Spanish and Nigerians, and with the
onset of recession in 2008 and a weaker pound, schools have turned their
gaze to South Korea, Thailand and Japan to tout for business. With boarding
enrolments now at about 68,500 the overseas contingent at some 24,000, some
37 per cent, constitutes a crucial share of that market, but such a transformation hasn't been entirely painless, not least the need to constantly upgrade
accommodation to satisfy the expectations of the global super-rich, all of
which has helped push up fees. Schools with a large overseas contingent
make much of their cosmopolitan diversity, but the exemplary work ethos
displayed by the Asians in particular has sometimes been offset by the dif-
ficulties they have encountered in adapting to British boarding-school life
and the ghetto mentality it has bred. Keen not to dilute the British brand and
alienate their home base, some schools have placed a limit on the number of
overseas pupils they admit, often around 10 per cent. Others talk of similar
restrictions but have quietly flouted that limit when their finances dictate.

With the popularity of British independent education at an all-time high,
many schools have opened branches overseas to keep up with demand, especially among the wealthy Asian elite but also with expats reluctant to live
apart from their children. By 2014 there were thirty-nine of these franchise
schools educating some 22,500 pupils, a figure that is likely to grow as more
schools head eastwards.

In 1996 Dulwich College blazed a trail by founding an international school at Phuket in southern Thailand as a means of raising its profile in a part of the world where it had traditionally recruited, and of raising revenue to fund its ambitious bursary programme back home. (Prior to 1976 and the abolition of the direct grant, 85 per cent of places at the school were funded by local authority scholarships.)

Deriving its inspiration from Anand Panyarachun, former prime minister of Thailand, an old boy of Dulwich, and financed by Arthit Ourairat, a former minister, the school, built in the style of its counterpart in south-east London, catered mainly for the local population who wore the traditional Dulwich dark blue and grey uniform.

In partnership with the Saha Union, a Thai confederate specialising in nuclear power, which provided financial support, Dulwich provided educational expertise, overseeing major appointments, controlling the curriculum and organising regular inspections. The arrangement worked well at first but when a dispute occurred in 2005 concerning Dr Arthit's demand for more control over school operations and his dismissal of the headmaster, Dulwich withdrew its licence.

By then Dulwich had opened a second school, in Shanghai, the prelude to further schools in Beijing, Suzhou and Zhuhai. It had support from the Chinese government, keen to provide first-class schools for European businesspeople helping to oversee the country's stupendous economic growth (although Chinese law prevented their children under the age of sixteen attending international schools). Later it was to open schools in South Korea and Singapore.

Another pioneer in the East was Harrow. Drawing on its close links with the Thai royal family, it established an International School in Bangkok for over 1,000 pupils, all of whom sported the traditional Harrow boater. Its success encouraged it to open another franchise school in Beijing in 2005, and a third one in Hong Kong in 2012, with boarding facilities for 300 of its 1,200 pupils.

In response to an insatiable demand for a traditional British education, a number of other schools have moved eastwards to set up satellites: Wellington in China (Tianjin and Shanghai), Bromsgrove and Shrewsbury in Bangkok, Brighton (two schools) and Repton in Dubai, Cranleigh in Abu Dhabi, Sherborne in Qatar, NLCS in South Korea (Jeju), Ellesmere in Qatar, and Marlborough and Epsom in Malaysia.

Unlike Harrow and NLCS, few of these franchise schools offer boarding but otherwise they run on fairly similar lines: a separate management, coeducation from three to eighteen, lower fees than their British counterparts and predominantly a British staff teaching a predominantly British curriculum, leading to exams in either the International GCSE (IGCSE) and A-level or the IB.

One exception to these international schools operating in the Gulf States and the Far East is Haileybury, which on the back of its large Kazakh contingent, became the first British school to open two schools in the oil-rich Central Asian republic of Kazakhstan. With support from Capital Partners, a Kazakh property company, Haileybury Almaty opened in 2009 and, although the locals found it difficult to adapt at first to the high expectations of the school, the president, Nursultan Nazarbayev, was impressed enough to request a second offshoot in Astana, the new capital. It opened in September 2010, complete with state-of-the-art teaching facilities and the British house system, catering primarily for the expat community, in contrast to Almaty with its predominance of Kazakhs.

With many independent schools full to capacity, the last two decades could be seen as a golden age for the sector, but the rewards have been unevenly distributed, reflecting the fluctuating fortunes of an increasingly divided society.

For highly selective day schools in the South and a few others such as Newcastle Royal Grammar School (RGS) and Hymers College, Hull, with their combination of large catchment areas and lower fees, the numbers have grown ever greater. Equally impressive has been the expansion of leading boarding schools. Aside from their name, most of these schools, situated in the prosperous South and patronised by a more traditional clientele, have been less affected by the 2008–13 recession than the majority of the sector. Indeed, for many of these people, in work, well paid and the beneficiaries of lower taxation and interest rates, these years have been ones of plenty.

Although governing bodies have been criticised by some former headmasters such as Martin Stephen (St Paul's School) for being inexperienced and unaccountable, many have become more diverse in membership, proactive and better trained for the role. Fully alive to the importance of appointing the right head, boards often employ recruitment companies or take the advice of former heads to help find the right person, with the result that botched appointments are less apparent than hitherto.

Although boards comprise a substantial number of people who lead very busy lives, they tend to be better informed about the school, which helps them hold the head to account, a critical imperative now that schools are complex businesses with turnovers of millions of pounds.

With the financial side of school life ever more important, power within the governing body has shifted towards its executive committee, a group of chartered surveyors and accountants who oversee the school's capital development, in league with the bursar. Where possible, the school roll has been expanded, tighter financial management imposed (sometimes in a rather high-handed way) and the business developed by the letting out of facilities during the holidays.

Although some schools, such as Christ's Hospital, Eton and Winchester, boast large endowments, they are the exception rather than the rule, so that major capital development has either to be paid for out of fees or by one-off appeals.

By the 1990s one-off appeals were dying out as alumni became less responsive to constant requests for money, especially from professional fundraisers unconnected to the school. Taking a leaf out of the US fundraising tradition, an approach that British universities had emulated for some time, schools began setting up foundation/development offices either side of the millennium and appointed professional development officers to explore new ways of fundraising. One approach adopted by Millfield School has been its Leavers' Gift Scheme whereby leavers pledge to make regular annual donations – however large or small.

Crucial to the success of school development has been not only the lead provided by governors, heads and staff in promoting their development plan, but also the cultivation of a close relationship with alumni, encouraging them to get involved either by advising current pupils about possible careers or by giving generously.

To help tap into this philanthropic support, contact via a comprehensive database or social media has become more frequent and alumni associations more active, hosting events and keeping donors well informed of specific new projects. More important has been the ability to seek out potential wealthy donors and approach them in a sensitive manner, flagging up projects of particular interest to them. According to the accountancy firm Crowe Clark Whitehill, in 2011 twenty-four schools raised more than £1 million each and sixty-nine over £200,000 each.

Leading the way is Harrow with its permanent staff of nine under its astute director of development, Douglas Collins. Aware that much of the big money is overseas in places such as Russia and China, Collins is a constant visitor to these countries and rarely returns empty-handed. Thanks in large part to his ingenuity, the Harrow Development Trust has raised some £60 million over the last twelve years.

These additional resources have given leading schools the best of everything in an ever more competitive environment. With schools becoming more homogeneous in what they offer, publicity departments have tried hard to find that niche in the market which enables them to steal a march over their rivals. Some heads, such as Martin Stephen, Andrew Halls and Tim Hands, have been the public face of the independent sector as a result of their views on education; other schools have opened their doors to the television cameras, although unflattering documentaries of Gordonstoun (1996), Ampleforth (2003) and Glenalmond (2009) proved counter-productive.

Richard Morgan, warden of Radley, gained much publicity in 1994 with his intention to make the school bilingual in French, a shrewd marketing ploy that didn't come to anything, and Felicity Lusk's fashion shoot in the *Daily Telegraph* on becoming head of Abingdon School in 2010 raised the school's profile, especially in Hong Kong.

The onset of league tables in the early 1990s benefitted those schools with a strong academic ethos, especially in London where competition for places has become ever more frantic. According to Susan Hamlyn, director of *The Good Schools Guide Advice Service* in 2014:

> We hear every day from parents who don't want 'a hothouse' and want their children to 'have a childhood and be happy' but when we send them a list of schools that offer a broad curriculum and take a spread of ability, they ask us about 'results' and whether the school sends a good number to Oxbridge. Nothing will have parents pushing faster past the house staff, SMT [Senior Management Team] and even a fearsome PA to hammer on the head's polished door than a set of exam results down a notch from last year's.[12]

Other schools, such as Norwich, Magdalen College School, Oxford, and St Catherine's School, Bramley, have seen their numbers grow rapidly in line with their rise up the league tables.

The IB has been used by some schools to help recruit overseas students. Tim Woffenden, a teacher at Haileybury between 1990 and 2004, recalls Barbara Glasmacher, the doyenne among agents sending German students to Britain, telling a delegation from his school in 1999, 'You start the IB Diploma: you will have twenty-four students in September', a lifeline to a boarding school then struggling with empty beds.[13]

New plush sixth-form boarding houses at Blundell's and Fettes have boosted recruitment; the excellence of their pastoral care has done something similar for Bradfield and St Edward's School, Oxford; while Brighton's decision to introduce weekly boarding has paid off handsomely.

One interesting innovation has been the introduction of diamond schools, in which pupils are taught coeducationally in both the prep school and the sixth form but independently between the ages of eleven and sixteen. Led by Dame Allan's School, Newcastle upon Tyne, and Forest School (which educates separately in its prep school), King's School, Macclesfield, Berkhamsted School and the Stephen Perse Foundation are among those that have followed suit, their argument being that pupils get the best of both worlds: the opportunity to mix socially and culturally while being educated separately.

Other schools have looked to sporting prowess to cultivate favourable publicity. Merchiston Castle School's great success on the rugby field since the mid-1980s helped transform its fortunes; Reed's School and Loretto have benefitted from their establishment of tennis and golf academies, respectively; while Plymouth College enjoyed a late surge of applications in August 2012 following the success of two of its swim scholars in the London Olympics, Tom Daley and Ruta Meilutyte.

Sport, and rugby in particular, not only helped define Llandovery College, one of the leading schools in Wales, it helped it through its darkest hour. With falling numbers and debts running to £4 million, the school, a nursery for Welsh rugby internationals, was brought to the brink of closure in July 2012. What saved it was the formation of a new company with new financial backers and a new board of trustees consisting of former pupils and local businessmen, alongside the wholehearted support of the parents and staff.

With the economic recovery of the mid-1990s heralding a decade of prosperity, the independent sector once again began to expand. By 2000 numbers had risen for the fifth successive year and 2002 saw a slight upturn in boarding, the first for fifteen years. This was attributed partly to the success of J.K. Rowling's *Harry Potter* and his nocturnal adventures at Hogwarts School, and partly to the growing number of two parents in full-time work who, faced with long hours and the pressures of commuting, had opted for boarding to give their children the care they couldn't always provide at home. Ominously, though, the fee increase of 7.5 per cent for 2001–02 was the highest for eight years as boarding fees reached £20,000, and the next year the rise was 9.5 per cent, the highest ever in real terms, an unwelcome development exacerbated by allegations of price fixing by fifty leading schools in breach of the 1998 Competition Act.

Following the uncovering of private correspondence relating to school fees obtained from Winchester College's private files and the leak of this information to the *Sunday Times*, the Office of Fair Trading (OFT), the government competition regulator, began an investigation into allegations of a fee-fixing cartel at Eton, Winchester and Westminster in June 2003.

When confronted with the allegations, the ISC admitted that it was standard practice for bursars at these schools to exchange commercially sensitive information about costs and fees. Until March 2000, the date when the 1998 Competition Act came into effect, schools were exempt from competition law and were free to exchange such information. That exemption was then removed without a debate in Parliament and without their consultation. Once they learned of this illegality, they stopped the practice in May 2003 and that December agreed to a code of conduct to avoid any further allegations of fee fixing.

In March 2004 the OFT widened its inquiry, compelling sixty schools to supply it with new evidence including their correspondence on fees, much to the indignation of the ISC. In a letter to John Vickers, director general of the OFT, its chairman, Jean Scott, expressed concern about the protracted nature of the investigation and treatment of a number of schools. They weren't a group of businesses conspiring to fix prices to the detriment of the consumer, they were non-profit-making schools openly following a long-established practice, unaware that the law had changed.

In September 2005, after one of the most extensive investigations in the

OFT's history, the ISC was found provisionally guilty of running an illegal price-fixing cartel that had pushed up fees. The findings were challenged by the latter, claiming that the schools were being held liable for a change in the law without them being consulted.

With neither side keen on a lengthy and debilitating fight, a settlement was reached in March 2006: forty-nine of the fifty boarding schools acknowledged that their exchange of sensitive information between 2001 and 2004 had breached competition law and accepted a nominal penalty of £10,000 each, well below the combined total of £50 million they could have been forced to pay. The schools also agreed to make ex-gratia payments averaging £60,000 per school into a new charitable educational fund designed to benefit pupils who attended the schools during the period the cartel was in operation. Although the ISC could derive some satisfaction from the fact that they had got off lightly and that the OFT made no reference to the exchange of information having any effect on the fees, the whole affair had done little to enhance their reputation. According to the *Daily Telegraph*, the schools had behaved foolishly and badly:

> Their defence that nobody told them that the law affected them is dubious in the extreme. Their governors include some of the most prominent and informed members of the Establishment currently at large. Given that these schools are the last bastions of the classical education, it might have been supposed that someone would have recalled that *ignorantia legis non excusat* — ignorance of the law is no excuse.[14]

In May 2007, to mark Tony Blair's ten years in power, *The Times* devoted its lead story to the success of the independent sector under his government. Despite Labour's pledge to improve state education and the ending of the assisted places scheme, the sector had seen its numbers rise by 40,000, and while the paper attributed this partly to growing affluence it also put it down to continuing deficiencies in the state sector: 'Academic standards have risen, but state school heads now focus on academic results to the exclusion of virtually all other aspects of learning.'

'Some twenty-five years ago,' its editorial opined, 'public school headmasters lived in fear of a Labour election victory because the party had pledged to abolish independent education. After ten years of Tony

Blair, their successors must be praying that this Government is endlessly re-elected.'[15]

Not everyone agreed with this verdict. According to Alistair Cooke, general secretary of the ISC between 1997 and 2004, the Blair decade was a wasted opportunity for the independent sector. It had shown no interest in exploring ways of making itself more accessible, for example attempting to win substantial sponsorship so that places could be offered on a wider scale. More important, it had made little effort to curb its fees. Between 2001 and 2006 average school fees had risen by 39 per cent compared to 18 per cent in average earnings. According to a survey by Halifax Financial Services in 2007, only thirteen professions could afford private education compared to twenty-three in 2002.

In a later study for the stockbroker Killik and Co in 2014, the Centre for Economics and Business Research analysed data and average earnings over the previous twenty-four years. Fees for private day schools had increased from £2,985 in 1990 to £12,700 in 2014, while fees for boarding schools over the same period had soared from £6,800 to £28,000.

Overall, fees had shot up by more than 300 per cent while wages had risen by just 76 per cent. Given this fourfold increase in fees, it follows that the type of family that could afford them had changed drastically. In 1990 average day fees and extras for one child would have accounted for 19 per cent of the average doctor's salary, 30 per cent of the academic's and 29 per cent of the accountant's. By 2014 those fees had risen to 36 per cent of a doctor's salary, 51 per cent of an academic's and 59 per cent of an accountant's.

With private education becoming increasingly unaffordable for the professional middle classes, the effects were to be felt in those institutions that had been struggling for some time. Ever since entering the independent sector many of the former direct grant schools in the Midlands and North, in contrast to their counterparts in the South, had struggled with recruitment. Many relied on the assisted places scheme (30–40 per cent of pupils were on bursaries in over fifty schools) but once the scheme was phased out they were left to their own devices. Severely under-capitalised, their attempts to upgrade their facilities to keep pace with the boarding schools and provide means-tested bursaries out of fee income led to significantly higher fees.

Given the squeeze on middle income families, these parents have become more wary of committing themselves to independent education, especially when they no longer see it as an automatic passport to a glittering future. Not only that, the establishment of private school chains such as Gems and Cognita offering a low-fee education, and the improvements in state education, not least sixth form colleges providing good A-level results, have given them viable alternatives.

In 2007 the Belvedere School in Liverpool and William Hulme's Grammar School in Manchester, two historic fee-paying schools serving inner-city communities, faced with ever-falling rolls, chose to become state-funded academies. The next year Colston's Girls' School and Bristol Cathedral School followed suit, their plight as much due to the surfeit of independent schools in Bristol as to the stagnation of the local economy. Thereafter the repercussions of the credit crunch and the Coalition government's financial cutbacks, which particularly affected public sector jobs and wages in the Midlands and the North, made a bad situation even worse. According to John Claughton, chief master of KESB, competition in his area and elsewhere has been intense:

> It's more vicious now for Manchester Grammar. I'm a governor there, and MGS and KES have suffered very similar fates. It's got colder, it's got hard to get bright kids in, the grammar schools have improved, people haven't got the money to send their children to independent schools.[16]

By 2014 twenty independent schools had opted to become academies or free schools, the former including Liverpool College, one of the founding members of the HMC, the latter including Bradford Girls' Grammar School and Queen Elizabeth's Grammar School, Blackburn. St Mary's College, Crosby, the Catholic school that educated Cardinal Vincent Nichols, attempted to do likewise in order to reconnect with the local community, but the Archdiocese of Liverpool refused to back its application because of the government's decision to impose a 50 per cent cap on the number of pupils admitted to free schools on the basis of their faith.

Traditional boarding schools of the smaller variety, especially girls' schools, with their inability to make economies of scale compared to their larger rivals, have continued to struggle. In 2002 Gordonstoun acquired the ailing North Foreland Lodge in Hampshire, the alma mater of Princess Alexandra and Queen Margrethe of Denmark, and planned to open a joint prep school to give it a base in the South. That never happened because, within little over a year, it had controversially sold North Foreland at a profit, contending that its financial position was so parlous it felt unable to give a long-term guarantee about the school.

Three years later, Bedgebury School in Kent closed, St Mary's School, Wantage merged with Heathfield School and Malvern Girls' College merged with neighbouring St James' School to become Malvern St James, all victims of falling rolls.

Another casualty was the high-achieving Alice Ottley School, forced to merge with the coeducational Royal Grammar School Worcester next door. 'I am a great believer in the benefits of single-sex education for girls,' headmistress Morag Chapman told Isabel Berwick of the *Financial Times*. 'But the principle of single-sex schools is coming low down after convenience for many families – they want one carol service, the same term dates, and they want to drop their children off at the same place. More and more families have both parents working and they need that convenience.'[17]

A particularly acrimonious merger took place in 2013 between Sedbergh, a traditional Northern boys' school for most of its history, and the culturally refined Casterton, a girls' school that counted the three Brontë sisters among its former pupils. In a part of the world where all boarding schools have struggled over recent decades, Sedbergh's decision to become coeducational in 2001 proved judicious but its gain was very much at the expense of its neighbour, Casterton. Between 2011 and 2013 the latter's numbers dropped by 25 per cent, causing a 14 per cent decline in income, a serious loss for a small school.

With Sedbergh looking to expand, including its junior school, and Casterton in retreat, the two governing bodies agreed to a merger, much to the fury of the Casterton parents, not least because of the failure of their board to consult them. Convinced that a new board and some energetic marketing could save the school, a group of disaffected parents called on the existing board to resign and took legal advice regarding seeking a High Court injunction to stop the merger. Foiled in their efforts, the parents were forced to back down and the girls paid an emotional farewell to their school in July 2013 before the merger went ahead. Forty-five of Casterton's remaining 123 girls transferred to Sedbergh that September, along with some of its staff, while Sedbergh relocated its junior school to Casterton.

Economic circumstances have forced other independent schools to make hard choices. Back in 2007 Leeds Girls' High School merged with neighbouring Leeds Grammar School, a boys' school, to become The Grammar School at Leeds, although teaching between the ages of fourteen and sixteen remains separate; in 2012 Bedford High School for Girls took a similar step with Dame Alice Harpur School becoming Bedford Girls' School, as did two neighbouring girls' schools, Central Newcastle High School and Newcastle upon Tyne Church High School to become Newcastle High School. Most fraught of all was the merger between Arnold School, Blackpool, and King Edward VII and Queen Mary School, Lytham St Annes, a decision that riled both sets of parents and which led to the headmaster of Arnold being assaulted at his home.

It is true that the decline of enrolments between 2009 and 2013 was only half that of the 1990s recession, but with the cost of a boarding school education rising above the average wage of £26,500 for the first time in 2013, the outlook for a number schools remains uncertain. In March 2015 St Bees, a coeducational boarding school in Cumbria, founded in 1583 by Edmund Grindal, Archbishop of Canterbury, signalled its intention to close at the end of the academic year because of dwindling numbers, a devastating blow not only to the staff and pupils but also to the local community.

In 2009 a report by Gavin Humphries, a market analyst for MTM Consulting, an advisory service for private schools, estimated that 190,000 pupils – some 30 per cent of those educated privately – would be priced out of the market over the next twenty years unless schools made drastic cutbacks such as increasing class sizes or stopping the teaching of minority subjects. Costs were being driven up by capital expenditure and investment in more teachers – up 50 per cent in real terms since 1981 as the teacher–pupil ratio fell from 12.6 to 8.3 in 2009 – although Humphries doubted whether the quality of education had improved by an equivalent 50 per cent over the same period.

'For too long we have all been guilty of trying to outdo each other with ever improving facilities,' admitted Patrick Derham, then headmaster of Rugby, in the *Daily Telegraph*.[18] 'Years ago, when my last child left boarding school, we couldn't help but notice that his room at school was actually rather more luxurious than the one he had at home,' recalled Martin Stephen in an article warning that the independent sector was becoming increasingly exclusive, just like in Victorian times.[19] Another to bemoan the growing cost of private education was the freelance writer Stephen Robinson, an alumnus of Westminster, forced to ponder his family's declining economic mobility. 'The truly annoying aspect of this is that there is absolutely no need for private school fees to be so astronomically expensive,' he wrote in the *Spectator* in May 2012. He continued:

> These schools offered first-class teaching long before they decided they must pamper their pupils, and impress the parents, with pointless drama centres and music blocks.
>
> And it has been a vicious circle. The more the schools try to appeal to the global superrich, the more the fees go up, so fewer of the native middle class can go, and the schools become even more dependent on Chinese and Russian oligarchs and criminals.[20]

In his recent book, *Lifting Our Heads*, Alex McGrath, headmaster of The King's School, Ely, argues that, at a time of fragile market confidence and greater competition from the state sector, a number of independent schools need to provide better value for money. Aside from getting more out of less committed teachers, he highlights the cost of having so many promoted posts and the growth of senior management teams. 'Senior managers spend huge amounts of time in meetings while being paid more than anyone else in the school. If that time is spent ineffectually, we are wasting money,' he concludes.[21] He also thinks that expenditure on advertising, computer equipment and contracting out services has lacked rigorous scrutiny: 'Looking at ourselves with honesty, we have been far too profligate, and we have wasted money in the past. We are also spending far too much on goods and services.'[22] If fees continue to rocket, as they have done over the previous two decades, the independent sector will be gravely weakened, he predicts. Affordability is the biggest single challenge it faces.

With the economy beginning to pick up, the annual Census of ISC Schools in 2014 reported 511,928 pupils – more than attended these schools in 2008 before the economic downturn. The revival isn't universal, however, for while London has seen a rise of 14 per cent in places since 2007, and the South-east and East Anglia by slightly over 3 per cent, the North has declined by 12 per cent during that same period. Whether that decline can be reversed depends to some extent on the fortunes of the regional economies but also on the ability of the sector to convince potential clients that it is providing value for money.

For all the genuine austerity, MTM Consulting has estimated that there are still some 1 million households able to afford private education but which have chosen to resist its blandishments owing to a mixture of ideological hostility, a satisfaction with the state sector and a perception that independent schools are alien territory to those who were educated elsewhere. 'A lot of prospective parents are rather wary about coming to see me,' Pat Langham, headmistress of Wakefield High School for Girls, told the *Telegraph* in 2008. 'They're afraid I'm going to have a plummy accent, or will expect them to curtsey or something. The fact is that I was brought up on a large council estate and didn't have any advantages other than being lucky enough to get into a good grammar school.'[23]

In an environment in which a private education no longer guarantees secure employment – although it helps – the independent sector is struggling to persuade potential clients that they offer value for money. According to John Fern, deputy head of KESB, a generational change has occurred among those parents who became wealthy during the 1990s. Unwilling to give up their comfortable lifestyle and foreign holidays, they will only go private when they can't obtain a satisfactory education in the state sector.

A similar trend can be detected in parts of Scotland. In East Renfrew, an affluent commuting district to the west of Glasgow, the excellence of its state schools led to a decline in those going private from 11 to 1.5 per cent in the decade before 2008. Not surprisingly, such a trend has caused vacancies in Glasgow's independent sector in contrast to schools in Perthshire such as Morrison's Academy, Kilgraston and Strathallan, which have benefitted from the indifferent reputation of local state schools.

Despite constant Mori polls since the 1980s showing that over 40 per cent of independent school parents are first-time buyers and repeated claims from the schools that they have changed out of all recognition, the image of a cloistered elite still persists. With an Old Etonian prime minister spawning many a cartoon alluding to his privileged education, and with many a story relating to private education accompanied by photos of tail-coated Etonians watching the Wall Game, it is easy to see why. While many in the independent sector, especially the former direct grant schools, resent this image, others are more philosophical, accepting that they are privileged and that they need to improve their communication with potential first-time buyers. According to Janette Wallis, senior editor of *The Good Schools Guide*, the one message that emerged from its 2014 edition was that too many admissions offices remain tight-lipped and inaccessible. 'I am hard pushed to think of any business that more rarely monitors or checks how their front-line staff are behaving,' commented Fiona Robinson, a senior *Good Schools Guide* consultant.[24]

Of the 284,000 households that visited an independent school but chose not to enrol, MTM found that, while the vast majority were greatly impressed by the facilities and atmosphere, they were less taken by the staff's ability to appreciate their particular concerns, not least value for money and whether their children would fit in. In order to win over nearly half of those 284,000 potential clients, MTM suggest that schools should make a greater effort to relate to the children, showing how their interests and aptitudes could flourish there. That said, word of mouth remains the best possible means of recruitment and, as Eton's Eric Anderson used to say to prospective heads: 'Run a good school and the rest will look after itself.'

Chapter 3

THE UNEASY PARTNERSHIP

When Richard Rhodes became headmaster of Rossall in 1987, tasked with expanding its roll, his reference to customers made little impact on his insular common room, apparently blind to the consumer revolution of the 1980s and the rise of parent power.

It had long been the tradition that parents and school had minimum contact with each other save for a few polite words with the housemaster on speech day. End-of-term reports would provide the most reliable indicator of a pupil's progress, but details about their inner life remained unknown and unsaid. In an age when communication was much less sophisticated, pupils, especially boys, volunteered little information to their parents, while the latter happily deferred to the school in the education of their children. That was how many schools preferred it. 'You were my ideal parent,' Malcolm Thyne, headmaster of Fettes between 1988 and 1998, told the clerk to the governors, Alasdair Fox. When Fox inquired why, Thyne replied, 'Because you always wanted the school to deal with any problem.'[1]

On his departure from Eton in 1963, the headmaster, Robert Birley, thanked his housemasters for keeping the parents away from him, and certainly many a school continued to view them as a mixed blessing. The novelist Jonathan Smith recalls that when he taught at Loretto during the 1960s there were no parents' evenings:

If any fool in the staff room ever suggested we should have them the usual response was 'Parents? Who the hell wants parents? What's it got to do with them? This is a private matter between the pupils and us. The next thing we'll have is the parents picking the teams.'[2]

Even when parents' evenings became the norm during the 1980s, the more aloof members of the common room rather resented them, not least the assumption that their professionalism was being questioned by ignorant outsiders. As a result they could be rather brusque in their approach.

By the 1970s greater affluence had bred more consumer choice and its relative absence in education persuaded the 1974–76 Wilson government to offer more consultation. It established the Taylor committee, which recommended parent governors, a recommendation accepted by the Thatcher government as part of its drive to make state schools more publicly accountable. With the independent sector susceptible to market forces, it too would have to respond to growing parent power, especially those financiers and self-made businesspeople new to private education.

With their meritocratic, materialistic outlook, these parents looked for a substantial return on their investment and weren't afraid to voice their disquiet when schools failed to deliver on the inflated claims they made in their promotional literature. Shoddy accommodation, bad food, compulsory rugby, lack of choice over subject options and poor exam results became familiar grievances. Teachers, once figures of great authority, had begun to lose their mystique, victims of 1960s iconoclasm and their own shortcomings. Aside from a growing concern about standards and discipline in many schools, teacher militancy in the late 1970s and 1980s had lost them public support. Some of these shortcomings were manifest in the independent sector and, as exam results assumed an ever-greater importance, those who fell short in the classroom became the object of parental disillusion. Even the more gifted teachers who taunted and repeatedly criticised pupils were singled out for their insensitive approach. Encouragement not carping was the new credo.

Gradually, as consumer power became ever greater – several heads were forced out primarily as a result of parental dissatisfaction during the early 1990s – schools latched on to the fact that parents needed more sensitive handling. Many had made great sacrifices on behalf of their children's education and were entitled to feel aggrieved when they weren't getting value for money. Yet too often schools either failed to inform parents if their child was floundering or brushed aside their concerns, attributing a lack of progress to pupil deficiencies, thereby absolving themselves of all responsibility.

More savvy heads, far from ignoring their parents, appreciated they were the school's most priceless asset and embraced them with open arms. Part of Dennis Silk's great success at Radley could be attributed to the excellent relationship he had with his parents, especially the mothers. He repeatedly sought their cooperation in his efforts to improve the boys' appearance and prevent them from drinking and smoking during the holidays, an appeal that sometimes fell on deaf ears.

Ian Beer, headmaster of Harrow between 1981 and 1991, was another who valued a close rapport with his parents. In his memoirs he recalled the suspicion of several of his housemasters when, on arriving at Harrow, he expressed his desire to address the parents of the new boys on their first day. He told his housemasters it was his business to get to know them, and following this innovation he instituted regular parents' meetings with the staff.

Other schools did the same and, with the falling rolls of the early 1990s illustrating the importance of consumer power, all heads awoke to the new reality. 'One thing is certain: in schools, parents are in,' wrote Jonathan Smith after thirty-three years teaching at Tonbridge, in 2000. He continued:

> In the independent sector in particular, where the mothers are inspecting every room and the parents have the buying power, the generic term 'Parents' is now quoted endlessly by heads. Far from being irrelevant, in these pupil-poaching days parents are The Big Issue. Parents are what it's all about. 'It won't go down well with the parents,' we're told. 'Parents expect nothing less,' we're told. 'Tell that to the parents,' comes the sharp reply.[3]

Now that most parents live closer to their children's schools and regularly attend matches, concerts and plays, schools are more hospitable than they used to be, laying on match teas and drinks at evening events. They have also become more adept at liaising with parents through frequent newsletters, questionnaires and website updates, as well as meetings to discuss subject choices, universities and careers. Some schools, especially London day schools, have responded to parental concerns about contemporary youth culture by organising seminars on matters such as parties, drugs and social media. Ann Butler, a former housemistress at St Edward's School, Oxford, recalls the great value of pastoral evenings there where parents, house staff and tutors would tackle case studies in small groups: 'It really helped communication and meant you could gently educate the parents who needed it, identify the ones who might overreact and so on. It made those difficult phone calls much easier.'[4]

In addition to written communication, schools, especially their senior staff, now spend much time responding to parental telephone calls and emails or meeting them in person to discuss their child's progress. Parents in turn have reciprocated by helping out with school trips and work experience, raising money and acting as the school's greatest cheerleaders on social media. Some have joined the governing body, although heads don't always appreciate this development as parent governors tend to pursue their own agenda.

While some teachers remain insufficiently receptive to parental needs, the fault isn't all on one side. Some parents can be patronising in their approach – 'the super-wealthy treat you as a member of their staff,' complained one housemistress – and intent on getting their own way. 'Parents who tried to pressurize me into pulling strings at Oxford and Cambridge got short shrift and did not like it,' recounted John Rae.[5] He admitted that if he gave an inch, the parents took a yard. Other heads have discovered that the choice of school prefects, lead roles in the school play and captains of the top teams has become much more contentious as a more competitive world has bred a more grasping, self-absorbed type.

In 2001, at a time when some school speech days were becoming tainted by vulgar displays of opulence, John Lewis, the then headmaster of Eton, wrote to his parents to advise them that the school's annual Fourth of June celebration was a private function for Eton boys and their families, rather than an occasion for corporate hospitality in elaborate marquees erected by commercial contractors.

Even before the current frantic scramble for places at London's top schools, the novelist Celia Brayfield noted how girls would be given a pony by their mothers for passing the entrance exam to St Paul's Girls' School, her old school. Now, the entire social life of some London parents is consumed by getting their children into the school of their choice. Against the advice of many prep schools, they increasingly rely on private tutors to cram their children with additional facts from the earliest of ages, in between whisking them from one organised activity to the next.

This relentless parental focus on private tuition is repeated right up to A-level, in addition to accompanying their children to university open days, overseeing their written applications and lobbying universities to get them in. 'I've had parents in my study who've said, "I want my daughter to go to Cambridge to study architecture,"' commented Jo Heywood, headmistress of Heathfield School. 'And I've turned to them and said, "Lovely – but what does your daughter want?"'[6]

According to Richard Harman, headmaster of Uppingham School, parents need to stop pressurising children or risk damaging them in later life. He accepted that exam scores were important but the hothouse atmosphere and the paranoia it created could be damaging:

> Instead of focusing on results, schools and parents must help children handle failure, develop different strengths and become resilient people who can make relationships with others, because that is what brings proper happiness and success.[7]

With this growing demand for success, schools have had to face more parental intervention, querying exam grade predictions, demanding special needs provision and seeking more individual attention for their children. Where teaching standards are still not up to the mark, parental frustration is understandable and most schools do try to resolve such problems in a tactful manner. Few would be quite as direct as Hugh Woodcock, former headmaster of Dulwich College Preparatory School, who, when berated by a mother about an uncomplimentary remark in her son's report, turned to the boy and said very quietly, 'Take your mother home, Edward, before I say something I might regret.'[8]

This intense one-upmanship has extended to the sports arena, where ambitious parents are driving their children toward sporting careers through additional training and fixtures. 'Too often I have had a promising young tennis player come to Repton aged thirteen whose parents are determined that he or she should play nothing else other than tennis in order to stand a chance of breaking through to the senior ranks,' commented former headmaster Robert Holroyd. 'The reality is that there are very few thirteen-year-olds who are truly good enough to warrant that level of specialisation at such an early age.'[9]

These competitive instincts manifest themselves on the touchline where the shouting and screaming of some fathers, anxious to relive their own schooldays, has led to occasional magisterial missives appealing for greater restraint at matches. Wycombe Abbey discontinued the parents' race at the school sports day because one father overdid it and had a heart scare, while the restaurateur Christopher Gilmour described the parent–daughter netball match at Downe House as unbelievable. 'Because I am big, I try not to bump into people, but I was surprised at the number of aggressive mothers and fathers who bumped into me,' he said.[10]

A particular bone of contention has been discipline. It would be wrong to suggest that the traffic has been entirely one way. Back in the 1980s in particular, parents blamed feeble housemasters for their lax discipline and laissez-faire attitudes for an insufficient work ethos and for misdemeanours that went undetected, but, increasingly, schools have found parents to be unreliable allies in the maintenance of standards. As children of the 1960s, a decade in which traditional values, including parental authority, were questioned, their attitude towards parenting has become much more informal and indulgent than their own upbringing. Their children are given more money, allowed to stay up later and talk back in a way that would never have been previously countenanced. Not only that. Some parents have adopted a more relaxed attitude to smoking, drinking and teenage sex and are trusting enough to give their children carte blanche to entertain their friends at home when they are elsewhere, with all too predictable consequences. When Patrick Tobin, principal of Daniel Stewart's and Melville College, Edinburgh, between 1989 and 2000, wrote to his pupils' parents asking them to ensure there was always an adult present when staging teenage parties following several notorious incidents, he was accused of interfering in matters outside his ken.

Vivian Anthony, secretary of the HMC and a former headmaster, wrote in *The Times* in February 1994:

In all these matters, schools are expected to maintain standards that others in society have abandoned. The time is ripe for a new Parents' Charter, one which stresses parents' responsibilities and the importance of their support for the school. Discipline cannot be maintained if parents appeal against every decision.[11]

Believing that their emotional closeness to their children guarantees them special access to their inner feelings, parents invariably accept their version of events when in conflict with the official line. Consequently, schools have had to become more meticulous in their disciplinary investigations, recording every incident, while ensuring that their procedures don't overstep the mark.

In face of this parental ambivalence towards disciplinary sanctions, schools that have kept serious punishments 'in house' have been less likely to court controversy. Part of the opposition to suspension has been the inconvenience inflicted upon parents as a result of having their children at home at short notice. Some have given no quarter while others have proved more understanding, which rather undermines the principle that punishments should be applied on an equitable basis.

Concern about parental double standards became ever more pronounced as time went on. In 1998 Patrick Tobin, when chairman of the HMC, told his colleagues that marital breakup was more serious than drugs and drink. 'It is the parents' generation that has the problems. They don't know where they stand on many issues,' he said.[12] Serious disciplinary problems could be traced back to divided homes.

Five years later, one of his successors, Graham Able, master of Dulwich, touched on this theme, berating the selfishness of divorced parents. 'It would be refreshing if society and the legal system concentrated more on the duties of parents to their children rather than their rights to self-gratification no matter what the cost to others,' he opined. The need for high-quality pastoral care in schools, he declared, had never been greater.[13]

He was followed by Mary Steel, headmistress of Abbots Bromley School for Girls and chairman of the GSA. She told its conference that year that many more parents were prepared to lie to get their children out of school commitments. A growing number paid lip service to independent school values and codes of discipline but were unwilling to live by them or instil them in their daughters. To nods of approval she said, 'An increasing number of our parents seem to see the issue of values as marginal and irrelevant, and that is where they seem to come from a different culture and actually from a different planet.'[14]

According to Martin Stephen, high master of St Paul's between 2004 and 2011, parents experience much more stress now as a result of working long hours and dysfunctional marriages, and they atone for any guilt they feel about neglecting their children by protecting them at all costs, which doesn't allow them to face up to the consequences of their actions. In 2006 a Marlborough parent who sued the school for expelling his child because of a notorious disciplinary record lost his case, the judge ruling that a private school had the right to turn customers away. Nevertheless, the growing threat of litigation, especially in cases of serious discipline, has made schools extremely wary of unduly alienating the rich and the powerful, sometimes to the detriment of their staff.

In a recent survey in *Attain*, the official magazine of the Independent Association of Preparatory Schools, the vast majority of heads named unreal parental expectations as the greatest frustration of the job. In a speech to the annual conference of the Boarding Schools Association in May 2010, Tony Little, headmaster of Eton, declared that the pressure parents placed on schools was little short of harassment, forcing some heads to resort to short-term solutions. These solutions could lead to longer-term problems, such as a greater preoccupation with exam grades or, in some cases, distorting disciplinary processes for a quiet life. According to Little:

> Our parents are indeed our customers, but they are buying into a distinctive philosophy of education; that is our strength. We should not be a pick-and-mix counter of unrelated choices. These days boarding schools are highly professional institutions; parents are paying us for our professional expertise. We should not hold back from telling them so.[15]

Yet for all their demands there can be no doubt that higher parental expectations have helped to drive up standards within the independent sector, primarily in the academic sphere but also in relation to facilities, accommodation, catering, sporting opportunities and better pastoral care. John Rae spoke for many when he admitted that parental complaints about incompetent teachers had helped him remove some of these types and, in more recent times, many a head has learned to be more ruthless in the interest of the pupils. According to Jill Berry, headmistress of Dame Alice Harpur School, Bedford, between 2000 and 2010, the vast majority of parents were supportive and even the demanding ones were usually motivated by a love of their children, a trait she thought preferable to those parents who were disengaged.

Similar sentiments were expressed by Bernice McCabe, headmistress of NLCS, who chides her staff when they complain about unrealistic parental expectations, telling them that she feels flattered that such types have chosen their school for their daughters. She says,

> I'm really sympathetic to parents who are incredibly aspirational for their children because I can see this in Korea [NLCS has a franchise school there]. That's why the Korean economy is so successful; that's why educational attainment is so high there.[16]

Others also have positive memories. Michael Meredith, an Eton housemaster during the 1980s and early 1990s, agreed with his parents that they could ring him at any time provided he could reciprocate, an arrangement that suited both parties.

Tony Beadles, ex-headmaster of King's School, Bruton, well aware that parents were his best recruiting officers, encouraged them to become more involved in the school and he forged a number of enduring friendships with them. Colin Niven and Norman Drummond viewed their respective headmasterships of Alleyn's School and Loretto in a similar light, grateful for the support they received from their parents, not least in the latter's case at Sunday chapel.

John Wright, a Glenalmond housemaster of nineteen years' standing, was astonished how much parents would share with him and, while he found them to be more demanding than had been the case, they were also understanding and appreciative.

At St George's School for Girls in Edinburgh, Judith McClure, headmistress between 1994 and 2009, tried to balance the total dedication of the parents with the broader interests of the school but overall felt that 'engaging with parents if you get it right is wonderful'.[17] According to Ian Davenport, ex-headmaster of Blundell's School, parents now have a greater understanding of the complexities of the school and their intervention worked to the benefit of both. 'In seven years, I have only been involved in one formal complaint or appeal of any kind with a parent,' commented John Claughton, chief master at KESB. 'I think our parents are more forgiving than down south: the litigious world hasn't come to us.'[18]

'We are unafraid of parents,' declared Cameron Wyllie,[19] head of George Heriot's senior school in Edinburgh, reflecting an obvious truth that if school and parents work together, the child will be the beneficiary.

Chapter 4

PRIMUS INTER PARES?

'The head is an autocrat whether he likes it or not,' wrote John Rae in his book, *Letters From School*, 'and if he does not like it he had better find another job. There are checks on his power but they are only as effective as he allows them to be.'[1]

In line with Herbert Asquith's famous remark that the power of the prime minister depended on the individual, Rae contended that a headmaster's power derived more from the force of his personality than the letter of the law.

In his *Anatomy of Britain*, written some two decades earlier, in 1962, the writer and journalist Anthony Sampson described the headmasters of leading independent schools as,

> awesome and formidable men, ... wielding immense power, maintaining exact if sometimes irrelevant standards ... figures of massive integrity and moral uprightness: a divorced headmaster is unimaginable. Their way of life combines monasticism with worldly ambition.[2]

Although their styles of leadership might differ considerably, most headmasters conformed to Sampson's description. Invariably sons of teachers, civil servants or clergy, they were scholars or sporting bloods, sometimes both, and dedicated themselves to their school as teacher, preacher, administrator and disciplinarian. With governing bodies, for the most part, non-interfering, common rooms reasonably placid and parents deferential, the restraints on their power were few, although the dismissals of Donald Crichton-Miller from Stowe in 1963, Anthony Chenevix-Trench from Eton in 1970 and David Emms from Sherborne in 1974 showed that no one was indispensable.

The 1980s and early 1990s saw the last of these old-style headmasters, a number of whom enhanced the reputation of their schools, such as David McMurray at Oundle, Martin Marriott at Canford and David Spawforth at Merchiston. Being a loosely knit federation of schools by the very nature of their independence, no one headmaster could claim to have dominated the HMC, but in terms of seniority, profile and charisma four stood out.

Perhaps the most admired headmaster of his generation, alongside Eric Anderson, was Dennis Silk, warden of Radley for a remarkable twenty-three years. Son of a medical missionary, Silk was an outstanding sportsman at Christ's Hospital and Cambridge, winning blues in both rugby and cricket. After learning his trade at Marlborough, where he became a housemaster, Silk was appointed warden of Radley in 1968 and turned a provincial back-water into the toast of the Home Counties.

Inheriting a school with ailing finances, lax discipline and a troublesome common room, the new warden soon made his mark by removing those boys unwilling to conform to his standards. Uncommitted colleagues were also sent on their way as Silk, in his determination to turn Radley into a family school, scoured Oxbridge common rooms for talented schoolmasters willing to give their all to the boys. In no time he assembled a formidable team, so much so that many of them went on to become distinguished head-masters in their own right, such as Chris Brown (Norwich), Peter Johnson (Millfield) and Michael Spens (Fettes).

Besides nurturing and encouraging his staff, Silk made a point of getting to know all the boys, often stopping them around campus and compliment-ing them on some accomplishment he had noted. Keen that they acquired the 'right habits for life', he went to great lengths to ensure that standards were maintained. Suzanne Farr, headmistress of Downe House between 1978 and 1989, recalled him ringing her on the day her school was entertaining a party of Radley boys for dinner. 'I have just had a look at the list of boys coming to Downe, and some young gentlemen on it wouldn't have been my first choice ... I think I shall come,' he said.[3]

A man of immense charm and courtesy, Silk developed an excellent rap-port with prep schools, but although a traditionalist himself he knew that Radley must modernise to enhance its appeal. Liaising with his great friend,

Micky Jones, the doyen of bursars, he gave over much time to fundraising and oversaw a transformation of the school's infrastructure, including the building of a new science block, arts centre and sports complex.

Although rather narrow in scope compared to an establishment such as Marlborough, the quality of Radley's all-round education persuaded parents to enrol in large numbers, their faith in Silk's alchemist touch rarely disappointed. By the time he left in 1991, the school had a twelve-year waiting list.

Another Cambridge rugby blue to make a difference was Ian Beer. Joining Marlborough on the same day as his close friend Silk, Beer followed successful headmasterships of Ellesmere College and Lancing College with his appointment to Harrow in 1981. A magnetic figure lacking nothing in self-confidence, he combined a robust muscular Christianity with a shrewd understanding of modern marketing as he roused Harrow from its slumber and trumpeted its many accomplishments. Although these accomplishments were less concrete than the image suggested, not least its indifferent academic record, Beer helped modernise the school's facilities and restore its reputation with its feeder schools. After his retirement from Harrow, Beer became chairman of the ISC and helped steer it through the turbulent waters of the 1990s as schools came under much greater scrutiny.

Even in death John Rae remains something of a divisive figure to many in the independent sector because of his apparent antipathy to much of what it stood for, in contrast to his sedulous promotion of Westminster.

For all his concern regarding social division, Rae loved the grandeur of Westminster and the opportunity to shape lives in that gilded universe. Although depicted as a radical figure during his lifetime, Rae's style of leadership appears in retrospect to be rather dated, as evidenced by his dislike of technology and meetings – although he was a very good chairman – and desire to be among his flock whenever possible. Despite his many forays into the media and the outside world, he in no sense neglected Westminster, knowing the name of every pupil and, when not teaching himself or watching from the touchline, he was consorting with them informally. 'Emotionally, I needed the boys and girls,' he later wrote. 'Just to be near them, to watch them talking, playing, fooling about, washed away the disillusionment I sometimes felt after a clash with the governing body or the common room.'[4]

Although alive to the need to raise numbers, modernise facilities and promote academic excellence, all of which he accomplished, Rae also understood the teenage mentality and how to relate to pupils so that, while he remained unstinting in his opposition to drugs, his general tolerance towards a number of their foibles helped create a school at ease with itself.

Rae also kept the independent sector in the public eye and, according to Eric Anderson, did it as well as anyone.

Anderson himself, later to be knighted for his services to the monarchy and education, numbered the Prince of Wales and Tony Blair among his pupils when teaching English at Gordonstoun and Fettes, respectively, before becoming headmaster of Abingdon School in 1971. His success there, and later at Shrewsbury School, not least his shrewd appointments, made him the obvious candidate to succeed Michael McCrum at Eton in 1980.

Imposing of height and distinctive of voice with his rich Scottish brogue, Anderson looked and sounded every inch a headmaster as he continued his predecessor's work of making Eton one of the best-managed and academically elite schools in the country. An efficient worker and able administrator, he reached sensible decisions with speed and equanimity, leaving him time to participate in many areas of school life. A naturally gregarious person, he and his charming wife Poppy were the soul of hospitality, helping to light many a warm fire in the Eton community, and while never one to shy away from a contentious situation, Anderson was remarkably popular for a headmaster, much admired for his wisdom and humanity, not least by the crop of current headmasters who learned their craft under him.

Through his teaching of the intellectual elite in the sixth form, Anderson came into contact with both Boris Johnson and David Cameron. On one occasion teaching the former, he wrote Business, Industry, Commerce on the board and asked them to spend a few minutes writing down what the words suggested to them. Boris wrote: 'These three words suggest to me that the Head Master dined in London last night.' 'Correct,' Anderson replied with a smile.[5]

He later declared that Boris was the most interesting person he ever taught, noting his penchant for performing and living on his wits, qualities he had previously detected in Tony Blair. On one occasion when acting the king in some scenes from *Richard III* in the cloisters at Eton, Johnson had failed to learn his lines, so had them pasted up behind various pillars, a bungling display, which, while amusing his peers, irritated Anderson.

As the economic malaise of the 1970s gave way to the brash, material-istic 1980s, education was increasingly viewed as a business and heads were expected to demonstrate entrepreneurial flair and business acumen, as well as more traditional values. When the cerebral Richard Bull retired as head-master of Rugby in 1990, the school's *valete* of him was as much an elegy to a more innocent era as it was to a man of integrity.

> In an age when public relations and high personal profile seem to be the only things that impress, it is indeed easy to overlook the more solid virtues of a natural modesty, compelling sense of duty and an ability to lead by unselfish example.
>
> He was a headmaster with a gentleman's style which might seem outdated in post-Thatcherite Britain.[6]

In the more uncertain climate of the early 1990s, heads became more vul-nerable to market pressure and the whim of governing bodies, as a number of high-profile departures indicated.

When Simon Hall became warden of Glenalmond College, the most blue-blooded school in Scotland, in 1987 he faced a dilemma. Although set in glorious countryside ten miles to the west of Perth, the school's isolated position had become an impediment in an age when boarding had become increasingly local. Despite the introduction of girls in the sixth form in 1990, overall numbers remained sluggish at 313 – there had been 384 boys four years earlier – and with a projected entry of only 44 for 1991, morale began to sag.

At the behest of the council, a survey conducted during the summer of 1990 pinpointed the main reasons for Glenalmond's plight. Not only were the facilities deemed to be antiquated, the school's marketing was also poor and the warden appeared unable to empathise with prospective parents.

Given these findings and the bad vibes emanating from Edinburgh din-ner parties about the school, the council felt compelled to act. In February 1991 the warden was asked to resign and left at the end of that term never to return to teaching, while his deputy, Jim Wainwright, on the verge of retire-ment, was given four hours to decide whether he would accept the position of acting warden. He did, and over the course of his four-term tenure helped revive the school's fortunes.

It was the misfortune of Helen Williams, high mistress of St Paul's Girls' School from 1989, that she should succeed the much-revered Heather Brigstocke who had lifted the horizons of the school and enabled it to scale great academic heights. In contrast to Brigstocke's cosmopolitan glamour, Williams' dowdy appearance and donnish style didn't inspire. Concerned that some girls were taking too many GCSEs, Williams proposed a limit of seven, freeing up time for more general courses to deepen their learning. Her proposal was supported by the governors but provoked outrage from many parents who felt that their children would be missing out on qualifications necessary to achieve high-paid jobs.

The unrest fed into a general perception that the high mistress wasn't officer material and, with influential parents adding to the furore, the governors, already concerned about her management style, took fright. In a blaze of publicity Williams was relieved of her responsibilities. She later told the *Sunday Times*,

> I underestimated the anxiety of the age and for this I am deeply sorry, for I hold nothing more dear than the responsibility of the school to enable all its students to realise their proper aspirations.
>
> However, nothing will change my commitment to the idea that a truly liberal education is much more than the sum of external examination syllabuses.[7]

Commented the *Independent*:

> Schools are quite like families: in good times they are warm, supportive, intimate communities, but when they argue, they turn cruel, claustrophobic and often quite irrational. In the particular case of St Paul's, the kitchen became too hot for Mrs Williams to remain. But there is a broader lesson: in this new educational climate, governors have a great responsibility to stay cool.[8]

The next casualty, weeks later, was David Cope, master of Marlborough, following a bruising six years at the helm during which the school had been dogged by a series of drugs and sex scandals. He admitted that he would be very glad to be free of what sometimes seemed 'relentlessly hostile, mischief-making publicity at the expense of the school'.[9] His resignation won him the sympathy of *The Times*:

> The simple verities of muscular Christianity, team games and cold showers are no longer enough to guide a head teacher through the moral maze posed by today's adolescents. David Cope, the Master of Marlborough, ... is merely the latest to wash his hands of a job that the conflicting demands of parents, pupils and governors have rendered almost impossible.[10]

In 1993 Eric Anderson, addressing the Annual General Meeting of the Governors Boarding Association, called his talk 'Feeling the Heat: Heads in the 1990s', and in October 1994, the *Sunday Times* reported that a record number of heads were being dismissed or retiring early because of the pressure of league tables, competition for places and parental demands. Ten years earlier one head in twenty moved on each year; now a new study of independent schools revealed it was one in nine as the philosophy of instant results associated with the corporate boardroom prevailed. 'The pressures have got greater,' lamented John Rees, rector of the Edinburgh Academy, soon to retire after only three years in the post. 'The ever increasing burden of paperwork demands long hours and makes it difficult to retain contact with the children.'[11] Headmasters tended to spend too much time worrying and not enough time enjoying the wonders of the achievements of the boys.

At the annual meeting of the HMC in 1994, its chairman, Roy Chapman, headmaster of Malvern, had excoriated those in high places for their lack of moral leadership. His attack came back to haunt his colleagues the following September when Peter Hobson, headmaster of Charterhouse, was forced to resign following press revelations of his meeting with a nineteen-year-old escort girl.

An enlightened housemaster at Wellington College and headmaster of Giggleswick School, Hobson had found managing the large, powerful Charterhouse common room a more taxing proposition and during his two years there had cut an increasingly forlorn figure. Whether the pressures of leadership contributed to his indiscretion is unclear but his ignominious demise overshadowed all his previous good work in the teaching profession.

'Public schools have always had skeletons in the cupboard,' declared John Rae, 'but they were expert at keeping them hidden. Nowadays the press finds them so quickly that they never get to be skeletons. Headmasters are regarded as fair game, like bishops or deans, because people are fascinated by the closed society and slightly pompous figures.'[12]

In October 1996 there was another leading casualty when Peter Wilkes, popular headmaster of Cheltenham, well-respected for catering for pupils of all abilities, paid the penalty for his school's disappointing A-level results that year. The abruptness of his dismissal stunned the school community and led to bitter recriminations. Wilkes' wife denounced the governing body for putting intolerable pressure on heads to raise academic standards, two governors resigned because the decision to dismiss the head was taken without their knowledge, and a meeting of over 600 disaffected parents called overwhelmingly for Wilkes' reinstatement.

Confronted with mounting anger, the governors agreed to an independent inquiry under Tony Higgins, chief executive of the Cheltenham-based Universities and Colleges Admissions Service (UCAS). His report cleared the governing body of dismissing the headmaster over league tables but criticised it for breaching natural justice and employment law. Although the president of the council felt obliged to resign, Wilkes, resisting overtures to stay and fight, chose to move on to another headship to prevent the school tearing itself apart. Within days of his departure the following summer, Cheltenham achieved its best performance in the A-level league tables to that date.

In comparison to former times when most heads had cut their teeth as housemasters or housemistresses, the current generation have risen by way of head of department and deputy head. (The current headmaster of Harrow and his predecessor previously ran day schools.) Although this experience has better prepared them for the administrative and managerial demands of the job, it has taken them away from the rough and tumble of the classroom, a regrettable development according to Eric Anderson:

> Schools in the future will not have some of the great figures of my youth: Frank Fisher [master of Wellington] a fantastic character who knew everything about schools, Walter Hamilton [headmaster of Rugby] and Tom Howarth [high master of St Paul's], a man of great ability and human qualities.[13]

These men weren't expected to spend undue time recruiting, fund-raising and reading a balance sheet. When Michael Mavor first met the bursar on becoming principal of Gordonstoun in 1979, he was told: 'Just leave the money matters to me and we'll get along famously.'[14] A majority were only too delighted to oblige, figuring that their priorities lay elsewhere. Now heads, as chief executives, cannot avoid the financial aspects of running a school, despite their lack of training for the job. Few emulate the commercial nous of David Levin, the recently retired headmaster of City of London School, who raised millions of pounds for means-tested bursaries from corporate boardrooms because of his understanding of business and how it worked.

According to Angus McPhail, warden of Radley, the biggest single problem confronting heads is that very few of them have had experience of marketing a school. Some schools have gone out of their way to appoint a corporate head but their business acumen doesn't always sit easy with the world of education. Like politicians, they talk constantly about the value of good public relations but their presentation skills can leave much to be desired. Too often they resort to the language of the corporate world with its jargon about mission statements, targets and quality assurance indicators rather than taking a genuine interest in the young. 'It is a business,' opined Norman Drummond, 'but if you have people with a business background they bring business values to educational problems. What room now for the modern inspirational leader if schools have become more like machines?'[15]

Another imposition, as with so many jobs, has been the bureaucratic overload. When Ian Walker became headmaster of King's Rochester, in 1986 there wasn't one paper on policy to deal with; by the time he left in 2012 there were over 1,000, an imposition that prevented him from teaching and coaching.

It was this excess of paperwork that persuaded a disillusioned Antony Sutch to take early retirement from Downside in 2002. 'It is a second-rate culture in which the bureaucrats protect their own jobs by creating more and more systems to measure everything,' he opined.[16] His views were shared by Gary Best on his retirement as headmaster of Kingswood School in 2008:

I won't miss the paperwork, the bureaucracy, risk assessment, health and safety, inspections that achieve very little. Those are things I won't miss.

I think if I had known the way headship would change because of the nature of the constant flow of stuff from the government, I suspect I would not have become a head ...[17]

In a less deferential age, heads often refer to themselves as *primus inter pares* ('first among equals'), stressing the sharing of responsibility with their deputies but also consulting with staff and redressing their grievances. One ex-headmaster of many years standing reckoned that staff management had become an increasingly arduous responsibility, so much so that he now rated the common room a more demanding body to deal with than either the pupils or the parents – not that he found them easy. Another head noted how staff now questioned their superiors in a way she would never have done when she was a young teacher.

It is a refrain that many heads would recognise as they have often baulked at cutting allowances, confronting under-performing colleagues and ultimately getting rid of them. 'I can think of no other walk of life, except perhaps the ordained ministry of the Church of England, in which it is possible for a lazy man to get away with so little for so long,' wrote John Rae.[18] For aside from the bad blood it can generate in the common room, especially concerning long-serving members who have seen better days, employment tribunals can be expensive and create unwelcome publicity as Eton discovered in 2006 when Sarah Forsyth, Prince Harry's former art teacher, won £45,000 compensation for unfair dismissal.

Yet for all the constraints upon them, those heads with a clear vision and forceful personality, and with the support of prominent members of the governing body, can still make a great difference. 'What does Lord Hanson do when he moves into a bad outfit?' reflected Richard Morgan, headmaster of Cheltenham between 1978 and 1990. 'He put in new management within six months. Unfortunately, you can't do it that quickly in a school, but I did end up with a staff whose average age, at thirty-three, was a lot younger than it had been.'[19]

Having overseen a major transformation at Cheltenham, Morgan set out to reform Radley on succeeding Dennis Silk. Perceiving the common room to be 'a bit staid, a bit bachelor and a bit too self-indulgent, especially in alcohol', he told them to work for the boys or leave. Many left, unable to cope with the exacting expectations, especially in academia, to be replaced with young heads of departments who oversaw a major improvement in exam results.

Few headships were as turbulent as Morgan's but, like him, those who have left a mark didn't shirk hard choices on assuming office: Edward Gould restored order at Marlborough after a period of unrest; Stephen Winkley halted Uppingham's decline and placed it on a more secure financial footing; Ian Walker shunned overtures from bigger schools to provide strong leadership at King's Rochester; Ian Davenport promoted a more positive 'can do' culture at Blundell's; Anthony Wallersteiner managed to rid Stowe of its unruly image; and Andrew Halls created miracles at Magdalen College School, Oxford, during his ten years there between 1998 and 2008.

Confronted with an ailing school living on its reputation as its numbers and academic results plummeted, Halls realised that the key to restoring its fortunes was reinvigorating the common room. Appointing Richard Cairns, currently headmaster of Brighton College, as his deputy, he introduced staff appraisal, and hard though the malcontents kicked against it, the majority came onside as parents liked what they saw.

By his last year, the school had jumped from 170th in the league tables to first, its numbers had risen from 510 to 700 and it became the *Sunday Times* Independent Secondary School of the Year in 2004. It was an accolade that Halls was to repeat at his new school, King's College School Wimbledon (KCS) in 2014.

Etched more firmly in the public consciousness are those headmasters whose performances have commanded the national stage.

An Old Etonian by virtue of winning a choral scholarship, and the first person in his family to be educated beyond the age of fourteen, Tony Little appears the very model of a provincial bank manager, with his unpretentious glasses and unassuming manner. Thoughtful and unfailingly courteous, he enjoys a favourable public profile but his urbanity shouldn't be mistaken for a soft touch since he is a man of forthright views.

Frustrated by the media image of Eton, which he sees as bearing scant resemblance to the place he works in every day, he is constantly surprised by the changing perceptions of the critics when they visit it. 'There is an element of hypocrisy over independent schools,' he declares. 'No one will stand up for them and yet many are keen to have their children in them.'[20]

Alarmed by the growing sense of measurement in education, he worries that bureaucratic intervention has stifled flair in the classroom and undermined trust in the teaching profession, as well as in the leadership potential of pupils, something which has always been essential to an Eton education.

Determined to make Eton more accessible to those of ability, regardless of their background, Little has overseen a substantial increase in the school's bursary fund to help make his vision a reality. He has also strengthened links with a number of state schools, most notably its sponsorship of Holyport Academy, a free school (part-boarding) that opened in September 2014, and has been a tireless advocate of the British independent sector on his many trips abroad, particularly in China.

Due to retire in August 2015, Little ranks, according to his provost, William Waldegrave, as one of Eton's greatest headmasters. His successor, Simon Henderson, headmaster of Bradfield, will be following in Anthony Chenevix-Trench's footsteps some half a century earlier, although unlike the latter, Henderson has previously taught at Eton.

A man not given to small talk, Barnaby Lenon, former headmaster of Harrow and chairman of the ISC, is a tough, no-nonsense type, unafraid to speak his mind.

After five years as headmaster of Trinity School, Lenon moved to Harrow in 1999 resolved to return it to its former glory. In keeping with the modern style of headship, he delegated much of the day-to-day running of the school to his deputy but wasn't averse to laying down the law when he felt so inclined. One summer holiday, without consulting his housemasters or senior management, he wrote a letter to parents stipulating that the school uniform would immediately revert to light grey trousers of an earlier vintage on the grounds that they looked smarter.

Overhauling the school entry system to introduce a more meritocratic one, he promoted a more exacting work ethic, brooking no sloppiness from a staff that held him somewhat in awe – unlike the boys – and, although some found his methods too abrasive, the results spoke for themselves. Harrow shot up the league tables to become a serious academic force for the first time in years, the arts flourished and sporting opportunities continued to abound.

With a fair wind at his back, Lenon was able to get his message across to one and all, including two successful television documentaries (a third followed after he left), that a Harrow education now compared with the very best. Demand for places surged, its traditional clientele blending with a more meritocratic multi-cultural elite.

Mention the name Anthony Seldon, master of Wellington, and it will elicit all kinds of descriptions, ranging from a true educational visionary to obsessive self-publicist.

The son of Arthur Seldon, an erudite pamphleteer who rose from poverty in east London to become a tireless proponent of free market economics long before it was fashionable, Anthony Seldon has excelled as a political historian, publishing weighty biographies of John Major, Tony Blair and Gordon Brown.

A small intense man who meditates every morning, Seldon is a gifted speaker who relates well to parents and pupils alike. An innovative thinker, he turned Brighton into a top-flight school before moving on to Wellington in 2006, ridding it of its uncouth image and transforming it into one of the most enlightened schools in the country. In addition to introducing full coeducation, the IB and self-awareness classes, he has established a Mandarin Centre, sponsored an academy and diversified the choice of sports without in any sense diminishing Wellington's proud rugby tradition.

By disposing of staff who didn't measure up, encouraging his common room to be enterprising in the classroom, and playing host to a glittering array of outside speakers, Wellington has undergone something of an intellectual renaissance.

A staunch advocate of education beyond the classroom, Seldon hasn't been slow to espouse these values to the state sector. He has also been a leading advocate of closer state–independent school relations, especially through the academy movement, an idea that has yet to commend itself to the majority of his colleagues. The fact that he has resorted to hectoring them over their reluctance to sponsor academies, as well as using his berth in the media to talk up Wellington at every conceivable opportunity, hasn't endeared him to all. Yet when he retires this year his legacy will be an enduring one – officially recognised by his recent knighthood.

Seldon's successor at Brighton was Richard Cairns, another maverick out of the same stable. Not averse to causing controversy, Cairns has spoken out against slipshod teaching, the endless obsession with capital development in the independent sector and its lack of partnership with the state sector. Cairns has continued Seldon's reform agenda by bringing in compulsory

Mandarin, introducing social etiquette classes and forging closer links with a community school in east London, leading to the establishment of the London Academy of Excellence. All this has generated much favourable publicity and, while Brighton's place in the sun has alienated some of its competitors, there can be no doubting its success under Cairns' leadership.

Aside from the ever-growing demand for places – boarding is at its highest since 1929 – Brighton's tolerant atmosphere has encouraged excellence across broad swathes of school life. Nowhere has this been more evident than in the classroom. Cairns' commitment to inspirational teaching has yielded outstanding academic results – 96 per cent A/B at A-level and a climb from 147th in its league table in 2005–06 to 18th in 2011–12.

Given its record, the *Sunday Times* named Brighton its independent school of the year for 2011–12, and again in 2013–14, precisely because of its achievement as the only school whose results had risen in seven successive years. A further accolade came Cairns' way when he was named by *Tatler* as its headmaster of the year in 2012.

The son of a Scottish soldier turned postman and a Dutch mother, Patrick Derham's story is a remarkable one. Raised on the naval training ship *Arethusa*, which prepared young men from deprived families for the merchant navy, his potential was recognised and he won a scholarship to Pangbourne College where he became head boy. 'My life was transformed by an opportunity to be sent to boarding school,' Derham later recalled. 'I'm living proof of the great Chartist slogan that education is a liberating force.'[21]

After Cambridge, where he gained a first-class degree in History, Derham taught at Radley under Dennis Silk, which provided ideal preparation for his headships of Solihull School, Rugby and Westminster.

A committed Roman Catholic, Derham continued the work of his predecessor Michael Mavor in restoring Rugby's fortunes so that the school once again stands comparison with the very best. With his interest in nineteenth-century history, Derham derived particular inspiration from following in Arnold's footsteps and his establishment of the Arnold Foundation, a charity offering fully funded bursaries at the school for those from a deprived background, has taken the school back to its charitable roots, setting a benchmark for other schools to follow.

As declining social mobility came to dominate the national debate, Derham constantly pointed to the Arnold Foundation as the way forward, not without encountering some scepticism from those opposed to private education.

In 2008 Derham entertained John Prescott at Rugby during the filming of Prescott's BBC documentary *The Class System and Me*, but although he found him good company there was no meeting of minds between these two former merchant seamen. 'Criticising what works is no way to fix what doesn't,' Derham later reflected. 'By imposing his class system on education, the former Deputy Prime Minister entrenches divisions between state and independent schools.'[22]

The retirement of many leading headmasters in 2014 and 2015 marks the beginning of the end of that generation who began their teaching careers in a more straightforward, less regulated era. The challenge facing their successors will be to ensure that, in coping with a more taxing economic and bureaucratic environment, they don't lose sight of the personal and educational values integral to all thriving school communities.

Chapter 5

MR CHIPS AS HISTORY

When George Chesterton enrolled at Malvern in 1936, he began a seventy-six-year association with the school that lasted until his dying day. The son of a cleric, Chesterton flourished there, becoming deputy head of school and captain of cricket. On leaving in 1941, he enlisted in the RAF and flew behind enemy lines during the war, participating in the D-Day landings and the ill-fated assault at Arnhem.

In 1946 he went up to Oxford and won a cricket blue during his final year, distinguishing himself as the university's leading wicket-taker. No academic, he returned to Malvern to teach geography and run the cricket, as well as playing for Worcestershire during the summer holidays. According to one of his protégés, Lord MacLaurin, a future chairman of Tesco and the England and Wales Cricket Board, Chesterton was a great coach in the way he moulded young talent and brought the best out of his teams.

After fifteen years as a dedicated housemaster, Chesterton became second master in 1973, his affability and integrity making him a universally respected figure.

Retiring in December 1982 after serving for one term as acting headmaster during an interregnum, he remained in close contact with the school and in 2012 was awarded the MBE for services to the community, receiving his award from the Queen two weeks before he died.

Chesterton's career accords with the traditional profile of many a second master at that time: loyal, long-serving members of staff who, administrative responsibilities aside, saw their role primarily as confidant to the headmaster and go-between in relations with the common room. Michael Charlesworth, senior master at Shrewsbury, his old school, between 1969 and 1981, recalled the pleasure he derived from getting to know every boy in the school, assisting the new masters as they settled in, as well as running the fives and teaching the top fifth form. Such was the *esprit de corps* of his 1969 class that, at the end of the year, they voted to meet again in fifteen years' time. 'So in 1984 a dinner was held and there round the table was every boy; they had been aged fifteen; now they were thirty. It was an occasion when I felt I was fortunate to have chosen schoolmastering as my profession.'[1]

Over time, as the governance of a school grew ever more complex, it became fashionable to recruit a young deputy head from outside to assume responsibility for its day-to-day running. Such is the importance of the deputy, especially in mastering the systems and procedures so intrinsic to a school today, that experience in this capacity is now the preferred route by which heads reach the top.

Just below the deputy head in the hierarchy is the deputy academic – the director of studies – and deputy pastoral. Together with the head of sixth form (in a day school), the bursar, director of marketing and director of development, they constitute the SMT. While different teams have different routines, most would reckon to meet once a week to check that all statutory regulations are being met and that the school development plan is being properly implemented. This arrangement has led to schools being run more efficiently than hitherto but such a narrow concentration of decision-making has detached them further from the common room. Michael Meredith recalls that, as a young master at Eton, he could influence the way the school was run. 'You'll be worked harder than ever before but as an assistant master you'll be listened to more than in any other school in the country,' the headmaster Anthony Chenevix-Trench informed him at interview.[2] He was as good as his word, always receptive to sensible ideas, especially Meredith's efforts to modernise the School Library. Subsequent headmasters implemented his ideas on the theatre, but now, according to Meredith, a young member of staff wouldn't gain access to the headmaster, their way being blocked by the SMT.

As academic attainment became ever more important so did the position of the director of studies, as a result of their responsibility for the timetable, subject options, staffing, the overseeing of departments, liaising with exam boards and, above all, exam results. More recently, many schools have offloaded a number of these responsibilities, especially classroom performance, on to a newly created position: head of teaching and learning.

When David Elleray went to Harrow in 1977 to teach geography, his head of department, Edward Gould, made it clear that he wouldn't interfere unless there were a riot or his results were dreadful. That was usual practice. Teachers were given considerable leeway to teach how they liked and were rarely held to account. It was only with the onset of league tables and review and development that heads of department began to show some teeth.

Whereas departmental meetings might have occurred once a term in previous times, they are now a weekly event with an official agenda. Aside from focusing on the syllabus, much greater attention is paid to how sets are taught, what resources are available and how pupils are assessed. With exam results the leading priority and with payment by results a reality in some schools, the incentive for departments to attract able pupils has become ever greater. Some are quite ruthless in deterring weaker pupils from choosing their subject, while others go out of their way to welcome all-comers and help them.

In this more competitive environment and with review and development becoming the norm, heads of department have played a much more proactive role in managing their colleagues, especially the younger ones or those who fall short of expectation. Whereas poor exam results were once quietly glossed over or attributed to the inadequacies of the class, it is the teacher and the department that now stand indicted, not least in conversation with the head and director of studies.

As the position of the SMT and heads of department has become more powerful, so that of housemasters and housemistresses has declined. Traditionally, they had been appointed on the basis of seniority and then left to run their houses in the manner they best saw fit, giving each house its own distinctive character. While some confined themselves to watching the boys play rugby or cricket, the majority made every effort to support the house in the round and get to know their charges. Those with a strong personality left a lasting impact, others were less suited to their role *in loco parentis*.

Much of the day-to-day running of the house was left to the boys. At best this gave them every opportunity to display leadership and responsibility, not least in coaching teams, fomenting a healthy house spirit. By the end of the 1970s, the prefects were less disposed to administer discipline, but there were exceptions and housemasters had to step in to ban excessive forms of house punishments and other initiation rites. Bullying, while less endemic than in previous times, continued to rear its head and, with solid academic endeavour confined to the minority, a system that had outlived its usefulness gave way to something rather different.

Instead of appointment by seniority, the position of housemasters from the mid-1980s became increasingly open to competition and merit, the occupants younger, better trained and more deferential to the head who appointed them. This wasn't mere patronage. Health and welfare inspection, child protection and university admissions have all necessitated uniform standards of discipline, procedures and supervision. Teams of house tutors now take responsibility for evenings in houses and academic progress, while the housemaster, when not seeing his charges, is closeted in his study responding to the constant tide of emails and phone calls from colleagues and parents. While no housemaster would dissent from the need to give every pupil the best care and attention possible, it has made the job much more taxing and this, along with many a spouse now working, explains why fewer staff crave such a position. Unlike their predecessors who used to serve out their twelve- or fifteen-year tenure, as well as running departments and coaching teams, the majority now settle for rather less, either because they move on to higher things or return exhausted to the ranks.

Although the make-up of the common room had begun to change in the mid-1960s, many still resembled a gentleman's club where members could read the newspapers, smoke their pipe and have a glass of sherry before dinner. Dan Hearn recalls the Haileybury common room on his arrival there in September 1965: 'The twenty-seven bachelors sat at breakfast in order of seniority. Silence was observed. Each member read *The Times* and only *The Times*.'[3]

'It was, for all its sociability and charm, an unquestionably conservative society,' wrote Patrick Tobin of his time at Tonbridge during the 1970s. 'There were Common Room cricket matches in lovely Kent villages and Common Room dinners during which the best wine flowed, but the young man who vomited his inebriation was given notice to leave.'[4]

Although Tobin felt slightly uncomfortable with the proprieties of the place – ladies withdrew after dinner, masters' wives were expected to help with the chapel flowers and any discussion about staff salaries was deemed to be vulgar – he ranked Tonbridge the finest school in which he ever taught, given the quality and commitment of its common room.

At its best the common room of that era comprised many staff to whom teaching was very much a vocation. Fortunate perhaps to have a private income – the Clifton car park contained a slew of Rolls-Royces and Bentleys post-war – or unworldly enough to forego material gain, masters dutifully accepted the low pay and austere living conditions for the rewarding life they led. Because a number of them had flourished at school themselves, the opportunity to share their passion for their subject or their sport wasn't one to be spurned. Consequently, fresh out of university, they returned to familiar territory and remained there for the rest of their careers.

One such character was John Gill, a larger-than-life bachelor who taught modern languages at Rossall for thirty-seven years before becoming secretary of the Rossallian Club. On being diagnosed with a terminal illness in 1996, he planned an elaborate funeral and when he died during the Easter holidays his body was preserved under cold conditions so that his funeral could take place when term resumed, with the entire school on parade to salute the funeral cortege on its way to a service in the chapel. 'This was an event unique in Rossall's history,' wrote its historian Derek Winterbottom, 'and the remarkable last fling of one of the school's great eccentrics.'[5]

Whether such an insular lifestyle dulled the staff's educational vision is a moot point. Jonathan Smith recalls that at Loretto the unspoken rule was that teachers gave their all to the job during term time and recovered their sanity in the holidays. It was only after he had left the school that he realised he had met no one outside it and barely knew Edinburgh despite its close proximity: 'In no time I was working too hard; within a year, despite a most helpful head of department, I had lost my sense of balance. I was 100 per cent for the school and in the school and thinking school.'[6]

There were those teachers who were unduly fastidious about petty rules and customs and who found it difficult to relate to the world outside, as Anthony Chenevix-Trench discovered when he tried to reform Eton during the 1960s. Conversely, there were many others whose rounded character and cultural breadth made them leaders of men. 'Almost all the teachers at Dulwich when I arrived were veterans of World War II,' recalled Nigel Farage, the leader of the UK Independence Party, about his time at the school between 1979 and 1984, 'tough opinionated, cavalier, articulate, outspoken and very good at their jobs. That is they amused and inspired. They made their lessons memorable.'[7]

'Many of the teachers at Westminster were an odd bunch, as great teachers often are,' recounted the journalist and author Harry Mount of his time there during the 1980s. 'Among them were stiff disciplinarians such as TJP (Tristram Jones-Parry), drunks, disappointed academics, non-practising pederasts and practising cradle-snatchers. ... All that mattered with these oddballs was that they had two qualities: high intelligence and the ability to keep control.'[8] Those he singled out included Jim Cogan, a Shakespearean scholar whose lessons were dominated by lively debate punctured by humorous interjections; Theo Zinn, the doyen of independent school classics masters, who could reel off vast tracts of Homer and Horace; and David Hepburne-Scott, a wonderfully original physicist with a passion for railways.

Given the diversity of characters in the common room, it isn't surprising that the standard of teaching varied enormously. There were polymaths whose erudition and wit were such that they infused their pupils with a lifelong love of Cicero and Shakespeare; there were old-fashioned form masters whose precision and patience helped many a laggard learn the basics in English-based subjects; and there were those who failed to pass muster either because they couldn't keep order or they had lost their spark in the classroom. Indolence often set in with age and, with teachers rarely held to account, a culture of inertia took root.

Part of the problem stemmed from the laxity of the appointments process. According to John Rae, most headmasters shared his dislike of this prime responsibility, which might well explain the rather casual way in which they went about it. Too often an applicant's credentials were taken on trust without ascertaining whether he could actually teach or relate to pupils, an oversight which has now been largely rectified.

As the old public school began to give way to the more meritocratic independent school during the late 1960s, these changes became reflected in the common room. The political biographer D. R. Thorpe started teaching at Charterhouse at a time when masters with private incomes were just declining. He recalled:

> I can remember a colleague saying to me 'Your salary won't take you very far, but you'll have your own resources to draw on.' As this belief that 'everyone'

had private incomes became increasingly untrue the bursars really did have to raise their game about pay.[9]

The social composition of common rooms changed a great deal following the appearance of two new groups: first, independent schoolmasters no longer with the resources enjoyed by their own parents and grandparents, often with several children, for whom the 10 per cent fees paid by staff were an absolute life saver; and, second, a new generation of grammar school and red brick university masters not entirely comfortable with the public school ethos. Thorpe recalls one snooty housemaster's wife saying to a younger member of this second category: 'Of course Charterhouse has a very different kind of intake in the Common Room these days.' 'Yes,' replied the patronised beak, 'they are much cleverer!' which was true.[10]

This change has continued apace over the succeeding decades as Oxbridge's meritocratic entry system weeded out many of the former public school 'bloods' destined for teaching. Not only are the majority of the staff now state educated, many of them have also taught in the state sector before transferring to the independent one, primarily because of the opportunity to teach smaller classes and enjoy greater freedoms. This has included an ever-growing percentage of women as coeducation became fashionable and single-sex boys' schools began opening their doors to them.

The reaction in the common room to the admission of women varied. Ruth Alinek was warmly welcomed on becoming the first female teacher at Aldenham School, and Ann Butler likewise at St Peter's School, York, helped by her prowess as a rowing coach. Less fortunate were Alison Webb, the first full-time woman teacher at Repton, who was expected to make the tea, and Helen Harrison, now deputy head of Fettes. She recalls walking into the Clifton common room as a new, twenty-two-year-old teacher and being greeted with, 'Who the hell are we employing now?' The fact that some of the women didn't greatly contribute to the sporting life of the school caused some resentment, but this shouldn't be exaggerated. The majority of masters, especially the younger generation, found them a welcome addition to enliven their rather monastic existence and, not surprisingly, romance often blossomed.

As the number of women teachers has increased in these schools so have those in promoted posts, especially as heads of department. In 2006 Denstone

College appointed Jane Morris to be its director of cricket, the first woman to run the sport in an HMC school; that same year Dr Jane Grant became 'master of college' at Eton, in charge of the seventy King's Scholars, the first woman 'housemaster' in its 566-year history.

In 2014 Harrow appointed Dr Susannah Abbott, a former footballer in the women's premier league, to be its first female 'housemaster', and in 2015 Gordonstoun appointed Dr Eve Poole, a former management consultant at Deloitte, to be its first 'chairman' of governors. Another former Deloitte consultant, Heather Hancock, has proved a very able 'chairman' of governors at Giggleswick. More women have also joined governing bodies and SMTs but they remain the minority.

Although Gwen Randall made history in 1994 by becoming the first female head of an HMC school, Framlingham College, and headmistresses such as Katy Ricks (Sevenoaks), Sarah Fletcher (City of London School) and Emma Taylor (Christ College, Brecon) have particularly impressed, there are still only a few of them overall, typical of the rather fusty image that still percolates the HMC.

Sarah Fletcher recalls that at one interview she attended for a head-ship, she was told that she was the best candidate but couldn't be appointed because the old boys wouldn't give donations to a woman; on another occasion she missed out because she lacked the physical stature. 'If you get a top post, you are labelled ambitious as a woman but if you are a man you are talented,' she remarked.[11]

The new intake of staff is extremely well qualified, well versed in the latest teaching methodology and comfortable with being assessed in the classroom. A number of teachers, however, with no experience of the independent sector, struggle with the ethos of extra-curricular demands, especially the supervision of games, with the result that schools have been compelled either to pay extra or rely on outside coaches. One headmaster who refuses to be bound by such thinking is Anthony Seldon, who insists that all staff at Wellington participate to get to know the pupils in a rounded way and understand everything the school has to offer.

Compared to their predecessors who were more accepting of low pay, teachers today expect to be properly remunerated and aren't afraid to press their claims with the head. (Research by the Association of Teachers and Lecturers (ATL) in 2014 suggests that pay is slightly better in the independent sector than the state sector, although additional allowances can boost their earnings.) Some 55 per cent of staff in the former belong to a union and when a national one-day strike was called in June 2011 over pension reform, a number walked out – unhappy with proposals that the teachers' pension scheme would no longer apply to the independent sector.

Part of this growing militancy results from the greater academic, pastoral and bureaucratic demands placed on teachers over the last two decades. Bureaucratic demands are particularly time-consuming and present an obstacle to their performance. When an ATL survey in 2006 revealed that 60 per cent of their members in the independent sector worked more than fifty hours a week, the *Guardian* called the findings shocking. Yet many teachers work harder than this, a point underlined the following year when an assistant housemistress at Malvern College won £12,000 compensation after working a staggering 121.5 hours a week for less than the minimum wage.

Given this onerous environment, teachers' greater family commitments (many of their spouses work full time), and the fact that fewer now live on campus, the opportunity for intellectual discussion has all but disappeared. John Byrom, an English teacher at Marlborough during the 1980s, recalls being asked by the master what he was currently reading and being invited over to the master's lodge that evening to discuss the book over a glass of whisky. 'I can't imagine that happening now and that is dangerous because if you are not reading you can't teach well,' he says. 'I do detect a slow growth in the superiority of action over thinking and I do worry that people now feel uncomfortable if they are not working.'[12]

Another casualty has been the restricted opportunities to socialise – some departments don't even come into the common room for break – not least staff cricket matches and Friday evening drinks. Michael Meredith recalls the dinner parties he attended as a young master at Eton which helped him get to know the community there and the way it worked. The fact that this tradition has died because the wives now work, he says, means young masters today know much less about the school and its traditions.

Those whose lives were centred very much on the school and were part of a harmonious community (though not always) have most cause to recall the pleasures of a more leisurely age, the intellectual stimulation, the diversity of character and enduring friendships. The modern common room may come across as rather utilitarian and colourless in comparison, lacking that same sense of loyalty to the school, but teachers compensate with their professionalism and sensitivity to the needs of individual pupils.

This commitment to the pupils doesn't always extend to the parents at a time when modern communications have raised expectations of a rapid response. According to Alex McGrath, heads and SMTs have grasped this reality more fully than many of their colleagues who complain about the added demands on their time. 'This failure to engage with the customer is now an unforgivable sin. In burying their heads, teachers compound problems further, meaning that parental interactions escalate more quickly and more frequently,' he notes.[13]

Having given some thought to this failure, McGrath concludes that teacher commitment is to the children and not to their parents, who they perceive as rather overbearing; he also sees their vision as an unduly narrow one, directed more towards their subject or their career than the school itself. Some of the heads who confided in him told of their failure to convince their common rooms that all of them had a part to play in promoting the interests of the school.

It has always been thus. Irked by one member of staff's reservations concerning the growing proportion of overseas pupils at Fettes during the 1980s, the headmaster, Malcolm Thyne, asked his critic whether he wanted his salary paid. According to McGrath, breaking out of the bunker and making staff more aware of financial realities – not least higher salaries pricing schools out of the market – should be the leading priority of heads. He also believes that more staff development should be directed towards their relationship with parents and that teacher appraisal should be more rigorous – with underperformance more starkly exposed. McGrath suggests that,

> Although we must reward staff adequately, we should be aware of what wonderful and exciting places our schools are in which to live and work. Our children are generally vibrant and exciting. They are a joy to teach, are well-mannered, and on the whole want to learn. This might well be reward enough for some teachers, and we must take great care that we do not over-reward them financially to the detriment of our schools and what they can provide.[14]

Chapter 6

TOP OF THE TABLE

When Michael Young wrote his seminal book *The Rise of Meritocracy* in 1958, he foresaw a new grammar school elite running the country, little realising that this elite would be eclipsed by the comprehensives which became the only route by which most children could rise up in the world. According to Anthony Sampson in *The Changing Anatomy of Britain*, the independent schools actually became the new meritocracy, competing much more systematically for Oxbridge.

'[T]oday the public schools can claim, with justice, to be in the forefront of new educational thinking,' wrote Peter Wilby in the *Sunday Times* magazine in November 1981. 'Most of the successful innovations in academic syllabuses over the past twenty years have their provenance in the public schools.'[1] He cited the School Mathematics Project and the Nuffield Science Teaching Project – which attempted to teach science through practical experiments – as examples and mentioned Bradford Grammar School's pioneering work in scientific engineering, Oundle's in electronics-computing and Marlborough's in A-level business studies.

At Eton during the 1970s, the headmaster, Michael McCrum, in the pursuit of excellence, decreed that entry should be solely by competitive exam, much to the chagrin of many Old Etonian families, and reformed the curriculum away from its classical domination, so that forty Etonians won awards to Oxbridge in 1979 and forty-seven in 1981, the highest ever. At Winchester half of its pupils went to Oxbridge, down from 70 per cent two decades earlier, but still the highest percentage then of any independent school, while Shrewsbury under Eric Anderson won forty-three Oxbridge scholarships, the majority in maths and science, between 1975 and 1978.

Yet this academic renaissance was by no means universal as a number of pupils continued to view Lloyds, Sandhurst or Savills as their future destiny, where background and character counted for more than intellect. On becoming principal of Gordonstoun, Michael Mavor remarked in his 1980 open day address that he didn't think that the boys and girls there worked hard enough. That same year only 37.5 per cent of Harrovians attained an A or B at A-level whereas 15.5 per cent attained an E and 18 per cent failed outright. Eleven years later, the A and B tally had risen to 55 per cent, but this didn't impress the *Harrovian*, the school magazine, which stated: 'Harrow appears to be thirty years behind the times, still attempting to produce "sporting gentlemen".'[2]

A similar dilemma bedevilled Repton. John Billington, former head of English, recalled that one of the aims of heads of department there during the 1970s was proving that academic work was as stimulating as games and that it should be taken seriously. Distinguished scholars such as James Fenton, later professor of poetry at Oxford, were accorded less recognition than was their due.

Rugby was another school stuck in the past. Max Wilkinson, of the *Financial Times*, returned to his alma mater in 1990 and discovered that the main reservation of the scholars was that few Rugbeians took advantage of what was on offer:

> 'There are a lot of mediocre pupils here,' said one girl. Indeed, though A-level results are respectable and the staff I met were all impressive, you don't hear many people calling Rugby a 'great' school these days. It has some empty places.[3]

Following the compilation of *The Good Schools Guide* in 1986, the authors Amanda Atha and Sarah Drummond commented on the general low quality of the teaching they had encountered. This was particularly the case in smaller, rural establishments where obtaining good staff was often harder. Aside from those dedicated scholars who lacked the personality to communicate their love of learning to restless teenagers, there were those to whom the art of teaching ranked well below their coaching of sport in their order of priorities.

Confined to teach in draughty classrooms comprising soulless rows of graffiti-ridden desks and devoid of teaching aids, pedagogy lacked variety and stimulus. Too often the teacher talked and pupils listened or took dictated notes with little interaction between them, aside from ripostes of magisterial sarcasm towards the form comedian. Written work often consisted of learning a list of facts, marking often lacked constructive comment and encouragement was in short supply. In an environment where tradition and conformity ruled there was little self-evaluation and departmental oversight so that bad results were very much the fault of the pupils and not those who taught them. 'I'm often asked to think of a teacher who inspired me,' commented Richard Cairns when recalling his education at the Oratory School in the early 1980s. 'I can't think of a single one. Teachers were late, they often seemed to teach the wrong things, and results didn't really matter.'[4]

Although exam results began to improve during the 1980s, nothing much changed until public accountability became the norm. The Education Reform Act 1988 requiring state schools to publish national test results annually, all in the name of raising standards and aiding parental choice, formed the backdrop to league tables in the independent sector, an idea that it had always opposed because 'dangerous comparisons' would be made. That isn't to say that competition had been entirely absent from the sector. Oxbridge awards and the number of places achieved there counted for something, especially among the more academic schools, but A-levels, O-levels and GCSEs remained rather a closed book. During August 1991 John Clare, education correspondent of the *Daily Telegraph*, phoned a number of heads to ascertain the proportion of their schools' A-levels that had been graded A or B. Intrigued by how many of the prestigious schools had performed worse than some of the others, he decided to place the results in a league table and the *Telegraph* published them on 29 August.

Top of its table was girls' school Portsmouth High School with 83.4 per cent A/B grades, followed by KESB with 81.2 per cent. Winchester, St Paul's, Manchester Grammar School, South Hampstead School for Girls, St Paul's Girls', Wycombe Abbey, King Edward VI High School for Girls, Birmingham and Haberdashers' Aske's Boys' School all also finished in the top ten.

Accepting that league tables didn't represent a hierarchy of teaching quality, much less of all-round merit, the *Telegraph* nevertheless suggested that, at a time of rising fees, the lowly position of some well-established schools – Repton with 50 per cent A/B grades, Marlborough 49 per cent,

Wellington 46 per cent, Clifton 45 per cent and Uppingham 44 per cent – would be a cause for concern.

'Perhaps open competition of this kind will smarten us all up, but there are also dangers,' declared Joan Clanchy, headmistress of NLCS, ranked twelfth in the tables. Citing an interview she had just conducted with a sixth-form girl about returning for another year, she said: 'I urged her that it was worthwhile and that I was sure she could make Cs next summer. But for the first time it occurred to me that her Cs might stop us thumping South Hampstead in next year's table.'[5]

'We are opposed to the publication of results in the form of league tables,' declared Fr Dominic Milroy, headmaster of Ampleforth and chairman of the HMC, a year later. 'The suggestion of a competition on the basis of results is invidious, misleading and alien to the true purpose of education.'[6]

Despite the irritation of the HMC at the 'gimmick' of league tables, parental interest was such that there was no going back. The newspapers had a major new story at a traditionally quiet time of year and all began publishing their own league tables, applying different formats. Part of the HMC's reluctance to publish stemmed from a fear that parts of the independent sector would be shown up, as David Tytler, *The Times*' education correspondent, expressed in 1993:

> There is equally no doubt that the tables are a concern to some independent schools where the results compare less favourably with state schools. The problem is particularly acute in the South East where there is enormous competition for boys between a number of independent day schools and increasingly successful state schools, particularly those that have become grant-maintained.
>
> For independent schools the question is stark: why should parents pay for something they can have for nothing?[7]

Three years later *The Times* was sounding a similar refrain as its league table highlighted the continued rise of academic state schools. 'The danger for some independent schools,' remarked John Rae, 'is that instead of developing a genuine specialism they will attempt to bluff their way through the crisis with talk of character, discipline and unspecified social advantages. But there is little to choose between a good independent school and a good state school so far as discipline goes.'[8]

These concerns and a growing recognition that parents were using league tables to help them determine their choice of school helped galvanise the independent sector into raising its intellectual sights. Whereas only two schools achieved an 80 per cent A-level pass rate at A and B in 1991 and fourteen at 70 per cent, those figures had risen to thirty and ninety-one, respectively, by 2002.

The debate about league tables and their trivialisation of education was bound up with a wider one concerning the future of public exams. As the validity of the A-level became increasingly questioned by educationalists and employers alike for its lack of breadth and the impediment it posed to wider access to higher education, the Thatcher government commissioned an inquiry chaired by Professor Gordon Higginson, vice chancellor of Southampton University. When Higginson reported in 1988, he argued that the A-level encouraged premature specialisation and recommended that a five-subject structure should be adopted akin to the Scottish Higher model. However, despite winning wide support, his report was vetoed by Thatcher following representations from leading figures in the HMC such as Peter Pilkington, the high master of St Paul's and an unabashed elitist.

Pressure to reform the A-level continued to be applied by the rest of the teaching profession, including the GSA. At an extraordinary meeting at Dulwich in June 1990, the HMC, already unhappy about changes to the A-level to bring it more in line with the skills-based GCSE, appeared uncertain regarding how to respond. Recognising that some reform was necessary to keep more pupils in school – the current AS-level wasn't achieving that – it rallied behind Eric Anderson's proposal to maintain the A-level but offer an additional range of intermediate courses post-sixteen to bridge the gap between vocational courses and the A-level.

To Anderson's disappointment his proposal was rejected by the government, but the HMC kept up its pressure for a more flexible exam that placed academic and vocational courses on an equal footing. While the future format of A-levels aroused fierce passion among politicians and educationalists, concerns about grade inflation gathered pace, a problem exacerbated by the number of commercial exam boards offering easier exams. At the HMC's annual meeting in September 1999, its chairman, James Sabben-Clare, headmaster of Winchester, remarked that A-levels had ceased to identify the brightest pupils and were doing little to nurture intellectual development. Syllabuses were shorter, grade boundaries had changed and rigid marking schemes had destroyed the essay. Twenty years earlier one-third of Wykhamists gained an A in history; that figure had now risen to three-quarters, although they were no brighter.

Disillusion with the A-level had seen some schools switch to the IB, which they regarded as the yardstick of excellence and now, on the eve of the revised modular structure, many feared a further devaluation of the currency. Philip Evans, headmaster of Bedford School, warned that unless standards were firmly set, there was a risk of the same grade inflation that had occurred with the new GCSE exams.

The revised A-level had its origins in the Dearing post-sixteen review set up by the Major government as part of its attempt to encourage more people to stay on at school and then go to university or college. Dearing recommended that A-levels be made broader and divided into two parts, each carrying an equal weight of marks: three units at AS-level, the first year of study, and three A2 units during the second year. Together, the six units would comprise a full A-level, although there was the option of receiving an AS-level qualification in its own right, a sop to those who couldn't cope with A-levels.

At the insistence of the Blair government, the new exam stressed breadth whereby students would be encouraged to take four or five AS-levels. The additional workload was of little concern to Tessa Blackstone, Minister for Education, when she announced the new exam in March 1999:

> It is, however, a fact that young people in England are taught for an average of around eighteen hours a week compared with thirty hours in other European countries. I do not believe that our youngsters are any less capable than those in other countries. Our reforms will ensure they are stretched to achieve their full potential.[9]

Acknowledging the benefits derived from the recent introduction of modules in A-level subjects such as maths and science, most notably the motivation for boys to work harder, the independent sector approved of Dearing's proposals, top academic schools aside, which worried that subjects would become less analytical.

A more pertinent criticism came from David Willetts, Shadow Education Secretary, who accused the government of failing to give schools enough time to prepare for the new exam given that they would begin teaching it in September 2000. His presentiments were amply borne out as pupils were swamped by the volume of content prescribed by the new curriculum.

The swelling chorus of discontent reached a crescendo in the summer of 2001 when the unprecedented number of exams caused havoc with the school timetable and with extra-curricular activities. (At Gresham's School, the annual tally of seven house plays was reduced to one house entertainment and university visits were cancelled.) On 30 May Jonathan Leigh, then-headmaster of Blundell's, writing in the *Daily Telegraph*, protested that British pupils were the most examined in the world and warned that the AS-level was turning schools into exam factories. In many schools the spirit of the lower sixth year had been broken, the pupils were fraught and the staff were drained. 'The workload is unrelenting and the benefits questionable,' he wrote.[10] His reservations echoed the views of many of his colleagues, including Nick Tate, new headmaster of Winchester and formerly chief of the Qualifications and Curriculum Authority (QCA), who stated:

> I don't think we [curriculum advisers] fully thought out all the available options. We added a new tier of exams and the amount of testing now needs to be reviewed. I did think it was the right approach, but it looks different when you are on this side of the fence.[11]

Calling the AS-level the least rigorous public exam ever imposed on British schools, the *Daily Telegraph* declared it was the culmination of the anti-elitist Left's long march through the institutions. 'Instead of creating worthwhile vocational exams for less academic pupils,' it wrote, 'these educational vandals are undermining Britain's one respectable qualification: the A-level.'[12]

Accepting that pupils had been unnecessarily burdened with a stressful workload, Estelle Morris's first decision on becoming Education Secretary in June 2001, was to ask David Hargreaves, chief of the QCA, to conduct an inquiry into the botched exam. His interim report a month later recommended some timetable changes to reduce clashes. The final report that December averred that the reforms had been implemented too hastily, but with no pilot schemes available to test the arrangements for A2, and with confusion among examiners over the standards expected, the potential for further trouble loomed.

The failure of the exam boards to anticipate the impact of higher marks in the AS resits only added to their embarrassment, as the marking of A2 brought a glut of top grades, a cause for concern as Sir William Stubbs, new head of the QCA, informed Estelle Morris in July 2002. It was to help avoid a massive leap in the pass rate that Ron McClone, chief executive of the Oxford, Cambridge and RSA Examinations (OCR), the exam board overwhelmingly used by the independent sector, overruled his chief examiners and adjusted the grade boundaries to keep standards in line with the previous year.

When the results were released on 15 August, the news that the pass rate had risen by a record 4.5 per cent drew the usual barbs about deteriorating standards, although pupil celebrations were tempered by disbelief at the alarming number of unaccountably low grades recorded by many an able pupil. At Wrekin College all but one of the fifteen English literature class had failed the synoptic module, which tests overall grasp of the course; at Epsom College forty-four English candidates had their coursework, initially marked internally, downgraded by 23 per cent; while at Dulwich College one student offered a place at Oxford and Yale received an unclassified, the lowest grade possible, for his history coursework.

On 1 September the *Observer*, alerted to these aberrations by a disillusioned parent, published a number of these rogue results and in the following week the newspaper was inundated with numerous other instances of candidates, sometimes whole classes, experiencing rough justice, victims apparently of grade fixing by the exam boards.

These allegations were primarily directed against the OCR, in whose marking a great discrepancy in modular results was evident, particularly in English and history. This particularly applied to coursework – assignments deemed worthy of a high mark by the schools had been graded unclassified. This distortion in the marking had not only deprived a number of pupils of the top grades they had been predicted, but also prevented them from gaining admission to their first-choice university.

As tales of bizarre grades abounded throughout both the state and independent sectors, the HMC worked closely with the member schools affected to collate the evidence. Citing evidence from some of the teachers who had acted as examiners and a QCA insider to support their claims of exam fixing, they threatened legal action against the OCR and the exam regulator until they received a full and satisfactory explanation.

Confronted with embarrassing press revelations, including a leaked letter from Ron McClone to Wrekin admitting that some grades had been adjusted – not an unusual occurrence with exam boards – and accusations of a political conspiracy against independent schools, Estelle Morris appeared all at sea in a storm that was partially of her own making. 'At the root of the debacle is the ridiculous fiction – invented by the Government, propounded by the boards and assiduously propagated by UCAS, the university admissions body – that an AS-level is equivalent to half an A-level,' wrote John Clare in the *Daily Telegraph*. 'But how could an AS-level possibly be equivalent to half an A-level,' he continued, 'when the Government, the exam boards and UCAS, from the very beginning, described it as the "easier half"?' If A-levels were to be saved, he concluded, either AS-level should be junked or made hard enough to warrant the description of half an A-level.[13]

On 18 September, following an unsatisfactory meeting with the three exam boards, the leaders of the Secondary Heads Association, representing the state sector, joined forces with the HMC and the GSA at a hastily arranged press conference to demand the remarking of 250,000 A-levels, accusing the boards of manipulating the results under orders from the QCA. 'QCA's role as a regulator is to ensure the boards follow agreed procedures,' declared Edward Gould, chairman of the HMC and not a man to be trifled with. 'Its brief does not extend to telling the boards what the outcome should be, nor should it attempt to influence the outcome.'[14]

Unnerved by the intervention of the schools, which had broadened the crisis into one focusing on trust in the credibility of the exam system, and under pressure from Number 10 to get a grip, Estelle Morris ordered an unprecedented remark of disputed exam scripts and the setting up of an independent inquiry into allegations against the QCA.

The next day, at a crowded press conference, a harassed-looking Morris denied any political interference in the marking of the exams but acknowledged that public confidence in the A-level had been badly undermined. It was for that reason she had asked Mike Tomlinson, former chief inspector of schools, to investigate allegations that the exam boards had manipulated the marks and to report back within a week.

While the leaders of the independent sector met Tomlinson to put fresh allegations of exam fixing to him and talk surfaced of replacing the discredited A-level with a new baccalaureate, the QCA announced the completion of its own review. Not only did it clear the exam boards of any wrongdoing, it also aggravated matters by blaming the teachers for misunderstanding the requirements of the new exam, a verdict that was greeted with universal derision.

Still blind to the rising tide surging at the QCA's door, Sir William Stubbs appeared on television to accuse Estelle Morris of pre-empting the outcome of the Tomlinson inquiry by contacting the boards about contingency plans should the inquiry recommend a complete regrading, a claim that Morris vigorously disputed. With relations between the two now severely strained, it wasn't surprising that, following the publication of the Tomlinson report, the Education Secretary dismissed Stubbs to 'restore public confidence in QCA', even though Tomlinson had acquitted him of anything unbecoming.

Introducing his report at a press conference on 27 September, Tomlinson called the exam debacle an accident waiting to happen, given the sheer complexity of the new system. Estelle Morris had been warned a year earlier but had taken no action. Sir William Stubbs had acted with total integrity in upholding standards but had left the exam boards with the perception that they should reduce grades. The *Times* later commented:

> He has paid the personal price of a dishonesty about the A-level that stretches back two decades. Politicians and officials retained the name of that examination and never ceased to wallow in the rhetoric of a 'gold standard'. In truth, though, the character and central purpose of the A-level has been changed enormously. It exists today as a highly imperfect means of directing as large a number of young people towards any version of higher education as possible.[15]

While Tomlinson completed his inquiry, Estelle Morris chose to fall on her sword. Reeling from delays in teacher vetting for the new school year and a failure to meet primary school targets, as well as the A-level debacle, she resigned at the end of October, declaring that she wasn't up to the job. She was replaced by Charles Clarke, a more rumbustious figure.

Following the A-level fiasco, Clarke asked Tomlinson to review the 14–19 curriculum and encouraged him to develop clearer and more appropriate qualifications, especially for vocational studies, in the hope that it would encourage more pupils to stay on at school post-sixteen.

Given time to sift through reams of evidence and take advice from the numerous parties, Tomlinson managed to win a broad consensus for his radical overhaul of the exam system, aside from the HMC and the other leading associations in the independent sector. They resisted the plans to scrap the A-level and GCSE but called for the demise of GCSE coursework and for the A-level to be made more challenging.

When Tomlinson reported in February 2005, he advocated a new overarching four-tier diploma that would take in existing academic and vocational qualifications. Throughout his inquiry he had liaised with Clarke and his vision for an integrated qualifications system was in line with government thinking, but Clarke's replacement as Education Secretary by Ruth Kelly, and an impending general election changed everything. With Blair more vulnerable in the aftermath of the invasion of Iraq and not wishing to be the prime minister who abolished the A-level, he instructed Kelly to reject Tomlinson.

Meanwhile, the independent sector continued to go from strength to strength. In 2003 the percentage of A grades at A-level achieved by its pupils reached 43 per cent and that figure continued to rise until it passed 50 per cent in 2009 – compared to just under 40 per cent in grammar schools and 20 per cent in comprehensives – revealing an ever-wider gap between the two sectors.

Alarmed by the growing difficulty experienced by universities in distinguishing among high achievers, the independent sector had pressed for the introduction of an A* grade, awarded to those with an average of 90 per cent in their A2 modules. Yet when it was introduced in 2010 the fact that 31 per cent of its students gained this new top grade meant it was only of limited help to university admissions departments.

Another important trend during these years was the disproportionate number of privately educated candidates studying maths, physics, chemistry and modern languages at A-level, whereas those in the state sector increasingly opted for new subjects such as drama, film studies and PE, rated less highly by elite universities.

In 2011 the overall pass rate at A-level rose for the twenty-ninth year in succession and while the A grade remained static for the first year since 1997, its percentage of 26 per cent contrasted dramatically with the 11.9 per cent of 1981, helped by the decision of the examiners in 1987 to stop awarding a set percentage of A grades.

This grade inflation provided powerful ammunition for those who argued that A-levels were a mere shadow of those of yesteryear. Numbered among the sceptics was Michael Gove, Education Secretary between 2010 and 2014. Convinced that the current exam system comprised too much assessment and too little learning and failed to prepare students for the demands of higher education, he sought a return to the linear exams of the 1990s. Modules would be scrapped and exams would be taken at the end of the two-year course; AS-level would be separated from the full A-level to form a qualification in its own right – taken either at the end of the first year or the second year of the sixth form.

The proposals attracted little support across the educational spectrum, the HMC calling them rushed and incoherent, driven by political considerations. Ditching AS-level meant returning to a narrower curriculum and would deter pupils from studying challenging subjects such as maths and French; it would also deprive universities of the most reliable indicator of a student's potential. In March 2013 the HMC made a formal plea to the Education Secretary to keep AS-level with the suggestion that it constitute 40 per cent rather than 50 per cent of the overall A-level to remove any incentive for able students who performed well at AS-level to coast through their final year.

The HMC's representations had little impact other than winning the concession that the AS-level wouldn't become as hard as the A-level.

As disillusion with the A-level grew, especially its inability to stretch the most able students, some schools began to look for a more challenging alternative. First, there was the IB, devised by an Oxford academic in the late 1960s to cater for a growing number of internationally mobile students. Based in Geneva, its independence from government protects it from grade inflation and it is now taught in over 140 countries.

The IB is a multidiscipline two-year diploma in which students select options from six required subjects – first and second languages, maths, science, humanities and the arts – three at standard level and three at higher level, with exams being held exclusively at the end of the second year of the sixth form. They also write an extended essay of 4,000 words of original research, undertake a theory of knowledge course and complete a non-exam module that comprises creativity, sport and community service.

Sevenoaks, a school with a strong international intake, became the first British school to introduce the IB, in 1977, and ran it in conjunction with the A-level until it switched completely to the former in 1999. By then, other schools such as Haileybury, Malvern and Rossall had begun offering the IB, and, in 2001, KCS followed suit, its headmaster, Tony Evans, declaring that nobody knew what an A-level meant any more. Bedford adopted the IB in 2003 and since then some sixty or so independent schools now offer both A-levels and the IB, with NLCS and Oakham offering the Pre-U (described below) as well.

One school that went its own way was KESB, convinced that its reputation for academic excellence had been undermined by modifications to the A-level. Searching for an alternative, the chief master, John Claughton, was encouraged by Tony Evans at KCS to convert to the IB entirely, and following extensive consultations with several IB schools, the common room and parent body, he did precisely that.

Although implementing it proved harder than Claughton had ever imagined, the staff and pupils were equal to the challenge by achieving most creditable results and reinvigorating the intellectual life of the school. In 2014 more than 25 per cent of the boys scored 40 out of 45 – higher than the equivalent of four A*s at A-level – and two boys, one of whom was Claughton's son Tom, achieved the very rare distinction of full marks.

With its independent thinking and creativity, the IB has been popular with teachers and pupils and valued by universities. It was also endorsed by Tony Blair in 2006 as an ideal qualification for the global demands of the twenty-first century. Yet the taxing nature of the diploma, especially its maths and modern languages components, means it is not to everyone's taste; moreover, it is prescriptive – scientists cannot study three sciences – time-consuming and expensive to run.

In 2013 KCS, the *Sunday Times*' IB School of the Year in 2012, acknowledging that the IB was proving an arduous assignment for some of its pupils and that Cambridge didn't like its maths – it preferred double maths at A-level – reintroduced A-levels.

Another alternative to the A-level is the Pre-U, devised by the University of Cambridge International Examinations in response to requests from a number of independent schools for a curriculum that was intellectually stimulating and rigorous. With its free choice of subjects – unlike the IB – its in-depth study and terminal assessment at the end of a two-year course, it resembles the A-level of yesteryear, except for its nine-point grading scale, its top grade superior to the A* at A-level and the obligatory Independent Research Report to promote independent thinking.

Although the first set of results at Charterhouse, one of the prime movers behind the Pre-U, caused some disquiet with a number of pupils faring worse than expected, subsequent results fully vindicated its switch to the new exam.

Some 150 schools, state and independent, are now registered to teach the Pre-U, including Winchester – the one school to have switched to it entirely – Eton, Rugby and Westminster, yet while they find it intellectually stimulating they remain very much the minority. The A-level, for all the criticism it has attracted, remains the overwhelming choice of the independent sector. According to Richard Cairns, it behoves the sector to improve the national examination system not to abandon it for alternatives that either fail to insist upon a proper understanding of their nation's freedoms, as did the IB, or, like the Pre-U, hark back to a golden age that never was.

Similar views were expressed by Barnaby Lenon, who, in a letter to *The Times* in October 2010, took issue with Anthony Seldon and his constant denigration of the A-level: 'Keen, in part, to promote Wellington's own "unusual" alternative curriculum, he selects aspects of the A-level system and uses these to imply that the whole system is bust.'[16]

Lenon accepted that grade inflation and the retake of modules were weaknesses but these could easily be remedied. Many of the syllabuses and textbooks were good and his own experience of teaching three A-level subjects informed him that, 'Dr Seldon's description of lessons as "mere instruction" is not one most of us would recognise'.[17] A-level enabled candidates to specialise in subjects they enjoyed. He continued, 'We know perfectly well that forcing all pupils to do French, maths etc in the 6 form would be demotivating for all but a small proportion.'[18]

As with the A-level, the GCSE, first introduced in 1986, has been mired in controversy as educationalists and successive governments have tried to devise an exam that caters for the greater number of pupils who now stay on at school post-sixteen. Traditionally, the academic elite, the top 20 per cent, had sat the O-level and the next 40 per cent the less academic alternative, the CSE, leaving the bottom 40 per cent without qualifications. In order to give every child the best opportunity to achieve to the highest level, the Thatcher government, following on from the initiative of the Callaghan government, replaced both O-level and CSE with the GCSE, an exam catering for the whole ability range with coursework assessment as its most prominent innovation.

Although coursework, in the help it gives to those who struggle with timed exams and its reward of individual effort, had many supporters, the fact that it was open to abuse either through plagiarism or through lenient marking (it was assessed internally) soon placed the integrity of the new exam under scrutiny. Critics complained that it presented fewer challenges to the most able and provided inadequate preparation for A-levels. One of the first into combat was Martin Rogers, former chief master of KESB, who told his school speech day in July 1989 that bright pupils were in danger of being bored to death by GCSEs. 'Many of the questions our boys faced this year are trivial; an insult to their intelligence and hard work,' he stated.[19]

Schools such as St Paul's Girls', Winchester and Manchester Grammar School toyed with dropping the exam in all but the core subjects as the gap between the two sectors widened during the mid-1990s.

The introduction of the AS-level raised fresh questions about the future of the GCSE as pass rates in the independent sector continued to soar, 53 per cent of its students gaining an A grade in 2002. 'It's like Boy Scouts collecting badges,' complained Tony Little the following year, after 90 per cent of Etonians achieved A grades. 'One has to ask what the educational value of it is.'[20] Increasingly, schools began to consider the IGCSE with its end-of-course exams as an alternative, believing it to be more intellectually challenging.

The following year St Paul's abandoned some GCSEs on the premise that they no longer prepared its pupils for A-levels. According to its high master, Martin Stephen, the exam, through no particular fault of its own, had always been confused about its role. 'Is it a leaving certificate representing a guarantee of minimum competence?' he said. 'Is it a qualifier for further and higher education? By trying to do both, it has managed not to do either terribly well.'[21]

With Manchester Grammar School switching to IGCSE maths, *The Times* called for a basic reform of English and maths, citing the opinion of the CBI, which stated that employers recruited workers with good grades in those subjects only to then find they lacked basic literacy and numeracy skills.

In 2009 Wellington introduced the Middle Years Programme of the IB for all members of its third form, after which they could choose whether to continue with it or switch to GCSEs or IGCSEs, and St Paul's introduced IGCSEs in every subject except for art. By then, nine out of the top ten schools in that year's league table offered IGCSEs, especially in maths, science and English, and one-fifth of independent schools offered some subjects, although Brighton soon returned to GCSEs, citing some very subjective marking and the end to coursework in GCSE maths.

Despite repeated attempts by the independent sector to persuade the Labour government to allow all schools to take IGCSEs, it wasn't until the advent of the Coalition government in 2010 that the exam was officially recognised, a further inducement for schools to switch.

In 2012, after comments by Michael Gove that exam passes couldn't continue rising each year, GCSE grades dropped for the first time in its history, but that statistic was overshadowed by a major row over the marking of the English exam by the three exam boards when a sudden shift of the grade thresholds led to thousands being denied a pass grade. In a damning report that September, the HMC alleged that the exam system had been undermined by a series of 'systematic weaknesses' including flawed marking, wildly fluctuating grade boundaries and ever-easier questions. Some one-fifth of teachers believed that as many as 25 per cent of candidates received the wrong grade each year and it called for an urgent investigation by the Office of Qualifications (Ofqual), the new exam regulator, to ensure that examiners possessed the necessary expertise to properly assess the work.

Despite a further overall fall in top grades in 2013, 60.4 per cent of independent-school pupils attained an A grade and 32 per cent an A* – four times as many as in the state sector – but what really stood out was the growing popularity of IGCSEs. Over the last five years their number has tripled so that they now constitute nearly 40 per cent of exams taken by sixteen year olds in the independent sector. At Bedales School, the opportunity now exists to abandon GCSEs altogether and take IGCSE core subjects in addition to the school's own assessed courses – approved by UCAS – an innovation in creativity that has proved popular with teachers and pupils alike.

Yet, as with A-levels, the independent sector has been by no means united about abandoning GCSEs. Back in 2000 Philip Evans at Bedford argued for its retention because it ensured a broad curriculum without which pupils might lose motivation; in 2007 Pat Langham, president of the GSA, declared that the independent sector should be part of a credible national system, otherwise educational apartheid would be the result; then, in 2011, Tim Hands, master of top-performing Magdalen College School, described GCSEs as a test of pupils' character and stamina because it forced them to work on their weaknesses:

> The fact is that in the old days, you could do well in the subjects that you were naturally good at, and secure a place at a top university. That's no longer the case. You won't get into a top university unless you have good grades across the board. ...
>
> The truth is that GCSEs are a better and broader set of tests, and more meaningful to employers and universities.[22]

It was important to keep a single set of tests that everybody could understand. Constant change wasn't helpful.

Whether the exodus from GCSEs gains further traction depends on Michael Gove's reforms. Thwarted in his plans to create a new English Baccalaureate certificate in core subjects, he vowed to clamp down on coursework and resits, make linear exams more challenging and introduce greater differentiation in the grades at the higher end. Yet whatever the nature of the reforms, due to begin in September 2015, they will be of little value, according to the HMC, unless the government tackles the inadequacies of the marking system, which has particularly penalised the most able, their pearls of wisdom undetected by inexperienced examiners. Following a record number of successful appeals in 2014 and an admission by Ofqual that 6 per cent of examiners were inadequate, the priority must be to entice a better type of examiner with higher remuneration and for Ofsted to provide greater scrutiny of the exam boards when unexplained marking patterns across a subject become evident.

Chapter 7

THE GREAT LEAP FORWARD

Perhaps the greatest achievement of the independent sector post-1979 has been its leap forward academically, led by schools such as Westminster and NLCS, where some 98 per cent of students achieve A grades at A-level. According to the Organisation for Economic Co-operation and Development (OECD), British independent schools are the best in the world and the gap between them and the state sector is the largest in any advanced country. Why this is the case has been the subject of much debate. Is it simply down to superior resources of the former and their ability to select or does it owe something to their ethos and high expectations?

Those who simply attribute it to resources would do well to remember that for many years privilege bred complacency and mediocrity, evident in the independent sector's inferior Oxbridge intake compared to the state sector (38 per cent to 62 per cent in 1969). It is true that the influx of many of the high-achieving direct grant schools to the ranks of the former in 1976 helped transform its fortunes, as did the availability of additional resources. Attractive new classrooms, art studios and science laboratories equipped with the latest teaching aids became the fashion, supplementing the ever-smaller classes – a pupil–staff ratio of 9 to 1 compared to 17 to 1 in the state sector. Although recent research by Alan Smithers and Pamela Robinson at Buckingham University suggests that smaller classes as a prerequisite for academic attainment can be exaggerated, there is no doubting the benefits, not least in giving pupils greater individual attention.

Although the independent sector has not been immune to the general shortage of teachers in subjects such as maths and science, its ability to offer more generous terms has helped it employ the pick of well-qualified graduates. According to the Sutton Trust, a teacher in the independent sector is seven times more likely to be an Oxford graduate and three times more likely to have been to a leading university compared to their counterparts in the state sector. Moreover, these teachers are much more likely to have a degree in the subject they are teaching.

The ability to select has enormous advantages, especially as demand for places has intensified at top schools. By no means are all independent schools selective, but even in the less academic ones the brighter pupils are able to generate an atmosphere conducive to good learning.

Highly motivated parents are crucial, especially now that they are more involved with their child's education. 'The parent has made a significant investment and in return expectations are great,' noted Bernard Trafford. 'The expectation is in itself an enormous motivation not only to the parent but also the child who signs up to the quest for success and the school that signs up in return.'[1]

'People still think that if you are in the independent system you are somehow dealing with rarefied pieces of humanity,' declared Jill Clough, headmistress of Wimbledon High School between 1995 and 2000 and subsequently of East Brighton College of Media and Arts, one of the most socially deprived schools in the country. 'They don't understand the exacting nature of the market and feeling completely accountable personally to parents.' She continued, 'There is an absolute driver going throughout the independent system that no child can be allowed to fail and you have to find all the different ways in which a child can succeed.'[2]

Of course, the tenor of the times and a strong work ethic on the part of many pupils have contributed greatly to improved results. The introduction of coeducation certainly helped, although certain boys' schools aptly embodied the virtue of *industria*. Stephen Jones, warden of St Edward's, Oxford, recalls going to Radley as a housemaster in the mid-1990s and being astonished by its prodigious work ethic and the amount of marking that he had to do. What really impressed him was this new idea that intelligence wasn't a fixed concept and that staff could make pupils better by raising their aspirations.

These aspirations were part of a wider commitment to all-round excellence pursued by the independent sector over the last several decades as the world has become ever more competitive. Whereas schools in the past lavished their attention on nurturing the elite, leaving vast pools of individual talent to go untapped, all pupils are now encouraged to aim high both in and outside the classroom. The number of plays, concerts, sports and societies has proliferated. Pupils qualify for the Duke of Edinburgh Award, participate in the Young Enterprise Company programme, raise money for charity, write articles for the school magazine, speak in chapel, escort visitors around the premises and teach in local primary schools.

Of course, educating the whole child has always been integral to an independent education but the sheer breadth of activity now on offer and the profusion of pupils benefitting from that experience is what defines the modern era. It is true that the growing importance of exams has led to some pupils shunning sport, especially during the summer term, but Jonathan Smith is surely right, as he states in *The Learning Game*, that this temptation should be resisted:

> Pupils are every bit as likely to succeed in exams, if not likely to do even bet-
> ter, if they take some exercise and enjoy sport. They may need the change of
> scene, the change of focus, the fresh air, the physical exercise, the fun and the
> farce, and – above all – the chance to forget themselves in play.[3]

A 2009 study of 508 private schools conducted by the ISC revealed a correlation between the number of extra-curricular activities offered and the proportion of pupils receiving top grades at GCSE, explained in part by the rise in self-esteem such activities promote, especially among boys. 'Boys really want a hinterland for their studies,' commented Andrew Halls. 'They don't want to work in a vacuum and need a sense of life beyond the classroom to make the classroom more palatable.'[4] Opined Martin Stephen, recalling the boredom and disillusionment of his own schooldays, 'If you create self-esteem of the right type in a young person they will achieve whatever their potential is.'[5]

In 2012 the All-Party Group of MPs on Social Mobility called for an end to a narrow focus on exam results and declared that school inspectors should evaluate schools on whether they provided extra-curricular activities. Success in life, they contended, was linked to confidence and social attributes such as leadership, teamwork and conversation, which independent schools instilled in their charges through extra-curricular activity.

In its June 2014 report *Going the Extra Mile*, Ofsted recommended that the state sector should learn from the independent sector by taking competitive sport seriously. From a study of ten independent schools and thirty-five state schools, it found that those with a strong sporting culture had similar expectations in the classroom, and both helped to cultivate an environment in which pupils excelled.

If self-esteem is born of success it also emanates from a caring atmosphere. Whereas in the past schools (boarding ones in particular) stressed character-building through hardship, the accent is now very different. In 2014 Tim Hands, master of Magdalen College School, told the *Sunday Times* that pastoral care was his school's primary concern: 'It's old-fashioned but our interest is in children being happy first and foremost, and academic, sporting, musical and artistic success follows from that.'[6]

On becoming master of Wellington in 2006, Anthony Seldon was asked by one of his parents to identify his leading objective. 'That the children are happy,' he replied,[7] presaging his introduction of well-being classes to make people believe in themselves. In 2013 James O'Shaughnessy, a former aide to David Cameron, told a Positive Education Summit at Wellington that research confirmed that schools that focused on character development turned out happier and more successful young people.

A crucial difference has been the changing attitude of the common room. Staff have shed much of their Olympian hauteur and formed much closer relationships with their pupils, helped by individual tutorials, school outings and overseas trips, and their inclination to encourage has proved more motivational than the carping of old. On returning to her old school, Wakefield High School, in 2007, the journalist Penny Wark recalled her time there as a pupil in the 1970s with scant affection because, some fine teachers aside, her foremost recollections were of a feeling that she didn't matter. Headmistress Pat Langham told her:

> You want them to succeed but, far more important, you want them to be happy. That's what changed about education since our day. What we do now is give girls confidence. ... It's my belief that every child has something about them and what matters is that they achieve their potential.[8]

It is a recurring theme throughout the sector. When asked to account for Brighton's spectacular advance in academic results under his leadership,

Richard Cairns highlighted the school's benign atmosphere, in addition to the excellence of its teaching:

> It is a very gentle environment, very tolerant. If children feel cared for and supported they will work hard. A good school does not focus just on good results but creates the right environment in which, as if by magic, children get results beyond their imagination.[9]

According to Barnaby Lenon, nurturing pupils' well-being was the biggest change he saw in his thirty-five years in the teaching profession: 'When I began I don't think the words "pastoral care" were uttered by anybody. Now it's central to life.'[10]

With good discipline, by no means always the case in the past, a more intimate feel to classrooms and myriad digital resources to provide more varied teaching, the willingness to learn has been enhanced. Leaning on the guidelines issued by exam boards, lessons have become better focused, work more consistently set, marking more informed and progress more frequently recorded. Monthly effort/attainment grades, form prizes and house competitions have all played their part in stimulating academic excellence, while contextual data has enabled schools to monitor more closely every child, especially those who are underperforming.

With more time given over in departmental and staff meetings to discussing pupil progress, every effort is made by tutors, heads of year, housemasters and housemistresses to turn their geese into swans. Sometimes this might mean employing sanctions such as detentions and daily report cards, but more likely a heart-to-heart chat or additional tuition.

While some schools have been very competent at teaching to the test, others have gone way beyond syllabuses and instilled in their pupils a real love of learning. One head who leads by example is Bernice McCabe who, prior to becoming headmistress of NLCS, spent twenty-three years in the state sector. A resolute opponent of fashionable learning techniques, she has placed her faith in highly motivated teachers, a depth of subject knowledge and persuading all her charges that their lives have real meaning. It was this credo that helped propel Chelmsford County High School, a grant-maintained grammar school, to the top of the league table for state schools, a feat which she subsequently repeated in the independent sector at NLCS.

'If maverick children can't succeed here, where on earth can they?' she likes
to tell her staff.[11]

'I was impressed,' declared Andrew Cunningham recalling his first day's
teaching there in 2006. He continued,

> No head I'd worked for before had ever made that kind of commitment. Heads
> like these create a special atmosphere that goes beyond the gleaming facilities
> and makes a school unique.
>
> Peer group pressure has a wholly positive effect when 50 or 100 young
> people who aspire to a top university are educated together. The pupils spark
> each other and compete in a wholly productive way.[12]

Another important explanation for the independent sector's surge in academic attainment has been the growth of public accountability through both
inspection and league tables. Following the Labour government's withdrawal
of its own official inspection in 1978, believing that it had no business maintaining educational standards free of charge for the private sector, the ISC
created its own system, the Accreditation, Review and Consultancy Service
(ARCS), in 1980, as a way of checking those schools applying for membership;
once accredited, schools were inspected on a ten-year cycle. HMC schools
were visited by Her Majesty's Inspectors (HMIs) every few years but because
they were under no obligation to publish reports cracks in a faltering edifice
could be shielded from public view.

This all began to change during the early 1980s when accountability
shook many schools out of their lethargy. Although the establishment of
Ofsted, HMI's successor, in 1992 didn't apply to the independent sector, the
HMC, sensing the way the wind was blowing in an age of greater transparency, decided to respond to changes in the state system. It thus fell to James
Sabben-Clare and David Christie, warden of St Edward's, Oxford, to set up
an inspection system on its behalf and geared to its needs. Training for staff,
with support from Ofsted, was set in motion and it was agreed by the HMC
in September 1993 that inspection for all schools should be accepted in principle as a condition for membership.

Its inspections began in 1994–95 with a similar framework to Ofsted, the
main difference being that inspection teams were staffed by retired heads and
practising teachers. In 1996 the ISC and HMC asked Ofsted to review their

respective systems and make recommendations for improvement. Ofsted's report, published in 1997, while complimenting them on the value of their reports and the expertise of their inspectors, urged them to be more critical in their evaluations. Keen to make its inspections as effective as possible, the HMC acted on Ofsted's advice and merged with the ARCS to form the Independent Schools Inspectorate (ISI). This new government-approved agency, under the leadership of a former inspector and overseen by Ofsted, inspected schools every six years and made its reports public.

During the first cycle of the new regime all schools in the ISC were inspected and every teacher observed at least once. In 2006 inspections became shorter and more streamlined but since 2009 it is normally every three years with less time in the classroom and more emphasis on welfare provision, a development much disliked by the independent sector because of the bureaucratic leviathan it has created. Yet with so much riding on a good inspection, schools have acted on their various recommendations and have become all the more formidable, as evidenced by the many favourable ISI reports of late.

During the late 1980s and early 1990s performance management was introduced to the teaching profession by a government which felt that too many teachers were failing their charges. In the business sector and in parts of the public sector appraisal was long in vogue and now, as the practice spread, teaching wasn't immune.

For the independent sector, where teachers had long been granted greater autonomy in the classroom, the innovation came as something of a jolt, and many reacted warily to the idea of being observed by their head of department or some other senior figure. Although some didn't survive this greater scrutiny, the sensitivity of most SMTs helped to win over the majority of the sceptics by stressing the positive side of appraisal, not least in terms of support and career development. Jonathan Smith, who experienced his first formal appraisal late in his career, became a firm supporter of it:

> In my late fifties I have learnt new things about myself and about how to do my job. It has made me want to improve and listen more. … While no system of development is perfect, and all schemes have their critics, professionally organised review brings colleagues together, face to face, in a formal setting, with the HoD [head of department] and the headmaster centrally involved.

Private dinner parties, pub chats, huddles in the corner of the staff room, walks around the grounds and late-night telephone calls cannot do this.[13]

Of course, all the professional training in the world cannot make a good teacher, let alone a great one. When Nick Clegg provoked a storm in 2013 by insisting that all teachers in the new free schools should have a professional qualification, he was taken to task by Richard Cairns. Cairns, an outstanding teacher himself, made great play of the fact that thirty-nine colleagues at Brighton lacked a formal qualification but that hadn't prevented the school from being one of the leading academic institutions in the country.

Cairns' comments were dismissed by Tristram Hunt, Shadow Education Secretary, who was educated at University College School, Hampstead (UCS). Speaking on the BBC's *Sunday Politics Show*, he claimed that being a teacher at Brighton was an 'easy gig' compared to being a teacher in a very challenging school where they needed to be well-qualified to teach effectively, a jibe that infuriated Cairns. Emboldened by the success of his policy of professional appraisal whereby pupils mark their teachers' lessons, Cairns believes that all schools should follow this practice in the quest to eradicate mediocrity from the profession.

Underlying all these changes has been the controversial introduction of league tables in 1992. Despite its domination of these tables over the years, the sector overall has never reconciled itself to them, at least in public. A poll of the HMC in 2002 found that over two-thirds of its members favoured their abolition and in 2008 some sixty schools, including Eton, Radley and St Paul's, refused to publish their results because of their conviction that the tables penalised schools who admitted weaker pupils. Their concerted opposition placed them at loggerheads with parents who found them informative, the media who used them to sell newspapers and the government which believed in greater accountability to raise standards – so why the continued hostility? Five main reasons can be cited.

First, while the ISIS league tables include all the pupils taking the exam in any one year regardless of age, the government version comprises only those who are fifteen years old from the last day of September, thereby excluding not only bright pupils taking the exam early, but also those older ones, mainly overseas pupils, who take it late. Despite the repeated protests of the independent sector that these omissions give a distorted view of a school's performance, governments of both persuasions have yet to redress this basic grievance.

Second, league tables take no account of a school's entry criteria, so schools that have worked wonders with the less academically able receive no credit. As Martin Stephen declared:

> Top schools agonise about dropping a place or two; struggling schools are branded as failures and their job of improvement made even harder. The claim is often made that league tables identify under-achieving schools. They might indeed spot the survivor in the sea, but instead of handing over a life-jacket, they hold their head under water.[14]

Third, in order to inflate their position, some schools resort to questionable tactics: keeping weaker pupils out of the sixth form, preventing others from sitting the more demanding courses or entering them privately. Fourth, they stifle creativity and imagination by teaching to the test, although this arguably relates more to the nature of syllabuses and means of assessment. Fifth, they are a very narrow indicator of a school's success. They reveal little about its ethos or the character of its pupils and their broader social, cultural, sporting and personal development.

All these reservations are valid enough, but, in an age of growing accountability, isn't it legitimate that parents should have the right to assess a school's exam results and identify the successful ones, especially since most of them are perfectly able to distinguish between different types of school? According to John Rae,

> What heads dislike about league tables is that they enable parents to compare different schools; and such unfavourable comparisons are taken personally by most heads ...
>
> It is not the misleading nature of the league tables which worries them so much as the publication of clear evidence that some schools and some heads are better than others.[15]

'Heads get really sniffy about league tables, saying they don't tell the whole truth,' remarked John Claughton of KESB, a school which had slipped down the rankings. He continued:

My problem is: they do tell a truth. One of the main criteria, which affects what my parents think, in whether they want their children to come here and whether we're doing a good job, is what results they get, and therefore, what universities they go to. I'm afraid that the *Daily Telegraph* league table does tell quite a material truth. If six years ago we were 78th, when once we'd been first, that means we are worse.[16]

Whatever broadsides heads have launched at league tables in public, few would deny in private that they have helped raise academic standards and forced schools to pay more attention to each and every pupil. 'If Inspection has probably been the greatest single factor in *guaranteeing* the quality of what goes on in independent schools,' wrote Nigel Richardson, former headmaster of the Perse School, 'has not league table performance sharpened up the collective act?'[17]

Norwich, Harrow, Rugby, Haileybury, Uppingham, Repton, Brighton and Cranleigh are among those schools that have seen a drastic improvement in their performance over the years, and even Wellington, for all Anthony Seldon's reservations about league tables, makes great play in its publicity of its leap up the rankings.

And yet for all its success in ridding many schools – state and independent – of the worst teaching practices, greater public scrutiny has also inhibited gifted polymaths from roaming over broad acres of education, instilling a great cultural appreciation in their charges. 'We've lost sight of the teaching and nature of education,' contends Ian Walker. 'What matters is learning how to learn and that teachers and pupils are engaged with the same love of learning.' He recalls that when he used to teach religious studies A-level at Dulwich he never taught the syllabus, and yet every year he would receive a letter from the examiners commending his pupils for their brilliance.[18]

In 2002 Tony Hubbard, chief inspector of the ISI, warned of too much spoon-feeding by the independent sector, which threatened to create a generation of unimaginative and impractical school leavers with little incentive to think for themselves, contrary to the uncertainties of the modern world. According to Jonathan Smith, there needs to be a reaffirmation of the primacy of lessons being taught in an interesting and exciting way.

One such exponent of this craft was Richard Stokes, an unconventional German teacher at Westminster who had a great influence on Nick Clegg, according to the latter's biographer, Chris Bowers. Shunning grammar for the most part, Stokes taught mainly through German poems set to music so that pupils would learn more about rhythm. His offbeat methods achieved outstanding results, but years later one of his refresher courses on Goethe's poetry pre-A-level was given short shrift by an Ofsted inspector.

After Stokes had explained to his pupils, in English, some of the finer points of Goethe's meaning – and also how Schubert had set Goethe's poetry to music – the Ofsted inspector approached him and told him confidentially that it had to be done in the target language, and that he should be explaining the finer points of Goethe's poetry in German, not English. Stokes thanked her for her contribution and continued his lesson in English, only for the inspector to intervene again. Escorting him outside, she insisted that he must adhere to the target language, at which point an exasperated Stokes suggested she stick to her role as an observer or did something else with her life, advice which so offended her that she complained to the headmaster, who, knowing of Stokes' prowess in the classroom, wasn't going to tell him how to teach. 'Westminster not only tolerated or condoned but actually encouraged the sort of teaching that stemmed from a teacher's soul rather than from a book that tells you how to teach,' Stokes added.[19]

Although more prescriptive than they used to be, independent schools still give enterprising teachers greater freedom to teach in their own individual style. During his final year at Rugby, Patrick Derham was observing one of his new English teachers and, impressed by the stimulating class discussion about gender stereotypes, asked him why he had ended the discussion prematurely. When the teacher replied that he needed to stick to his lesson plan, Derham assured him that he was now in a school in which he could afford to take risks.

The freedom of the independent sector to use resources as it thinks best, employ additional staff, teach a broader curriculum, impose its own disciplinary code, meet particular needs and promote independent thinking have all been central to its success. According to Rod MacKinnon, headmaster of Bristol Grammar School,

> The secret of independent schools, as I discovered first hand from being on both sides of the fence, is the freedom we have to focus on what really matters in a child's development at school. We thrive precisely because we do not

have to respond to the latest educational whim from a centralised education bureaucracy; well-meant initiatives perhaps, but all too often the product of muddled thinking.[20]

In 2008, in research commissioned by the HMC, Alan Smithers and Pamela Robinson asserted that independent schools were more successful than state ones because they had the freedom to tailor their teaching to the needs of their pupils.

In October 2010 Katharine Birbalsingh, deputy head of a south London academy, rose to prominence following a speech she delivered at the Conservative Party conference exposing the failings of the state educational system. What particularly concerned her was that teachers there, many of whom she rated highly, were too much in thrall to the prescriptive model of Ofsted inspectors: 'Rather than allow our teachers to be excellent in their different and innovative ways, some teacher-training institutions and some schools attempt to squash all ingenuity out of teachers, and make them into parrot-like machines churning out whatever skill-based nonsense they have been brainwashed with.[21]

Having observed a number of classes in a private school where pedagogic exposition gave way to a class discussion, she wrote that no teacher in the state sector would dare to teach the way those teachers did. 'Yet the children were so well taught that they seemed to know everything about the subject,' she said.[22]

Given the diversity of children, classes and schools, she reckoned that the freedom to choose what lesson was appropriate, what teacher might work best and what curriculum was best suited was imperative if the system was to provide real opportunities for all. 'The public school boys who run Britain aren't doing so because they were all considered to be the same at school: they run Britain because their teachers had the freedom to choose and, perhaps in the end, that is what it is to be a good teacher,' Birbalsingh concluded.[23]

A similar conclusion had been reached a few years earlier by Andrew Adonis when surveying those comprehensives suffering from the dead hand of local councillors and central bureaucracies. State regulation was a poor substitute, if any substitute, at all, for good teaching, good leadership and good governance school by school, he opined. Inventing the concept of independent state schools, Adonis later wrote that 'Everything about academies is in the DNA of the successful private school: independence, excellence, innovation, social mission'.[24]

Whatever the case for mixed-ability teaching as a means of giving every child an equal chance in a socially inclusive environment, this philosophy has become less fashionable as results have continued to disappoint. Bernice McCabe entered teaching in the state sector in the 1970s as an egalitarian idealist but discovered through experience that teaching O-level English in mixed-ability classes wasn't feasible:

> I had lots of doubts in the 1980s. The prevailing ethos in the playground was not to do well academically. Boys were particularly susceptible to pressure from their peers not to work hard.
>
> In the teaching profession the unions really held sway. There were terrific divides in the classroom between people who wanted to carry on running lunchtime clubs and do things to get the children going and those who felt it was unpaid skivvying.[25]

Even as setting became more acceptable in the state sector and exam results began to improve – in some schools quite dramatically – reservations continued to be expressed about the prevailing intellectual culture. In 1999 the Labour-dominated House of Commons Education and Employment Committee declared that successive governments had neglected the most able pupils. According to its chairman Malcolm Wicks:

> As a nation, over the last twenty years we have focused on overall standards of performance and quite properly have been concerned about children who are doing less well. That means there is a danger that Britain's brightest children sometimes get a raw deal ...[26]

In 2013 Sir Michael Wilshaw, chief inspector of schools, raised concern that non-selective state schools were failing to help the most able pupils achieve their potential:

> Too many non-selective schools are failing to nurture scholastic excellence. While the best of these schools provide excellent opportunities, many of our

most able students receive mediocre provision. Put simply, they are not doing well enough because their secondary schools fail to challenge and support them sufficiently from the beginning.

It is a serious concern that many non-selective schools fail to imbue their most able students with the confidence and high ambition that characterise many students in the selective or independent sector.[27]

Confronted by the new meritocratic ethos of the 1970s and 1980s, the independent sector reinvented itself as the model of scholastic achievement at a time when academic standards overall were slipping. Wealth and selection aside, much of that renaissance came about as a result of sound governance, hard work, high aspirations and communities working together for the benefit of each and every pupil. The sector might still be slated for its elitism but it is an elitism based now as much on intellectual achievement as social privilege, a conundrum which university admissions offices have yet to resolve.

Chapter 8

A CLASS APART

Despite the rise of new universities there is no doubt that Oxford and Cambridge continue to exercise a great hold over the independent schools, especially the more academic ones. The winning of places there is still essential to a school's reputation and any success will feature prominently in a head's report on speech day. It's not simply the gilded world of honey-stone quadrangles, immaculate lawns and May balls that gives Oxbridge a special allure, it remains the passport to joining the elite. A report by the Social Mobility and Child Poverty Commission in August 2014 revealed that 75 per cent of the senior judiciary, 59 per cent of the cabinet, 57 per cent of the higher civil service and 50 per cent of diplomats were Oxbridge educated.

As academic attainment became more important during the 1970s, the independent sector began competing more intensely for Oxbridge scholarships and entry. Leading schools such as Eton, Winchester and Westminster enjoyed a close relationship with Oxbridge, their headmasters dining at high table in various colleges and reciprocating in kind to the admissions tutors. Colleges wanted the schools' intellectual elite and schools were only too happy to oblige, provided the colleges took some of their lesser lights too. Such academic bartering, according to John Rae, was one of the reasons why Oxbridge found it difficult to reduce the number of successful applications from top independent schools (although sporting bloods were increasingly rejected).

If that wasn't enough, Oxford's brief dalliance with the decadent lifestyle of an earlier generation following Granada TV's screening of Evelyn Waugh's *Brideshead Revisited* in 1981 seemed only to affirm its image of outdated privilege, much to the consternation of a new generation of classless dons who hankered after wider access. 'Dons prowl the countryside like medieval friars searching for brains, while sixth-formers from comprehensive schools are welcome on visits and reassured of the accessibility and normality of the place,' declared Harry Judge, director of educational studies at Oxford.[1] In his opinion this emphasis on meritocracy was the greatest change in Oxford's 700-year history, although in truth the effect was still a limited one.

With the admissions procedure becoming ever more complex as each college did its own thing – some applicants, mainly from the state sector, were offered conditional places based on interview – a committee was set up under Sir Kenneth Dover, the renowned classicist and president of Corpus Christi College, in 1982, to establish a more uniform system. After twenty-seven meetings over six months, the committee decreed the end to entry scholarships and exhibitions at Oxford and also to post-A-level entry, which favoured the independent sector with its seventh-term specialist teaching. From 1986 the Oxford entry exam would either be a fourth-term exam pre-A-level, the option favoured by the majority of independent schools, or a conditional offer based on A-level results.

Although the independent sector disliked the Oxbridge exam intruding upon A-level courses, it adapted to the new realities with a more rigorous approach. Greater attention was given to Oxbridge open days, choice of college and subject and an applicant's personal statement. Additional general studies classes were organised and attendance at school societies was encouraged in order to help candidates gain greater educational breadth.

This thoroughness soon began to pay off. Applicants from the independent sector actually rose from 45 per cent in 1986 to 50 per cent in 1995 as an Oxbridge degree became ever more sought after with leading employers. Confronted with this unwelcome statistic, Oxford abandoned the written exam in 1996 and required instead the submission of two pieces of work and an interview – with entry conditional on top A-level grades. The decision unsettled the HMC, which feared a lottery. 'The increased emphasis on interview when this is the only method of selection is tending to favour those who kiss the Blarney Stone over those with the biggest brains,' declared Martin Stephen.[2]

After Cambridge abolished the entrance exam in 1985, independent schools increasingly began to devote greater attention to interview technique, not least the need to avoid overblown academic claims on their personal statement which they then couldn't back up in discussion. Subjected to searching interrogations by their teachers, and often by outsiders, many a candidate honed their skills to the point that most – although by no means all – could hold their own at interview.

In 1998, following a notorious incident in which a Cambridge don ridiculed at interview the accent and intellect of a girl from an Essex comprehensive, unease with the admissions procedure grew. Dr Gerard McCrum, Emeritus Fellow at Hertford College, Oxford, opined that the interview should be banned because it was a covert form of selection that allowed the university to accept a disproportionate number of privately educated candidates based on the assumption that they were more socially poised and interested in current affairs. With researchers from the Cardiff Business School arguing that these candidates were better able to realise their potential because of the more rigorous teaching they had received than state school pupils, more Oxbridge colleges resorted to an admissions policy of positive discrimination. Several years earlier, in 1995, *The Times* had expressed its concern that this discrimination could harden into 'politicised class war'. Many private pupils came from working-class families who were either benefitting from assisted places or were making great sacrifices to pay school fees. A good many state school entrants were the products of sophisticated middle-class parents who were topping up inadequate schooling with the best private tutors that money could buy.

Such a policy drew no apology from Richard Barnes, senior tutor at Emmanuel College, Cambridge, one of the colleges with the highest state-educated intake, when the question of positive discrimination resurfaced in 2000 in light of the Laura Spence affair. He stated:

> Independent school pupils may have got the best grades but it is potential that we are looking for. I have had a furious reaction from some independent schools. We are far from infallible but we believe the pupils we have accepted have more potential. It is not just a question of exams.[3]

The spat continued the following year when, following a survey of 10,000 students in the independent sector, headmasters complained about the 'rude, abusive and arrogant treatment' of their pupils by admissions tutors. Their complaints were given short shrift by Alan Ryan, warden of New College, Oxford, who contended that interviewing was less intimidating than in the past:

> So we are now frightening the upper classes after upsetting all the poor devils from comprehensive schools? Surely this is just trying to climb on the band-wagon that the maintained sector has been travelling on for years.
>
> Interviews are a rotten business, but the truth is that it is a rough life and we had all better get used to it.[4]

As some parents began withdrawing their children from fee-paying sixth forms and transferring them to the state sector to boost their Oxbridge chances, Tim Hands tried to allay the anxieties of his colleagues when he sat in on Oxbridge interviews during December 2004. Impressed by their attempts to be impartial through the introduction of interview panels (as opposed to a solitary individual), and attempts to score objectively every piece of work, he concluded that in terms of time, data, scrutiny and individual attention its admissions system was far superior to any other university. 'There is no significant evidence of discrimination against independent pupils by universities, whatever the individual anecdotes occasionally reported,' he wrote in *Conference and Common Room*.[5]

The pressure on Oxbridge to open up to all-comers continued. Peter Lampl, founder of the Sutton Trust, compared Oxford's outreach programme as inadequate in comparison to top American universities – not surprising, given the resources of a Harvard or Yale – and David Lammy, Minister of State for Higher Education between 2008 and 2010, accused Cambridge of recruiting in China but not in Middlesbrough or Hackney, his constituency.

With research from Cambridge demonstrating a strong correlation between A-level performance and degree, regardless of what school attended, the universities stood their ground. According to Chris Patten, chancellor of Oxford, standards needed to rise before his university admitted more state pupils, while Alison Richard, vice chancellor of Cambridge, taking exception to undue government interference, declared that universities weren't engines of social justice.

In 2011 the Oxbridge debate was reignited by the Sutton Trust's revelation that four independent schools – Westminster, Winchester, St Paul's and St Paul's Girls' – and one sixth-form college, Hills Road, Cambridge, monopolised places there. These five schools sent 946 students to these two universities over a three-year period between 2007 and 2009, more than the 927 admitted from 2,000 other schools and communities nationally. In all, privately educated pupils were seven times more likely to get into Oxbridge than those from the state sector. Given the similarity in architecture and atmosphere between independent schools and Oxbridge colleges, it was hardly surprising to Peter Wilby that eighteen year olds from Northern comprehensives felt uncomfortable in such privileged surroundings. In order to widen entry from the state sector, he proposed that Oxbridge should identify, at fifteen, the two or three most academic pupils in each school and not only nurture them over the next three years but also allocate to this pool a fixed proportion of its places. That proportion, he suggested, should begin at 70 per cent and rise to 90 per cent.

With the growing debate on social mobility given added urgency by the coming to power of an Old Etonian prime minister and the tripling of tuition fees, Oxbridge came under renewed pressure from the Coalition government to promote wider access. They responded by pointing to their expensive outreach work encouraging a broader range of intake – state school applicants were up 80 per cent over the previous decade – and their summer schools to help these pupils prepare for university entry. The fact that many teachers in the state sector actively discouraged their pupils from applying to Oxbridge, believing they would struggle in such a privileged environment, didn't help.

Further controversy was fuelled in 2012 as figures supplied to the *Guardian* from Oxford under the Freedom of Information Act revealed that privately educated pupils who achieved three A*s were 9 per cent more likely to be offered a place compared to their state counterparts with the same grades. Invited to explain this discrepancy, the university said that it made offers on predicted grades, aptitude tests and interviews, and state school pupils were inclined to apply for the most competitive courses such as medicine and law, whereas independent school pupils predominated in less competitive subjects such as the classics.

Talk of wider access by universities, as Cambridge recorded its greatest growth in state-educated entrants in thirty years for 2012–13, induced an emotive outburst from Anthony Seldon the following January. Irked that only twenty Wellingtonians of the sixty-two interviewed were due to receive

Oxbridge places, he told the *Daily Telegraph* that discrimination against independent school pupils had become 'the hatred that dare not speak its name'.[6] Yet, in a year when eighty-nine pupils from Westminster gained entry to Oxbridge, this hardly appeared to be the case. The truth was that as competition intensified each year, the chance of succeeding gradually diminished (80 per cent of those applying fail to win a place). The fact that the independent sector has continued to send a disproportionate 42 per cent to Oxbridge suggests that its commitment to excellence has barely been undermined by all the talk of social engineering.

The ongoing controversy over Oxbridge admissions has also applied to the other twenty-two elite universities known as the Russell Group. With this growing competition, not least from overseas students, independent schools found that fewer of their pupils were automatically accepted to the most sought-after universities such as Durham, Bristol and Edinburgh. Unhappy that eleven of the Russell Group, under pressure from the government, had set specific targets, the HMC met Les Ebdon, director of OFFA, in 2012 and urged him to scrap all targets.

Yet despite this mild form of discrimination towards those from lower socio-economic groups practised by some universities, it could hardly be said to be widespread. According to the Sutton Trust, the proportion of privately educated students admitted to the top thirteen universities actually rose from 32 to 33 per cent between 2002 and 2007. Furthermore, research at Durham University in March 2013 found that state school applicants needed one grade higher than independent applicants to receive the same offer, the discrepancy apparently similar to that at Oxbridge where the former applied for the most competitive courses.

Confronted with this evidence, Ebdon told the universities that they had made little progress in the drive to recruit more under-represented groups and they should set more stringent admission targets. They responded that this wouldn't solve the real problem of too few state-educated candidates applying and achieving the right grades. More emphasis needed to be placed on nurturing those of real ability, something the target-driven culture – geared to rewarding those of middling ability – didn't encourage.

With university admissions getting no easier and the options becoming wider, independent schools no longer simply rely on the general expertise of their university liaison office; tutors and departments are also expected to dispense specialist advice. Tony Little has admitted that the failure of a top Etonian mathematician and true Renaissance figure to gain entry to Oxford has radically altered the school's approach to university entrance. On inquiring why its mathematician failed to get in, Eton was told that its reference to his prowess as a concert pianist and tennis player led the university to believe that he wasn't a serious enough mathematician. Reluctantly accepting that Eton had done this boy a disservice, Little now tells Etonians that all they need to get into a top university are paper grades. He concluded, 'The line is: what a boy says about himself and what we say and what we write about him must be focused on the course he is applying for, and nothing else.'[7]

Following the imposition of tuition fees in 1998 and the Laura Spence controversy that raised awareness of the American university system, British students began heading across the Atlantic in greater numbers. With elite institutions such as Harvard and Yale seeing themselves as global universities, their well-oiled marketing machines scoured the world in search of the brightest and the best. At a time when their universities reigned supreme in world rankings, they received a positive response from many independent schools, especially top London ones such as Westminster and St Paul's Girls'. 'They see themselves operating on a worldwide stage,' declared Clarissa Farr, high mistress of the latter. 'Our students still see Oxbridge as very desirable but other pinnacles are appearing beyond those mountains.'[8] Vicky Tuck, principal of Cheltenham Ladies' College between 1996 and 2011, concurred: 'Some of the girls see their life prospects being enhanced by going to a good US university.'[9]

With competition intense at Ivy League universities – only 7 per cent of students pass into Yale and Princeton – the American option isn't for everyone, but for successful applicants the lavish facilities, breadth of courses and personal attention they receive in class have opened up untold opportunities. As Anthony Seldon noted in 2009:

> The attractiveness of US universities is more and more apparent to British families and students. The US system is better resourced, has a lower pupil–teacher ratio, and there's far greater celebration of achievement. ... US universities celebrate you playing the clarinet or being a netball star whereas British universities couldn't care tuppence about it, with some exceptions.[10]

Increasingly, they judge everyone by exam results alone.

The cost of studying at a top American university can be dauntingly prohibitive but its hefty endowment funds often provide means-tested bursaries for British students from families with middling income. Given that these were the people hardest hit by the rise in tuition fees to £9,000, the option to study in the US has become increasingly attractive. 'But there is also a growing demand for employers, in a tough jobs market, for students with better cross-cultural understanding, with a global outlook,' wrote Phil Baty, editor of the *Times Higher Education* World University Rankings, in April 2011. 'So study abroad can not only be cheaper, but may also help graduates stand out in the jobs market.'[11]

In addition to the 3,000 privately educated Britons now studying in the US, a significant number have turned their gaze towards Europe, and Maastricht University in the Netherlands in particular, with its low fees, lower entry requirements and courses in English (although there is little in the way of clubs and societies). It is a trend that is likely to continue.

Chapter 9

THE CULTURAL AWAKENING

As independent schools broadened their curriculum and gave more expression to individual talent, the arts came into their own. Although these schools had boasted gifted artists and musicians in times past and staged some memorable productions, cultural activity was broadly confined to the elite. Michael Charlesworth recalled that the higher the standard of music at Shrewsbury, the fewer the boys who participated, and John Thorn had similar experiences at Winchester when headmaster there, the school's superb orchestra playing a Beethoven symphony to a mainly adult audience. Following the appointment of a dynamic new director of music, chamber music groups proliferated and the two chapel choirs attained a new level of excellence. With Thorn's encouragement, the school staged four operas during his time there (1968–85) and in spite of their imperfections, which aroused plenty of criticism, he rated them a triumph:

> They seemed to me to proclaim what boarding schools, lucky enough to have some talent seven days a week, could do, and what, in our century, they were about. The 'message' of the *Magic Flute* and *Fidelio* – the value of constancy, and the superiority of love over systems and of freedom over tyranny – was once a message public schools ... rarely seemed to convey ... The old-style public school had justified itself in the courage its ex-pupils showed in many wars and in the administrative skills they brought to the old empire. In a world without major wars of that kind and in a Britain without an empire, a new

justification was required for their strange institutional ways. In a striving for excellence in great art I felt we were finding some of that justification.[1]

With more heads such as Thorn willing to raise the banner of artistic expression in their schools and more pupils keen to participate in a more culturally expressive age, there has been a flowering of artistic activity. New theatres, concert halls and art studios have sprung up and more time has been devoted to plays and concerts, their ability to build confidence and fuel imagination increasingly recognised.

Art, now embracing sculpture, photography, print-making, embroidery and ceramics, has not only become a very popular subject, it has also become an extremely successful one, as evidenced by superb exam results and by the quality of work adorning campuses. Many more alumni now have successful careers as architects, fashion designers, artists and photographers.

Although music has remained a minority academic subject compared to art and drama, it prospers in every other sense. Helped by music scholarships, the number of choirs and instrumental ensembles has expanded, with greater emphasis on dance, jazz and rock, while informal lunchtime concerts have nicely complemented formal school concerts in cathedrals and concert halls, not least on exotic overseas tours.

Under its illustrious director of music Ralph Allwood (1985–2011), one of the finest trainers of young choirs in the country, the Eton Chapel Choir toured the world and released numerous recordings, and half of the 1,300 boys learned a musical instrument. 'As with the school itself, Allwood suffers from widespread and jealous muttering that he "should be producing this kind of result, given the resources he has," ' wrote Richard Morrison, chief music critic of *The Times*. 'But it isn't his budget that persuades sixteen-year-old boys that singing is cool. It's his charisma, and the fact that he sets them challenges that they know would stump many adult choirs.'[2]

One of the greatest challenges during Allwood's time featured the attempt of Alex Stobbs, one of Eton's foremost music scholars, to conduct J.S. Bach's epic choral *Magnificat* before an audience of several hundred in College Chapel. For not only had Stobbs chosen a fiendishly difficult piece but, more important, he suffered from a virulent form of cystic fibrosis, a life-threatening condition that slowly destroys the lungs and digestive system, and impaired hearing.

A chance encounter between Allwood and the award-winning film-maker Stephen Walker led to a Bafta-nominated Channel 4 documentary, *A Boy Called Alex*, which charted the highs and lows of Alex's three-month assignment to realise his ambition. Twice chronically ill during rehearsals, only vast doses of medication, the unstinting support of home and school – Eton paid for a part-time nurse – and a sheer love of music kept him going. Overcoming all his travails, he rose to the occasion magnificently as the performance in March 2007 was rated a great success.

Winning a choral scholarship to King's College, Cambridge, Alex featured in another Channel 4 documentary in which he conducted the renowned Rodolfus Choir in a performance of Bach's *St Matthew Passion* at London's Cadogan Hall. Surviving further bouts of dangerous illness, he graduated with a 2.1 in Music in 2012.

The growing importance of drama has been recognised by its place in the curriculum, both at GCSE and A-level. It has given greater confidence to pupils performing in public. Not only has the number of productions mushroomed, not least at house level, but so has the variety, with plays that challenge as well as entertain.

No school has been more successful in nurturing theatrical talent than Eton. Although the staging of plays there had always appealed to the pupils, the school authorities tended to adopt a rather disparaging attitude towards drama, deeming it to be rather decadent and pointless. The fact that Eton didn't have a theatre puzzled Anthony Chenevix-Trench on becoming headmaster there in 1964. With his support, and that of the bursar, a new multi-purpose theatre, the Farrer Theatre, was built, opening in 1968. Unfortunately, the splendour of its surroundings wasn't matched by corresponding standards in acting. A number of lacklustre performances were subjected to ridicule by the iconoclastic audiences of the late 1960s, a situation that convinced the authorities that something more professional was required. Directors with previous acting and drama experience were appointed, school plays were taken ever more seriously and the opportunity for boys directing their own plays abounded.

During the 1980s, under a new director of drama, Robert Freeburn, a triennial School Play Festival featuring plays written by masters and boys was established, house plays became the norm and under the expertise of directors such as Michael Meredith, Bill Rees and Angus Graham-Campbell talented actors now had the opportunity to play a variety of parts. Only the indifference of the audiences continued to disappoint, a major reason for Freeburn's departure in 1987.

Under his successor, Peter Broad, girls from local schools were drafted in to play female parts, a house drama cup was instituted, giving many Etonians their first experience of acting and the Double Edge Drama theatre company was founded with the sole purpose of taking quality plays to the Edinburgh Fringe. Improvements were also made to the Farrer Theatre, such as dressing room facilities and the introduction of computerised lighting.

A further boost came with the appointment of Simon Dormandy, a former Royal Shakespeare Company actor, as director of drama and head of theatre in 1997. His brilliance as an organiser and director set new standards of excellence. Convinced that drama was a superb way for adolescents to explore their entire being, Dormandy treated Etonians as professionals, inspiring a vintage generation during his fifteen years in charge. Already during the 1980s Eton had produced Damian Lewis and Dominic West; now they were followed a decade later by Eddie Redmayne, Tom Hiddleston, Harry Lloyd, Julian Ovenden, Harry Hadden-Paton, Nyasha Hatendi, Tom Palmer and Tom Stourton.

Dormandy's influence was particularly profound on Redmayne, an Oscar winner in 2015 for his mesmerising portrayal of the disabled physicist Stephen Hawking in *The Theory of Everything*. A lover of drama from an early age, Redmayne's delicate features combined with his total dedication and capacity to play all types of roles marked him out as somebody special. According to Dormandy, 'The first time I met Eddie, he was in the very first production I did, my own adaptation of *A Passage to India*, he played the female part and I knew as soon as I met him that he was exceptionally gifted.'[3]

After subsequently directing him in *Henry VI*, Dormandy brought him to the attention of Mark Rylance, artistic director of Shakespeare's Globe Theatre, in the latter's search for a teenage Viola to play opposite his Olivia in an all-male production of *Twelfth Night* at the Middle Temple Inn in January 2002. Unfazed by such elevated surroundings, Redmayne's Viola won much critical acclaim with a performance that gave him his first major break in his professional career.

With facilities and directors the envy of many a professional company and possessed of a natural swagger that lends itself to a commanding stage presence, Etonians are more fortunate than most. They also take their drama very seriously, often rehearsing well into the night. Some twenty-five shows, many written and directed by the boys themselves, are produced each year and with theatrical agents often lurking, especially in Edinburgh at the Fringe, Eton's current reputation for turning out stars for the stage and screen is set to continue.

Although no school can emulate Eton with the range and quality of its thespians, a number have played their part. One such school is Harrow, with its proud Shakespearian heritage and famous Elizabethan stage, graced by the presence of the screenwriter and film director Richard Curtis during the 1970s. In more recent times the school's drama department has helped launch the careers of Benedict Cumberbatch, star of the BBC series *Sherlock*, and Laurence Fox, best known for his leading role in the British television drama series *Lewis*.

As a young actor in an all-boys' school, Cumberbatch found himself playing female parts until his voice broke, beginning with Titania, the fairy queen, in *A Midsummer Night's Dream*. 'Cumberbatch was every inch the Fairy Queen,' commented the *Harrovian*. 'His ringing tones filled Speech Room and he displayed a mature control of gesture and movement that promises much for future productions. What most impressed here was the sense of danger this young actor breathed into the fairy kingdom.'[4]

With the lead roles of Willy Loman in Arthur Miller's *Death of a Salesman*, Petruchio in *The Taming of the Shrew* and Arthur Crocker-Harris in Terence Rattigan's *The Browning Version* to follow, Cumberbatch was serving notice of his brilliance as a communicator. According to Martin Tyrrell, Harrow's former head of drama, he was the best schoolboy actor he had ever seen.

Cumberbatch's junior by a year was Laurence Fox, son of James Fox and nephew of Edward and Robert, one of the great acting dynasties. Something of a free spirit, he, unlike Cumberbatch, derived little pleasure from his time at Harrow save only for his acting and his rewarding relationship with Martin Tyrrell. Perceiving him to be a kindred rebel with his tatty linen jacket and his smoking in school, Fox credited Tyrrell more than anyone else, including his father, for laying the foundations of his successful career, learning more from him about acting than he did from his time at RADA:

> He was passionate, committed and inspirational. ... I can remember many
> late evenings when he would go over and over plays that we were studying,

bringing them to life, fuelling us with the passion that he had for the work himself. He had a way of energising his students, bringing out the best in them. I never once detected a moment of apathy or boredom in him.[5]

Founded by the Elizabethan actor Edward Alleyn, Dulwich's association with the stage dates back in time and has recently nurtured the playwright Michael Punter and the actors Rupert Penry-Jones and Chiwetel Ejiofor, the latter Oscar-nominated for the part of Solomon Northup in the critically acclaimed film *12 Years a Slave*.

The son of a middle-class Nigerian family who came to Britain to escape from the Biafran War, Ejiofor's return to the country of his birth for a family wedding ended in tragedy when the car he and his father were travelling in collided with a lorry. His father was killed instantly and Ejiofor spent ten weeks in hospital with severe head wounds. Learning of his father's death from his mother, the first question he asked her was whether he could stay at Dulwich. When his mother said he could, he replied, 'Then we have to struggle on.'[6]

A voracious reader of literature, Ejiofor thought that acting was the most fantastic way of expressing himself. Playing Angelo in *Measure for Measure*, aged fifteen, he found the part to be particularly intoxicating – 'an expression of sexual anger, rage and manipulation'.[7] According to actress Sally Hawkins, then a pupil at the neighbouring James Allen's Girls' School (JAGS), who played a member of the Venetian court, Shakespeare was his forte, while to Peter Jolly, Dulwich's head of drama, Ejiofor was very talented from an early age. He had an ability to take directions and was a great team player. Not surprisingly, he won the school drama cup. Winning a scholarship to the London Academy of Music and Dramatic Art, Ejiofor was cast in Steven Spielberg's *Amistad* at the age of nineteen, a fortunate break from which he has never looked back.

At Tonbridge, Jonathan Smith recalled the occasion in 1997 when he and his colleague Lawrence Thornbury, a professional actor, were holding auditions for a production of *Macbeth*. With a long list to choose from, they were able to offer a couple of small parts for young boys. One afternoon a boy in his first year asked if he could audition for Macbeth and, if not, Macduff. His request was granted and immediately his captivating performance left everyone entranced, not least Smith himself, who thought him much better than many of the professional actors he had worked with at the BBC:

> His voice, a voice to die for, his range, his focus and his intelligence, they all hit me. Lawrence and I looked at each other, eyes widening but trying to hide our responses.
>
> The other boys and girls stood still. Whatever this boy's age, they all knew that they were watching someone extraordinary ...
>
> We cast Dan Stevens as Macbeth, and everyone in the production, even the most disappointed of his rivals, knew it was the right decision.[8]

Smith went on to direct Stevens, later of *Downton Abbey* fame, as Thomas Becket in *Murder in the Cathedral* and Prince Hal in *Henry IV, Part 1* during his time at Tonbridge and is credited by his protégé for curbing his rebellious instincts with words of wisdom and encouragement. Stevens later recalled,

> In the oddness of the public school system, English and drama were my salvation. Jonathan and Lawrence made the English department feel like a special place; they also recognised my passion for acting and were able to channel the various problems I might be going through as a teenage boy on to the stage. It helped a lot.[9]

Another school where the arts have flourished is Bryanston. It was there that the actress Emilia Fox, daughter of Edward Fox, and her brother Freddie were educated, the latter having a play specially written for him called *A Risky Business* in which he played the headmaster.

And not only the men have prospered. Women have been nearly as successful. Westminster produced Helena Bonham Carter, where she acted alongside Nick Clegg in *The Changeling*, and Imogen Stubbs; St Paul's Girls' – Emily Mortimer, Rachel Weisz, Olivia Grant and Clemency Burton-Hill; Badminton – Rosamund Pike; Bedales – Minnie Driver; Headington – Emma Watson; Wycombe Abbey – Sally Phillips and Rachael Stirling; and Woldingham – Carey Mulligan.

Although Rachael Stirling, daughter of Diana Rigg, had misgivings about boarding school, she acknowledged that it was the perfect place to catch the acting bug. Spending much time in the Lancaster Arts Centre at Wycombe

Abbey, she took part in anything that helped her overcome acute homesickness. The quality of the plays they put on varied but 'some of the drama was awesome'. She continued:

> My school believed in the power of our young imaginations, and in the ability of drama to engage them. It taught us to have confidence in our creative selves, not to be afraid of what we don't know. And it encouraged us to be curious all through life and keep learning as we went.[10]

From a young age Carey Mulligan had wanted to act and her chance came in school productions of *The Crucible*, *Return to the Forbidden Planet* and the musical *Sweet Charity* in which she played Nicki. According to Judith Brown, head of drama at Woldingham, she was very talented and natural:

> Carey had an inner confidence and knew she could succeed, but was incredibly modest about her ability. That was the lovely thing about her.
>
> If she didn't get a lead role, she was happy to be in the chorus. She wanted to learn about all aspects of production, from being an assistant to the director of Sweet Charity to helping with the First Year drama workshop.[11]

A highlight of her time there was a visit to see Kenneth Branagh in *Henry V*, and he inspired her so much that she wrote to him asking for advice. Branagh's reply through his sister was polite but fairly non-committal. Nor did she receive great encouragement when she sat next to Julian Fellowes, the film director and screenwriter, at lunch following a talk he gave to the school about the production of *Gosford Park*. On hearing of her theatrical ambitions, Fellowes advised her to marry a banker.

Rejected by drama school three times on leaving school, Mulligan recalled her encounter with Fellowes and managed to contact him through her ex-headmistress. Impressed by her perseverance, Fellowes invited her to dinner at Le Caprice, along with several other aspiring thespians, and his wife Emma took an immediate shine to her. The next day Emma rang a number of agents and casting directors and facilitated a meeting with a casting assistant, which in turn secured Carey an audition with Joe Wright, director of a film adaptation of *Pride and Prejudice*. After several auditions she landed the part of Kitty Bennet, the beginning of a glittering career on stage and screen, most notably for her roles in *An Education* and *The Great Gatsby*. Despite her success, Mulligan kept in touch with Woldingham, accompanying a school party to the local cinema to see *Pride & Prejudice* when it was released.

The independent sector has been well represented among the young, talented female playwrights who have come to the fore during the last decade. Polly Stenham (Wycombe Abbey and Rugby) became the toast of the West End for her play *That Face*, a visceral dissection of a rich dysfunctional family, which opened to glowing reviews in 2007, and *Tusk Tusk*. She heads a list that includes Anya Reiss (Francis Holland School), Lucy Prebble and Ella Hickson (both of Guildford High School).

While educating musicians, playwrights and actors has long been a tradition of many of these schools, nothing has quite emulated the rich vintage of the last three decades, itself a reflection of the greater priority they have given to the arts. This cultural output (in comparison to the decline of drama in the state sector), the rising expense of drama school and their social connections helps explain the current domination of the privately educated on stage and screen. It is a trend that has raised concern among the likes of Dame Helen Mirren, Sir Peter Bazalgette, chairman of the Arts Council, and Chris Bryant, Shadow Minister for the Arts.

In January 2015 Bryant told the *Guardian* that 'we can't just have a culture dominated by Eddie Redmayne, James Blunt and their ilk' who went to boarding schools. Blunt retorted, bitterly, that no one at Harrow had helped him break into the music industry and at every stage his background had told against him. Rather than engage in the politics of envy, Blunt stated, Bryant should celebrate success as the Americans did, a charge that the Cheltenham-educated Bryant denied. He wasn't denigrating Blunt's success, he explained – he had even contributed to it by purchasing one of his albums – or Redmayne's; he simply wanted everyone with artistic talent regardless of background to have the same opportunity to shine.

This nurturing of theatrical talent by independent schools was also viewed with some ambivalence by Boarding School Beak in the *Daily Telegraph* in February 2014:

> I must have spent dozens of tedious hours in school theatres over the years, stifling yawns and trying not to fall asleep. Great plays have been spoiled for

me by overexposure, as many schools often seem to put on exactly the same shows: tried-and-tested favourites like *Grease*, *The History Boys* or *Les Misérables*.

What's more, we beaks have to give up our rare and precious evenings off to watch these plays. I used to try and pretend I'd been, when I hadn't, nodding sagely in class the next day in all the right places. But the pupils very quickly rumbled that ruse. No matter what you think privately, your role is to sit there smiling approvingly.[12]

While acknowledging the educational value of drama and its ability to instil greater confidence in shy pupils, the columnist regretted the fact that it was the socially precocious who tended to gain all the main parts.

Sensible adults could also lose their sense of proportion, according to Boarding School Beak:

Yet to hear some of the hyperbole from purring parents, you'd think we had just witnessed the opening night of *Waiting for Godot*. … And that's why, while I applaud the current success of public school actors, I still groan inwardly every time the posters spring up for the school play.[13]

Chapter 10

PLAY UP, PLAY UP AND WIN THE GAME

Amid the euphoria of Team GB's success at the London Olympics in 2012, controversy raged over David Cameron's comments that too many state schools paid insufficient attention to sport and that too many medal winners were privately educated. It had been the same in 2008 at the Beijing Olympics, especially in sports such as rowing, sailing, shooting, hockey and tennis. The fact that 50 per cent of the medallists there had come from just 7 per cent of the population was one of the worst statistics in sport, according to Lord Moynihan, chairman of the British Olympic Association. He insisted it should be a priority to make sport a more accurate reflection of society.

In fact, the true percentage of independent pupils who won medals at the Olympics was 37.8 per cent in Beijing and 37.3 per cent in London, with rowing leading the way, and the great triumphs of Sir Chris Hoy (George Watson's) in cycling, Sir Ben Ainslie (Truro School) in sailing and Alistair Brownlee (Bradford Grammar School) in the triathlon.

The domination of the independent sector hasn't been confined to one sport. The England rugby revival of the early 1990s was led by Will Carling of Sedbergh, with a back line that included Rob Andrew and the Underwood brothers, all of Barnard Castle School, while their victorious World Cup XV of 2003 contained a significant number of privately educated players: Jonny Wilkinson (Lord Wandsworth College), Lawrence Dallaglio (Ampleforth), Lewis Moody (Oakham), Will Greenwood (Sedbergh) and Mike Tindall (Queen Elizabeth Grammar School, Wakefield). More recently, the team has been captained by Chris Robshaw (Millfield) and coached by Stuart Lancaster, a former head boy at St Bees.

It isn't just England. Finlay Calder of Stewart's Melville captained the victorious Lions in Australia in 1989; three of his successors as captain of Scotland during the 1990s were David Sole and Rob Wainwright of Glenalmond and Gavin Hastings of George Watson's, while Wales' 2012 Grand Slam included Alun Wyn Jones and George North of Llandovery College.

After the amateur captains of the 1960s such as Peter May, Ted Dexter and Colin Cowdrey, English cricket seemed to be heading in a more democratic direction with people such as Ray Illingworth, Graham Gooch and Mike Gatting in charge. The pendulum then swung back beginning with Mike Atherton (Manchester Grammar School) and Nasser Hussain (Forest School) down to Andrew Strauss (Radley) and Alastair Cook (Bedford). What's more, whereas 92 per cent of Gatting's team in 1987 were state educated, half of Cook's team are privately educated, as are some 30 per cent of county cricketers.

Even football, a working-class game for over a century, has seen the return of privately educated players, led by Frank Lampard (Brentwood School), James Beattie (Queen Elizabeth's Grammar School, Blackburn), Quinton Fortune (Forest) and Johnny Gorman (Repton).

This sporting elitism seems at odds with the oft-proclaimed demise of the cult of athleticism in the independent sector, but that loss of mystique has been replaced by a new intensity as sport has become more of an industry. 'The successful transformation of athleticism, which was hostile to academic achievement, into the new sporting ethos, which complements the schools' pursuit of academic excellence, is remarkable,' wrote John Rae.[1]

Although academia assumed a greater importance during the 1970s, sporting acclaim was still the priority for many a boy, with fixtures often intruding into class time, much to the fury of non-sporting staff, and taking precedence over other activities. Sporting bloods still held sway, especially in rugby. Will Carling recalls that, as a new boy at Sedbergh, he was taken down to the First XV pitch and told that the school hadn't lost for five years. 'It was surreal,' he said. 'Everything was designed to magnify the status of those who eventually represented the First XV.'[2]

When the likes of Sedbergh and Ampleforth were playing at home, the whole school would turn out to watch and a victory for the Fettes First XV would earn them a standing ovation as they entered the dining hall for supper. Those awarded their colours were the proud recipients of a special blazer and scarf and the object of veneration from many a pupil, including a number of girls who gained kudos by going out with a member of the XV.

Few events matched the cachet attached to house rugby as teams practised all hours and gave their all in matches that lacked nothing in passion. One Rugby housemaster was so proud and delirious of his boys becoming Cock House in 1980 that he gave each of them a bottle of champagne.

Athletic prowess remained a powerful attribute for those holding high office in many a school hierarchy, as George Osborne, a non-sporting intellectual, discovered at St Paul's in 1988. When proposed by Peter Pilkington, the high master, as captain (head boy), the opposition from the sporting lobby in the common room was so vociferous that Pilkington felt compelled to back down and choose a more conventional candidate, compensating Osborne with the position of vice-captain.

As the 1980s progressed and the bloods in the common room became a dying breed, sport lost ground to the broader extra-curricular programme that all schools were now promoting. School journals devoted less coverage to team sports, the First XV attracted smaller crowds and lengthy absences from class for matches became less tolerated given the growing importance of national exams. 'Increasingly, our school teams are not returning home unbeaten,' reported the NLCS magazine in 1981. 'Some girls no longer find that being members of school teams is important to them. Music lessons, part-time jobs and weekends away from home are all attractive alternatives to Saturday morning matches.'[3]

In addition to sport's declining hold over school life, its character changed as individual sports became more fashionable. A number of more liberal schools such as Abbotsholme, Bedales and Gresham's had pioneered this greater choice based on health and fitness-related programmes. By the millennium all schools had come to accept the concept of 'sport for all' with an ever-wider programme, and the opportunity for every child to participate and represent the school. School assemblies not only celebrated the achievements of the top teams but also the C and D XIs in the various age groups.

With parents demanding better facilities for their ever-higher fees, all-weather pitches and sports halls comprising fitness centres, swimming pools and weights rooms became the new priority. Roger Uttley, former England rugby international appointed to Harrow as director of physical education in 1982, recalled that lessons then took place in the original Archibald MacLaren gymnasium, 'hardly larger than one badminton court and equipped with traditional wall-bars, Swedish beams, and Olympic gymnastics apparatus. Changing facilities were minimal, there was a primitive homemade weights area, and that was about it.'[4] Within four years he was in charge of a brand new sports hall and a 25-metre indoor pool.

With the wider sporting curriculum and the principle of equality of entitlement, schools have come to rely on outside specialist coaches to provide expert tuition and PE specialists to teach the subject to GCSE and A-level, as well as help coach senior teams. Overseeing this burgeoning sporting empire with a substantial budget is the director of sport, often a former professional or international player. As the job has developed in importance beyond mere administration, the occupant is now likely to be part of the SMT with responsibilities for marketing as well as sport.

Although those indisposed to team sports may not be denigrated as in former times and given greater freedom to opt out, these sports are still highly prized by schools for their ability to foster resilience and team spirit. With the advent of professional coaches and the favourable publicity that accrues to a school as a result of winning a prestigious cup competition or tournament, the emphasis on winning is greater than ever. Schools proudly parade their sporting accomplishments on their websites, in weekly literature and on special public occasions such as speech day or open day.

Pre-season training for senior teams is seen as obligatory and training thereafter is never less than intense. Although some traditional fixtures have been terminated because of logistical problems, teams, with the possible exception of cricket, play as much as they ever did, especially if they experience a successful cup run.

Overseas tours have become very popular and, as well as providing opportunities for extensive practice, the experience of playing against hardened opponents in countries such as New Zealand and South Africa has helped raise the bar.

One tour which brought less happy memories was Harrow's cricket tour to Sri Lanka in December 2004. On Boxing Day, the boys were practising in front of the pavilion at Galle on the southern tip of the island when they heard people screaming and saw a mass of water surging towards them.

They managed to scramble to the top floor of the two-storied pavilion from where they witnessed a second wave deluge the ground. Within a couple of hours the water had receded enough to enable the party to make their way to the Galle Fort Hotel — their hotel had been devastated — only to learn that the stepfather of one of the boys had been killed while helping his wife escape from the tsunami as they made their way to the ground in a bus. Overall, 31,000 Sri Lankans lost their lives in the disaster. With the tour at an abrupt end, it was particularly poignant for Harrow to return to Sri Lanka in December 2013 and visit Vidyaloka College, the eminent boys school in Galle that it had helped rebuild.

In their desire to boost recruitment and win competitions, most schools now offer sports scholarships or general scholarships that take sporting ability very much into account. This development has helped create a group of elite schools, especially in sports such as rugby, football and hockey, but also in some of the more individual ones such as tennis. That in itself has generated controversy.

At their best, sports scholarships have enabled many athletes, including Olympians and rugby and cricket internationals, to realise their potential by having access to top facilities and coaching that otherwise would probably have been denied them. Not only have these awards contributed to national sporting success, with all the pleasure that this brings, not least at the 2012 London Olympics, but schools themselves have also benefitted by the example that these elite athletes set to lesser mortals. Struggling teams in particular can derive real inspiration from the performance of one or two leading players.

More problematic are those schools that recruit sports scholars simply to win without instilling in them the broader educational ethos. Aside from contravening the spirit in which the game should be played, there is something unsatisfactory about a pupil who has represented the school at junior level being shunted aside in favour of some burly South African prop whose loyalty to the school can be somewhat transient. Such an arrangement detracts from the team ethic if the fortunes of that team are simply down to individual brilliance rather than collective endeavour.

A policy of 'buying in', especially at sixth-form level, can also damage relations with trusted opponents on the circuit, especially those that don't provide sports scholarships. Some fixtures going back years and renowned for their keen rivalry have become so one-sided that those on the receiving end have refused to continue playing.

It is invidious to point the finger at certain schools for milking the sports awards system as the majority do so in one form or another, but clearly some do so much more extensively. That is their right but to expect other schools to compete on an uneven playing field, especially at rugby where the physical cost can be considerable, is tantamount to wishful thinking. Isn't it time that the HMC came up with guidelines similar to the Daily Mail Cup regulation in rugby whereby each school is limited to playing three new sixth formers?

In a more competitive culture that celebrates winners, the undermining of sporting ideals, so evident in the professional game, has seeped through to school sport. It would be idle to pretend that there once existed a golden age wherein Corinthian values reigned supreme. A mass brawl between Eton and Radley took place at Henley during the 1950s and Dr Robert James, on becoming headmaster of Harrow, was appalled by the unruly behaviour of his first Eton–Harrow match at Lord's in 1954. Tales of biased umpires and referees and other aspects of gamesmanship weren't unknown, but they were the exception rather than the rule. Many masters in charge of rugby and cricket were men of the highest integrity who taught their teams to uphold the very best of sporting ideals, and the friendships formed off the field helped cement the excellent spirit in which matches were played.

According to Anthony Seldon, no school exemplified hospitality and good manners better than Tonbridge,

> … with a tradition laid down by the great Michael Bushby and John Gibbs, both outstanding sportsmen who were dominant forces at Tonbridge for the last thirty years of the twentieth century. Teams were always met off their coaches by captains, the players were always well looked after, taken to meals and to changing rooms. The parents were always treated courteously and well, and match day was a deeply civilised and civilising event. This is sport at its very best.[5]

To some the Tonbridge model remained sacrosanct while to others it appeared somewhat dated. John Rae, keen to transform Westminster's rather casual attitude towards sport, appointed a new master in charge of football and gave him confidential instructions to make the boys more combative.

Following their instructions to the core, the First XI began to play with more aggression, much to the dismay of the master in charge at Winchester when the two schools played out a 1–1 draw at Westminster in 1983. Incensed by the physical tackling of the Westminster team, the Winchester master accused his opponents of playing like professionals. 'This is not what public school football is,' he complained to Rae as they went into the pavilion for tea. 'I make soothing noises because he is our guest and is clearly very angry,' wrote Rae in his diary. 'I can hardly tell him that what he objects to is a direct result of my policy.'[6]

Although schools' football has had its problems, its standards of sportsmanship now compare favourably with schools' rugby. In December 1997, following an ill-tempered encounter between Cranleigh and Eastbourne College in which some of the former 'brought a seething brutality to the second half', according to *The Times*, the headmaster of Cranleigh cancelled his side's tour to South Africa the following summer;[7] then, in 2007, fixtures between Wellington and Marlborough were suspended in the wake of allegations that a member of the Wellington XV bit an opponent's ear in the scrum.

A sign of declining standards was the sight of coaches questioning referees' decisions from the touchline. After Ian Walker, headmaster of King's Rochester, confronted one visiting master in charge for abusing the referee and being generally objectionable, he wrote to that master's school banning him from setting foot on King's soil again. 'I wonder if we Headmasters are sufficiently assiduous in ensuring that bad sportsmanship is squashed,' he declared in *Conference and Common Room*. 'I know a number of Masters-in-Charge of First XV rugby on our circuit whose behaviour is always, to say the least, reprehensible.'[8]

Walker had a point. Too many schools have turned a blind eye to such demeanour as the will to win has become ever more imperative, not least by professional coaches imported from the leagues. Parents, too, have been party to unedifying scenes on the touchline. Anthony Seldon, when deputy at St Dunstan's College, Catford, observed a father physically assaulting the opposition coach for putting his son on the pitch; he thought the boy should have been rested as he had an important county trial the next day. According to Seldon,

The example that parents give matters greatly. On touchlines over 25 years I have seen the full spectrum, from the magnificent to the disgraceful. Some schools seem to 'educate' their parents much better on how they should behave. No doubt it is part of the tradition built up over many years.[9]

It isn't just rugby that has had its problems. Cricket has been tarnished by bad language, intimidation of opponents and dissent towards the umpire. In June 1997 a rain-affected match between Radley and Marlborough ended in acrimony when Marlborough, subjected to abusive taunts by the Radley fielders, delayed its declaration, leaving its opponents with no realistic prospect of victory. Radley apologised for its behaviour but Richard Morgan, the warden, announced that it was in the best interests of both schools to suspend all sporting fixtures between them.

An equally unedifying encounter took place a few weeks later at Tonbridge when the school traded insults with Grey High School, Port Elizabeth, in what one master present called the most unpleasant match he had ever witnessed. The master in charge of cricket at Tonbridge, Paul Taylor, noted that 'Grey were competitive to a degree our players had not seen before and one of our boys was drawn into that.'[10] He commented further:

> The difficulty is that you are asking boys to play very competitively and aggressively and intimidate through actions and not through words. Teaching that line is very difficult when they see what goes on in the professional game.
>
> Schools cricket has got a lot harder in the past ten years and with that there is a danger, we are well aware of, of losing the line.[11]

'There is no question that the prevalence of sledging [personal abuse to intimidate an opponent] has increased markedly over the past five years,' opined Neil Gamble, headmaster of Exeter School and Devon cricket official, 'and that has percolated down to schools, because once the school season is over boys go and play in leagues around the country. There is a lack of chivalry and honesty.'[12]

At the gathering of the HMC later that year the chairman, Michael Mavor, asserted that such uncivilised behaviour shouldn't be tolerated. Its sport sub-committee drafted a code of conduct imported from professional sport, which was later accepted by all its members. The guidelines stated that it was the responsibility of heads to ensure that the high standards of conduct in school sport were maintained, to stamp out gamesmanship, intimidation, bad language and dissent by banning pupils who abused opposition players.

The code has been more honoured in the breach than the observance by some schools, the result being that standards of behaviour have varied enormously since then. In 2006 Robin Marlar, president of MCC (Marylebone Cricket Club), incensed by the inane chatter in a match between Brighton and Harrow, his old school, marched onto the field and demanded that both sides abide by the spirit of the game. The 2013 edition of *Wisden* drew attention to the serious abuse of umpires, even involving adult coaches, with David Graveney, former chairman of the England cricket selectors and the ECB (England and Wales Cricket Board) national performance manager, expressing surprise that umpires were prepared to stand at all. 'Behaviour on the field is often exemplary,' remarked Paul Bedford of the ECB, 'but it is noticeable that, if an incident does happen, masters in charge and coaches are less inclined to act than in the past.'[13]

Not all schools have been prepared to ditch sporting ideals in the pursuit of victory. Anticipating an excellent season for his First XV in 1991–92, headmaster of Clifton, Hugh Monro, a former Cambridge rugby blue, declared that he would not want an invincible XV since this would encourage aggression to the detriment of the values of the school. One game away from an unbeaten season, however, he did send the team a note wishing them every good fortune. They won the game and the headmaster was the first to congratulate them, not least for the impeccable way they had conducted themselves throughout the season.

In 2001 Hurstpierpoint was playing its arch rivals Ardingly in a local cup match and needed six to win off the last ball, at which point one of its batsman swung lustily to leg. The ball soared over mid-on and went many a mile, although no one seemed sure whether it had cleared the boundary before bouncing. With the result hanging on this imponderable, both sides agreed in the spirit of the game to a replay.

Finally, when the fourteen-year-old Jonathan Bairstow scored an undefeated 167 for St Peter's, York, against Ampleforth in 2004, his opponents to a man sought him out afterwards and shook his hand, typical of an establishment that has always known how to win and lose with grace.

In a world that has placed considerable pressures on teenagers, it ill behoves schools to add to these pressures by placing an undue emphasis on sporting success. Competitive school sport is a serious business but not so serious that it should cause coaches and players to lose their dignity or sense of perspective. Although the writer Rudyard Kipling disdained the cult of athleticism that dominated the public schools at the end of the nineteenth century, his much-quoted lines about treating triumph and disaster the same still resonate.

Chapter 11

SPORTING PRODIGIES

While the choice of school sport has greatly expanded over the last couple of decades, rugby continues to maintain its hold as the most prestigious, not least in the professional era when its growing intensity at club and international level has been emulated in schools.

Aside from the growing importance of sport to a school's marketing, the lure of intrinsic rewards for those able to play rugby professionally has brought a new competitive edge, none more so than in the Daily Mail Cup (now the NatWest Schools Cup), the largest school competition in the world. With the game becoming ever more physical and built around robust defence, the great emphasis on size has inevitably placed those of a lighter build at a disadvantage, especially their susceptibility to injury. A study carried out in six Edinburgh schools by Professor Allyson Pollock, then director of Edinburgh University's Centre for International Public Health Policy, in 2009, found that a young rugby player faced a 17 per cent chance of sustaining an injury, typically concussion – mainly from tackling – or a fracture. Concussion was under-reported because it wasn't monitored properly, she claimed, and consequently parents weren't fully aware of the risks posed by their children playing rugby.

Rugby governing bodies have tried to counter this disturbing trend by insisting on better medical training for referees and coaches, and a significant medical presence on match days. In Scotland, following several serious spinal injuries in school matches between 2007 and 2009, its governing body, the Scottish Rugby Union, decreed that no one could play in the front row in under-18 rugby until they were seventeen, and those under sixteen couldn't play until they had passed a grip, height and weight test.

Even this stipulation hasn't alleviated concern in schools and parents about safety, however. In 2012 Glenalmond announced that it was suspending fixtures against Strathallan and Loretto following a massive imbalance in size during the previous year's encounters; and in 2013, Wales' oldest schoolboy fixture between Christ College, Brecon, and Llandovery was cancelled, because the latter was deemed to be too strong for the former.

In 2002, with generous backing from the National Lottery, the RFU (Rugby Football Union) established fourteen rugby academies to help train the elite players of the future. A number of schools have links with these academies: Oakham School with Leicester Tigers; Bedford with Northampton; and Whitgift School with Harlequins – which can help these players progress to the next level, but the narrow intensity of an academy can conflict with the broader interests of the school. While some schools enable their pupils to give priority to their academy commitments, others aren't so keen and this clash helps explain why the RFU now wants its elite players in further education colleges so it can fully control their development.

On an extremely competitive circuit featuring Durham School, Barnard Castle, Queen Elizabeth, Wakefield, Woodhouse Grove School, Bradford Grammar School and Stonyhurst, no greater rivalry has existed than that between Sedbergh and Ampleforth. 'Relative to our physique at the time, the fitness sessions were brutal and as tough as anything I've done with England,' wrote Lawrence Dallaglio of his time at Ampleforth.[1] His coach, John Willcox, a former England captain, was a tough disciplinarian who had the forwards out every break in their school uniform for line-out practice and was meticulous in his preparation. During these years (1987–88 and 1989–90) Ampleforth was unbeaten, but while rugby retained a certain kudos, its aura, compared to that of Sedbergh, began to wane in the professional era.

With legendary names such as Wavell Wakefield, John Spencer and Peter Kininmonth numbered among its rugby pantheon, Sedbergh's devotion to the game knows no bounds. During Will Carling's three years in the First XV between 1981–82 and 1983–84, the last as captain, the school lost only twice. Much of that success he attributed to the master in charge, Kerry Wedd:

> Kerry was an excellent coach, very progressive. He liked attacking rugby, as most school sides do. He was very keen on fitness and modelled his sides around fast, elusive backs who had good back rows to go with them.

When I was there we just weren't used to losing matches. I never thought I was going to lose and it makes a hell of a difference to your play.[2]

With Will Greenwood, Phil Dowson and James Simpson-Daniel, all future English internationals, following Carling at Sedbergh, its XV not only became too strong for Ampleforth but also for almost every other school, and by the millennium the team was increasingly travelling all over the country to find meaningful opposition. Between 2005–06 and 2009–10, they were beaten only twice, by Millfield and Colston's – and there was no stiffer opposition than that.

Any school side that contained Rob Andrew and Rory Underwood was bound to flourish and the 1981–82 Barnard Castle XV set standards for others to follow. In 2003–04, under Lee Dickson, later England's scrum half, it had its best side for fifty years and reached the final of the Daily Mail Cup, only to lose 30–28 to Oakham.

The following year they were again runners-up, this time to Colston's, and then, in 2006–07, having seen off Wellington in the semi-final, they lost 24–23 to a late try to Warwick in an absorbing final, a result which led to church bells ringing out across the town of Warwick in celebration.

Another Northern school to excel is Woodhouse Grove. In 2013 it was the winner of the inaugural Daily Mail Schools Rugby Trophy, launched in conjunction with schoolsrugby.co.uk, which organises the merit table for games played in the autumn term, after an unbeaten campaign of twelve matches. Sedbergh was the runner-up.

Although not quite as competitive as the Northern circuit, the Midlands is no pushover, with Rugby, Oundle, Uppingham, Bedford and Oakham leading the way, the latter winning the Daily Mail Cup in 2002–03 and 2003–04.

Down in the South-west, the quality of Bryanston, Sherborne, Blundell's, Clifton and Downside has been overshadowed by Colston's and Millfield, which, along with Wellington, Sedbergh and Llandovery, are in a class of their own. Unlike Llandovery and Sedbergh, Colston's entered the Daily Mail Cup and was dominant to such an extent that it won it for six successive years between 1994 and 2000, three times against Queen Elizabeth, Wakefield, barely conceding a try during that time.

In 1999, in order to give state schools more of a chance, the organisers of the competition introduced a rule that prevented schools from playing more than three players who had joined at sixth-form level. The stipulation aggrieved Colston's, which denied that the majority of its players were on scholarships. Following its victory in 2000, it withdrew from the competition, citing the personal abuse to which its players had been subjected and its unwillingness to exclude some of its players for cup matches. Colston's compensated by expanding its fixture list to include the very best in Great Britain and Ireland and when Llandovery beat it 13–7 in 2001, it was the school's first defeat in four years.

In the South, Cranleigh, Epsom, Eastbourne and Radley have all enjoyed impressive winning sequences and, in 1995–96, Tonbridge went unbeaten for the first time since 1949, the prelude to a vintage era between 2003–04 and 2006–07 when it won every school match.

No school offered more rigorous opposition than Wellington as it lifted its rugby to a new and unprecedented level in the 1990s. Between 1997 and 2001 it won fifty matches in a row against British schools, and in 2008–09 became the first school to accomplish the double by winning the Daily Mail Cup at both under-18 and under-15 level, inflicting the only defeat of the season on St Benedict's School, a record that won St Benedict's the accolade of *Rugby World*'s School Team of the Year.

Wellington's professional ethos antagonised some of its opponents and, with some schools cancelling fixtures against it, Anthony Seldon decided that it should withdraw from the under-18 competition, 'an unpopular decision with the players and parents, though most understood the logic'.[3]

The absence of Wellington gave opportunities to others. In 2010–11 Whitgift beat Newcastle RGS in the final of the Daily Mail Cup, thanks in part to the efforts of Lawrence Okoye, the British discus thrower turned American footballer, and Marland Yarde, who made his England debut in 2013. The next year Whitgift won again, seeing off Oakham 45–24 in an entertaining final.

Whitgift's achievement in retaining the cup was eclipsed by neighbours Dulwich, which won it for three years in succession. Probably no school could emulate the mighty Dulwich XV of 1997–98 comprising David Flatman and Andrew Sheridan, future England internationals, which won fifteen matches out of fifteen with a phenomenal points record of 827 for and 47 against. According to Peter Allen, the Dulwich coach, he had never seen one player inject such fear in the opposition as did Andrew Sheridan with his combination of size, strength and speed, all of which brought him twenty tries.

Having gone through 2012–13 unbeaten, Dulwich lost convincingly to an outstanding Epsom side in 2013–14 but it richly compensated by overwhelming Warwick in the NatWest Schools Cup final with a scintillating display of running rugby. Entering the Cup in 2011, Dulwich remained unbeaten until losing to Bromsgrove in the 2014–15 final.

In Scotland a tight-knit circle of Edinburgh schools plus Glenalmond, Strathallan, Dollar Academy and Dundee High School make almost every match seem like a local derby. While the big day schools such as Stewart's Melville, Edinburgh Academy and George Watson's perennially provide stiff opposition, they have found it difficult to establish any supremacy over Merchiston.

Set in a rut in the early 1980s, Merchiston's revival owed much to the arrival of Frank Hadden, later the Scottish head coach between 2005 and 2009. Working in tandem with a team of experienced coaches throughout the school and concentrating on developing core skills, he developed an attractive style of fifteen-man rugby that was not only spectacular to watch but also devastating in impact. Soon Merchiston teams were beating all comers, often by embarrassingly large margins, and were forced to seek stronger opposition south of the border. During this period eight Merchistonians went on to play for Scotland, including Peter Walton, Duncan Hodge and Craig Joiner.

The school that came closest to emulating Merchiston was Dollar. From 1997 when the independent sector joined the Bell Lawrie (now the Brewin Dolphin) Scottish Schools Cup, Merchiston and Dollar were champions for seven out of the next eight years before others got in on the act with Stewart's Melville and Edinburgh Academy winning twice before large, enthusiastic crowds at Murrayfield.

Yet for all the excitement and quality of many a final, the cup lacks breadth in that no more than half a dozen schools stand a realistic chance of winning. Few Scottish state schools play rugby in any depth, exposing the narrow foundations on which the game in Scotland is based.

As part of its attempt to give the game a lift, the Scottish Rugby Union has tried to form a league and a cup competition embracing schools and clubs, but its efforts have failed owing to a conflict of interests between the various parties.

Although schools cricket has been less affected by change than rugby, it is a very different game from what it was in 1979. With the exam season encroaching ever further into its domain and the growing attractions of other sporting options, it has had to fight hard to maintain its status. The coming of the AS-level proved particularly pernicious because, with candidates increasingly opting out of cricket to revise, fixtures, especially mid-week, have been cancelled or makeshift teams concocted at the last minute.

It was partly to revive interest and partly in response to developments in the professional game that schools have increasingly resorted to limited overs. In 2002 Oundle began a trend by introducing coloured clothing, black balls and white sightscreens for its mid-week matches, and 2010 saw the introduction of the Schools' National Twenty20. Some schools have instituted local leagues to give further meaning to their fixture list and even traditional friendlies are now overwhelmingly limited-over games, normally 50 or 55 overs at senior level and 30 or 35 at junior.

With this new form of cricket have come restrictions for the number of overs for each bowler – partly also on grounds of health and safety – quicker scoring rates, more agile fielding and a greater sense of enjoyment. But with some 75 per cent of schools' cricket now limited overs – games against the clubs still tend to be declaration cricket – and with Twenty20 likely to expand its tentacles still further, this is all rather to the detriment of the longer form of the game, which teaches boys how to build an innings and bowl sides out. Take away the option of the draw, sterile though this can be, and many limited-overs matches can diminish in interest once the side batting second loses early wickets or gets badly behind the run-rate.

Despite the heroic efforts of the cricket charity, 'Chance to Shine', to introduce it in primary schools, the withering of the game in the state sector has helped account for the large number of privately educated county cricketers. Leading the field in nurturing future professionals is Millfield, proud winners of the Lord's Taverners' under-15 trophy on fourteen occasions, whose alumni include Ian Ward and Ben Hollioake of Surrey, Craig Kieswetter of Somerset and Simon Jones of Glamorgan. With such talent to draw on, it isn't surprising that Millfield has been the team to beat in the South-west, although Taunton would run them close, given their enviable record.

Taunton's neighbours, King's College, Taunton, has been another school to have stood out and never more so than in 2009 when it was *Wisden's* School of the Year with a side that contained Jos Buttler, England's current wicket-keeper, and Alex Barrow and Craig Meschede, both of Somerset.

While Felsted with John Stephenson and Nick Knight, two future England cricketers, to the fore, proved obdurate opponents during the 1980s, two North of England schools carried all before them during that decade: Manchester Grammar School, led by Mike Atherton and John Crawley, and Durham, sustained by an abundance of runs from the Roseberry brothers.

Another school to flourish was St Peter's, York, not least between 2004 and 2008 when Jonathan Bairstow, son of the former England wicket-keeper, David Bairstow, was a member of the XI. An outstanding all-round sports-man, he won the inaugural *Wisden* Young Cricketer of the Year in 2007 for averaging an incredible 218 from eight completed innings.

With a team boasting Robin Martin-Jenkins, later of Sussex, and Andrew Strauss and Ben Hutton, both of Middlesex, it is perhaps unsurprising that Radley was a feared opponent during the early to mid-1990s. Another future Middlesex player, Jamie Dalrymple, ensured that its legacy continued between 1997 and 1999 when it was unbeaten.

Tonbridge was Radley's equal in its dedication to the game and its record has ranked among the best in the country, a fact supported by its domination of the Cricketer Cup, a competition for the old boys of thirty-two leading schools. Part of Tonbridge's allure has been its association with the Cowdrey family, from Graham Cowdrey's accomplishments during the early 1980s through to his nephew Fabian in more recent times.

A devotee of the game from an early age, Fabian placed a lot of pressure on himself to live up to the expectation that goes with the Cowdrey name. It is much to his credit that his record at Tonbridge, particularly during his last year, 2011, when he scored his 3,000th run for the school and averaged 83, emulated that of his father Christopher and grandfather Colin.

Not to be outdone by the Cowdreys, Ed Smith, who played for England against South Africa in 2003, made hay on Tonbridge's excellent wickets dur-ing the mid-1990s and left with an average that has never been exceeded. In his recent book, *Luck*, Smith compared the school's sporting facilities with the very best he had experienced, its twenty nets more than any profes-sional team he had played for and the smoothness of its outfield second only to Lord's.

Although reduced from its two-day format to one in 1982, the fact that Eton still plays Harrow at Lord's, a tradition dating back to 1805, making it cricket's oldest fixture, still gives the occasion a special allure. Recovering from a fallow period during the 1970s, Eton was more than Harrow's equal over the next two decades, ensuring that the latter had to wait until 2000 to record its first victory over its old rivals in twenty-five years. The move to a limited-over format in 2001 gave added meaning to a fixture that all too often had ended in stalemate. Between 2002 and 2004 Eton won three on the trot before Harrow turned the tables in 2005, beginning a seven-year unbeaten run, helped by the inclusion of Sam Northeast, later of Kent, and Gary Ballance, now an England player of note.

It says something for Bedford and Brighton that they were the only two schools to lower Harrow's colours during their vintage 2004–08 period, but then both schools are renowned cricketing establishments. Ever since Neil Lenham, later of Sussex, galvanised the school during the early 1980s, Brighton has been wonderfully consistent on a strong circuit featuring Lancing, Eastbourne and Hurstpierpoint. In 1999, in a side that contained Matt Prior, the future England wicket-keeper, it chalked up twenty victories, the most by any school since 1980.

As befitted a school that liked to challenge convention, Brighton made history by including Clare Connor in its 1993 XI. A dogged opener, she fended off everything the pacemen could throw at her: hit in the ribs against Christ's Hospital, she spurned the opportunity to go off, determined to prove that women, if good enough, could mix it with the men. Within two years Connor was to play for England's women, beginning a notable ten-year career that culminated in her leading the 2005 England team to victory over Australia, the first success against their oldest rivals for forty-two years. Numbered among her team was fifteen-year-old Holly Colvin, who became the youngest-ever England cricket international, male or female. That summer she and Sarah Taylor had followed in Connor's footsteps by playing for the Brighton XI, an innovation that shocked the former captain of Sussex, Robin Marlar. He called it absolutely outrageous that girls should play competitive cricket with older boys. 'If there's an eighteen-year-old who can bowl at 80 mph and he's been brought up properly then he shouldn't want to hurt a lady at any cost,' he said.[4]

Marlar's remarks were dismissed as anachronistic by John Spencer, a former Sussex player himself and the Brighton coach, who reminded him that there were laws of discrimination in place now. 'Robin has a rather quaint sense of chivalry which I don't think many girls would regard as necessary – both Taylor and Colvin are a lot tougher than many boys who have played for me,' he said.[5] According to Roger Nicholson, Brighton's director of sport, the disdain with which many leading boys' sides first greeted them soon turned to embarrassment as hubris got the better of them:

> The big lads would take one look at Holly, a little spinner, and come striding down the wicket to smash the ball out of the ground. The spin would fox them and Sarah behind the stumps would whip the bails off, smile sweetly, and tell them, 'You just got out to a girl'.[6]

Such was the girls' success that Sarah Taylor was voted the Cricket Society's Most Promising Young Woman Cricketer for 2005, ironically receiving the trophy from Robin Marlar. The next year Holly Colvin headed the Brighton bowling averages, a feat she repeated in 2007, the year when the school won a memorable match against Eastbourne. Chasing 307 in fifty overs, Brighton needed two to win off the last ball with their last pair somehow managing to run two to mid-off.

At Bedford in 1998 a fresh-faced music scholar turned up to nets on his first day and made an instant impression with the cricket coach, the ex-England batsman Derek Randall, who marvelled at his superb balance and temperament. Asked to play for the MCC against the school the next year when the former was one short, Alastair Cook obliged with a century and from there never looked back, scoring seventeen centuries for Bedford and collecting a bat in school assembly each time for his achievement. As a sixteen-year-old, Cook put on 242 with his partner James Stedman to beat Tonbridge by ten wickets in a two-day match; then, in his final year, 2003, he scored two undefeated double-centuries with an average of 160.

For many years Bedford Modern was a force to be reckoned with, none more so than in 1999, its best ever season when Monty Panesar topped the bowling averages. In 2013 its batsman, Kyle Cunningham, hit six sixes off one over against Haileybury as he raced to 99 off 35 balls. Another school in that area to have attracted attention of late is Stowe, its most prolific batsman being Ben Duckett, who in 2011 was the leading batsman in the country.

Elsewhere in the Midlands, Malvern, Rugby, Oakham, Uppingham, Repton, Oundle and Shrewsbury have consistently performed to standard, turning out cricketers of the calibre of Chris Adams (Repton), Will Jefferson (Oundle) and James Taylor. It says something about Taylor that he began his five-year stint in the Shrewsbury XI with a six and ended it in 2008 with an average of 179, earning him the accolade of *Wisden*'s Young Cricketer of the Year. Not satisfied with scoring a century during the afternoon, he frequently could be found honing his technique after prep at 9pm.

While Scottish cricket is a notch below the general standard south of the border it lacks nothing in enthusiasm and intensity, no more so than at Merchiston, its record in the last decade among the best in the country. Evidence of its resilience was provided in its traditional two-day match against Edinburgh Academy in 1986 when, having followed on 121 behind and left its opponents a mere 26 to win, Merchiston bowled them out for 24.

In an age when cricket has lost some ground to other sports and to the exam system, it is a tribute to the cricketing fraternity in the independent sector that it has kept the flame burning, producing so many outstanding players. A team consisting of Alastair Cook, Andrew Strauss, Mark Butcher, Mike Atherton, Nasser Hussain, Joe Root, Matt Prior, Stuart Broad, Chris Jordan, Simon Jones and Monty Panesar would give any England team a good game.

Sport's growing diversity has seen the welcome revival of football. Despite playing a significant part in the formation of the Football Association (FA) back in the 1860s, most independent schools turned their backs on the game when it went professional, deeming it to be grubby and socially inferior, a view that prevailed until very recently, especially among the old rugby-playing establishment.

During the 1970s a new breed of football-playing master made efforts to introduce the sport at rugby-playing schools as it gained a cult following among the boys. At Harrow, David Elleray, later a renowned international football referee, faced intense opposition from his colleagues in his efforts to re-establish football after its demise there in the 1920s before gradually gaining the upper hand. At Haileybury the footballers were confined to a waterlogged pitch miles from anywhere but through the pioneering efforts of Nigel Prentki, master in charge, the fixture list began to expand until one was secured against the much-fancied Charterhouse, and on a wet, windy day in 1981 they beat them 9–0.

That memorable victory helped raise football's status at Haileybury despite animosity from some of the old guard in the common room who administered detentions to boys caught playing with a football in the rugby and cricket terms. According to Oliver Petersen, captain of football in 1998–99, it was the success of the teams of the mid-1990s and their attacking style that finally won over the sceptics. 'It was rewarding to see some of the rugby masters showing up at the First XI soccer games, too, and investing heavily in the team's success, even bringing it up in class time, when chit-chat was previously reserved for rugby and cricket,' he said.[7]

With an improvement in the quality of pitches, the introduction of a scout from Tottenham Hotspur and an evening five-a-side league that proved highly popular with players and spectators alike, not least with the girls who were soon entering their own teams, football went from strength to strength.

Haileybury's experience mirrored that of many other rugby-playing schools as they responded to the rising demand for football. Not only was the English premier league winning ever more converts among the middle class, many first-generation pupils were reared in footballing households rather than rugby ones. With rugby perceived to be increasingly danger-ous and subject to possible litigation, schools such as King's Ely, Brighton, Dover College and City of London switched to football, although King's Ely was later to have second thoughts, ironically once a female head had taken over. By 2002 more than half of HMC schools were playing football and resources have been invested in professional coaches, improved playing surfaces and sophisticated training techniques. Links have also been estab-lished with various football academies and after a century with barely any independent school representation in professional football there has been a slow drift back with Johnny Gorman making his debut for Northern Ireland while still at Repton.

The inauguration of the Boodle & Dunthorne Cup, the independent schools FA's Blue Riband competition, in 1992–93, has helped generate interest and raise standards from the time that Forest beat Charterhouse on penalties in front of 1,600 at Fulham's Craven Cottage. Although no school dominated during the first decade, the leading contenders were inevitably those schools with a proud footballing pedigree: Bury Grammar School, Ardingly and Brentwood. In 2004–05 Queen Elizabeth's, Blackburn became the first team to win the cup three times and in 2012 Hampton School became the first to secure a cup double at under-18 and under-15 level.

In 2005–06 King's School, Chester, defeated the favourites Millfield to lift the cup for the second time, a feat also accomplished by Shrewsbury. Three times defeated finalists, Charterhouse's luck finally turned when it beat Millfield on penalties in 2007–08; then, three years later, despite chants of 'Nineteen Prime Ministers' from the Etonian supporters, it beat Eton 2–0, echoes of the 1881 FA Cup final when the Old Carthusians beat the Old Etonians by the same score.

As football's popularity surged through the independent sector so the entrants to the Boodles Cup have risen to over sixty, one of whom was Millfield. Making its debut in 2004–05, it became the first four-times winner and the first to retain the cup when it defeated Bradfield 6–1 in 2014.

Another sport to advance its profile has been hockey. Always something of a poor relation to rugby, in particular, and football, various changes such as the substitution of astro-turf pitches for grass, lighter sticks and changes to the rules, especially the end of offside, have made the game faster, more skilful and more exciting. As popularity for the game has soared, schools have responded by increasing their fixtures, employing more coaches and entering more cup competitions. Coaches often video training sessions and players are expected to log on to assess their performance and make comments online.

Amid the elite-playing hockey schools such as Dean Close School, Cheltenham, Cranleigh, Trent College, Whitgift, Ipswich, Worksop, Kent College, Canterbury, and Repton, three stand out: Kingston Grammar School, which has won the National Schools Championships eight times since 1979, Millfield and St George's College, Weybridge. At under-16 level, St George's have topped the bill with seven triumphs, followed by Kent College with four and Trent College with three.

Rowing may well be confined to schools that have substantial resources and proximity to water but recent Olympic success in the sport has highlighted the contribution made by the independent sector. Very significant changes have taken place in the competitions that are of the greatest interest to the majority of rowing schools. The Special Race for Schools at Henley, dating back to a more privileged time when it enabled a limited number of schools to avoid the clash with A-levels, quickly disappeared when A-level exams were set earlier in the year. At much the same time the National

Schools Regatta (NSR) was brought forward to the end of May to avoid the bulk of exams.

In International Junior competition the race distance was increased to 2,000 metres for boys and girls with the aim of encouraging more endurance training, which was thought to be more beneficial for young athletes; the NSR followed suit, which tied in with the longer races at Henley and the Schools' Head of the River was progressively extended to the full 4.5 mile course from Chiswick to Putney.

At the other end of the age range the Amateur Rowing Association (ARA), the governing body in England for rowing, voted to stop sweep-oared races for under-14s in order to encourage more sculling (rowing with two oars) and to assuage concerns about spinal problems in the young. This has led to a great upsurge in sculling competition for both schools and clubs, not least at the NSR and Henley. So nowadays young athletes all start off in sculling boats and will later train for longer races.

Following the trend set by the senior internationals, the emphasis is now on endurance work both in the gym and on the water; this is regarded as more effective and it is common for athletes to train all year round.

Training and selection is much more scientific and objective and assisted by monitoring equipment on the boats and the ubiquitous rowing machines. In the 1970s the ARA started the coach education schemes so now there are many more top-flight coaches. The leading schools don't just buy the best equipment, they also hire the best coaches and Eton has its own rowing course, which hosted the 2012 Olympic regatta.

As regards equipment, the obvious change is that wooden boats and oars have largely vanished in favour of plastic composites that offer higher performance and lower maintenance. At St Edward's, Oxford, the first eight won the Special Race in a borrowed plastic boat, so the governors gave the head coach, Bill Sayer, the money for a new plastic eight in which they won the Head, the NSR and the Princess Elizabeth Challenge Cup (PE) at Henley in 1984. When Sayer moved to Shrewsbury in 1998, they still had many wooden boats but now the whole fleet is plastic and the eights are German and American. All this is, of course, very expensive and has required a lot of fundraising, but Henley wins tend to unlock the purse strings.

Although the number of school regattas has abounded, the triple crown of the Schools' Head, the NSR and the PE remains the ambition of every rowing school. With competition fierce, no school has attained complete ascendancy on the water, although Eton's record post-1979 places it in a class of its own. Aside from its domination of the NSR, it has won the PE eight times, followed by Hampton and Abingdon with four wins each and Pangbourne College and St Edward's with two each, the latter's win in 1999 something of an upset.

In the heats against favourites Hampton, the St Edward's fourman, Rik Lancaster, caught in heavy traffic around Henley, looked likely to miss the race until he took drastic action. Jumping out of his car, he crossed several fields, persuaded a boatman to ferry him across the river and flouted Henley protocol by running through the stewards' enclosure in full rowing kit to join his crew just in time. Beating Hampton, St Edward's accounted for Abingdon in the semi-final by again coming from behind, despite facing the worst of the elements, and winning the final against St Peter's College, Adelaide.

Although Radley and Shrewsbury only won the PE once each during this era, both remained formidable opponents, the former losing out to Abingdon in the semi-final in 2011 and in the final in 2012. Under the American Todd Jesdale, one of the best rowing coaches in the world, Shrewsbury won three School Heads, the NSR and the PE in 2007 when they beat Brentwood College School, the Canadian national champions, by a foot in a race where the lead changed seven times.

In recent years Abingdon has emerged as the monarch of the river by winning the Schools' Head, the NSR and PE in 2012, and the PE in 2013 for the third successive year, a feat not accomplished since 1948, and in record time.

Although other rowing schools don't quite match the standards of the above, Dulwich, King's Canterbury, King's Chester, King's Worcester and Shiplake have turned out their share of rowing internationals and Olympic medallists. Among the many triumphs in recent Olympics, few can match the men's coxless four winning gold at Athens in 2004 with a crew that comprised Matthew Pinsent and Ed Coode of Eton, Steve Williams of Monkton Combe School and James Cracknell of Kingston Grammar School.

With Olympic success has come a surge in rowing's popularity and because it is one of those sports that can be taken up at a later age, there is every reason to believe that it will begin to lose its elitist image. For the moment, however, the independent sector continues to dominate as British rowing looks to build on its recent triumphs.

Although blighted by obsolete media images of sport as a vigorous male activity less suited to girls, this perception is beginning to change following the recent success of British female athletes at the London Olympics, and that of the England women's cricket, hockey and rugby teams.

With greater parental support, an unprecedented choice of sports available and access to quality coaching, girls' sport in the independent sector has received a shot in the arm. Elite performers receive additional support and links between schools and sports governing bodies and clubs have been strengthened, thereby smoothing the path of the talented few who aspire to national honours.

With its greater exposure through Sky Sports, netball remains the leading girls' sport played in both the state and independent sectors, the proliferation of leagues and county tournaments giving added meaning to school matches. Although some girls play netball over two terms, the majority of independent schools play during the Easter term, the bigger ones fielding as many as sixteen teams in a block fixture.

With professional coaches instilling more 'professional' direction and greater levels of fitness, games lack nothing in intensity, especially at top level. Liz Robertson, netball coach at Epsom, recalls a match against one leading rival last season when, in addition to the mistress in charge and the coach, there were two other members of staff with clipboards making notes on every pass, a disconcerting spectacle that prompted one of her best players to say, 'You wouldn't do that to us, would you, Liz?'

Following years of supremacy by Croydon High School in the National Schools Netball Competition, Bromley High School, The Grammar School at Leeds, King's Worcester, Wakefield High School and Repton have emerged as worthy successors, but none can match Bromsgrove's achievement of five championships in the last eight years.

Although lacrosse is a growing sport at the grassroots and university levels, it lacks the television coverage, club structure and Lottery funding that has benefitted hockey and netball. Consequently, it remains the preserve of a relatively select group of independent schools with their historic rivalries in a game noted for its speed, strength, skill and tactical nous. Amid the growing number of tournaments, nothing compares with the annual two-day National Schools Lacrosse Championships every February at which some fifty schools compete. Recent winners include Guildford High School, the Lady Eleanor Holles School (LEH), St Swithun's School, Winchester, Wycombe Abbey, Downe House, St Catherine's, Bramley and, most impressive of all, the Godolphin School, Salisbury, three time winners between 2009–10 and 2013–14.

As with boys' hockey, sports scholarships, more intensive preparation and superior playing surfaces have lifted the standard of the girls' game, none more so than at Repton under Martin Jones, former Great Britain international. In addition to winning numerous indoor tournaments, they were six-time national champions between 2004 and 2010 and have been well represented at international level. During England's series of matches against Germany in November 2013, five Old Reptonians played for England and one for Germany.

Although rather overshadowed by Repton, Dean Close, Trent College, Wakefield High School and Arnold School have all enjoyed success, while Kingston Grammar School ended Repton's unbeaten run in 2011.

Repton's girls have also excelled at tennis, second only to Queenswood School, and the school has been a pioneer, along with Wycombe Abbey, in the development of girls' football, one of the fastest growing games, helped by the wide appeal of the Premier League. The FA now sponsors girls' coaching and organises an under-18 eleven-a-side competition, won in 2014 by King's, Taunton, while Bradfield hosts an annual six-a-side tournament every October with competitions at under-13, under-15 and under-18 level.

Girls' cricket and rowing are also on the rise, with Felsted leading the way with the former and Headington and LEH with the latter.

Away from the main sports, schools have established a reputation in others too: Bolton for water polo, Brentwood for fencing, Gresham's and Uppingham for shooting, Millfield, Kelly and Plymouth for swimming, and Whitgift for the modern pentathlon.

It must be accepted that, as a result of the encouragement and commitment shown by their sports coaches and teachers, those fortunate enough to be privately educated start with a massive advantage denied to many of their counterparts in the state sector. Pupils in state schools have been sold short by the lack of time given over to sport and the paucity of many of the amenities. It can only be hoped that the recent efforts of many independent schools to share their facilities and coaches with local communities will not only give more of these children the chance to play sport and enjoy it but to also go on to excel at the highest level.

Chapter 12

THE BATTLE OF THE SEXES

Few changes shook the ordered world of the English public school more than the introduction of girls – as from humble streams mighty rivers begin to flow. Most schools attributed the admission of girls to educational conviction – it was natural and reflected modern society – but while coeducation did win a growing number of converts over time, idealism invariably came second to financial considerations. What suited the school didn't always suit the girls, which meant they often missed out during the transition, but with growing opportunities for women and changing work practices, coeducation has increasingly appeared the norm, much to the detriment of many a girls' school.

With its austere surroundings, robust discipline and veneration of rugby, the typical public school seemed totally unsuitable for girls. Bedales, it is true, had been coeducational since 1898 and Millfield from 1939, but neither of these schools was a member of the HMC. In 1968 Marlborough, under its progressive master, John Dancy, embarked on a new direction by admitting girls into its sixth form. Encouraged to innovate by Bernard Williams, the renowned moral philosopher and fellow member of the Newsom Commission, Dancy, keen to consolidate the liberal reforms of the 1960s, needed little persuasion. His motive appeared to be a genuine educational one, unlike most of those who followed suit.

Although John Rae attributed his awkward relationship with girls long after his schooldays to his single-sex education and vowed to free the next generation from its curse, his prime motive for admitting girls into the sixth form at Westminster in 1972 was to boost numbers and raise academic standards. With rocketing fees and boarding becoming less popular, recruiting girls was one way of schools recouping lost revenue. Rugby, Cheltenham, Stowe,

St Edward's, Oxford, Fettes, Haileybury, Charterhouse, Repton, Uppingham, Lancing, Wellington, Oakham, Gresham's, Rydal and Bryanston were among the forty or so HMC schools that admitted girls in the sixth form during the 1970s, Bryanston quickly moving to full coeducation. 'I would judge our first motive to have been the survival and enlargement of the school or the college with less than total regard for the good of our neighbours or even of our newly recruited girls,' Peter Watkinson, headmaster of Rydal, told a London symposium on boarding education in March 1984. 'It was a move founded on convenience rather than conviction,' he continued, 'but shortly afterwards we began to defend it on ground of principle. Our priorities have remained those of boys' schools and our male hierarchy has not been challenged.'[1] His case for coeducation rested on the argument that it gave the girls better and fairer opportunities.

The trend towards coeducation continued through the 1980s and 1990s as the slump in boarding education showed no sign of abating. 'Not only were we not getting the girls,' explained Stuart Andrews, headmaster of Clifton, 'but we weren't getting their brothers either, because parents were looking for a school to which they could send all their children.'[2] 'A lot is made of the philosophical and moral reasons for going coed,' declared Andrew Cunningham, sometime head of the sixth-form girls at Cranleigh. 'The simple truth is that, for many parents, the ease of sending "little Johnny and Joanna" to the same school makes sense, same drive, same drop-off, same term dates, same matches, same holidays.'[3]

When Charles Bush, headmaster of Eastbourne, disclosed that parent pressure was the prime motive behind the decision of his school in 1995 to admit girls at thirteen, he was taken to task by Martin Fisher, deputy at Downside, in a letter to *The Times*. It wasn't the job of a school to mirror society, contended Fisher, nor the job of a headmaster to follow whatever trend is then in vogue. His priority was to decide what was educationally desirable.

In 1996 Fr Leo Chamberlain, headmaster of Ampleforth, declared coeducation to be inappropriate for a school like his. 'I know other places are doing it, but I don't see us doing that here. I think girls and boys perform better when they are educated separately.'[4] Four years later, in 2000, after a difficult few years in which numbers had dropped, the monks had second thoughts. 'We believe that the unique qualities of an Ampleforth education can be just as valid for girls as for boys,' Chamberlain wrote to parents, explaining the decision to admit girls into the sixth form. He went on to say that, in a changing world where a young man's first boss might well be female and a young woman had to make her way in a career, there was precious little guidance on these matters either at university or in business. 'We think it will help both boys and girls if they learn at school to work and be at ease.' He also acknowledged that Ampleforth parents had requested the change, especially given the absence of any Catholic independent girls' school in the North of England.[5]

Discovering that the arrival of girls didn't mean the end of the world, Ampleforth soon went further by moving to coeducation at thirteen in 2004, the year before Downside took the plunge. Having ended its brief experiment with girls in the sixth form in 1987 on the grounds that it was inappropriate for unmarried religious celibates to look after girls and cope with their problems, the school, now overwhelmingly lay and looking to boost its roll, reconsidered the matter. The monks said special prayers after compline every night for a month and when the decision was taken there wasn't one dissenting voice.

With Sedbergh going coeducational in 2001, the boarding schools standing out against the zeitgeist were few and far between. Those that did tended to be the larger, more affluent schools that had less trouble filling their roll. When Charterhouse discussed going fully coeducational in 1989, the housemasters supported the move, declaring that it was natural and would attract talented girls. The heads of department, on the other hand, thought otherwise, believing that thirteen wasn't a suitable age for girls to change schools and that the quality of their sixteen year olds would decline because few would now come. With the common room split, the governing body looked at a number of coeducational schools and, finding that they lacked academic rigour, remained with the status quo.

On taking over at Radley in 1991, Richard Morgan was told by the council that accepting girls wasn't an option partly because parents had deliberately chosen a single-sex school and partly because there was no space for them. At Tonbridge, faced with the choice of taking girls and building a new boarding house or spending £1 million on a new church organ, the authorities decided on the latter. 'We have the finest church organ of any school in the country,' headmaster Martin Hammond told the *Financial Times*.[6] Girls could be a civilising effect on a school, he declared, but so could a church organ, especially one tailor-made by Marcussen, the renowned organ-building company.

At Winchester, Ralph Townsend, on becoming headmaster in 2005, instigated consultations about taking girls but discovered no great desire for change, while Barnaby Lenon's biannual survey of parental attitudes at Harrow found the overwhelming majority in favour of keeping the school single-sex. With Eton as popular as ever – four applications for every one accepted – that is the way these top schools are likely to remain until such time as the market dictates a change of direction.

As girls' schools became vulnerable to smash-and-grab raids on their territory by boys' schools, they weren't slow to register their disgust. Back in the late 1970s, Elizabeth Manners, headmistress of Felixstowe College, had caused ructions by denouncing headmasters as male chauvinist pigs using totally unscrupulous means to entice pupils, and her colleagues, while more restrained in their language, continued to express similar sentiments. Freda Kellett, headmistress of Birkenhead High School, wrote in the *Sunday Times* in November 1984,

> There is real anguish about this in the girls' schools. ... Parents imagine that if their girls can go to a big public school, then that is the best thing for them in the sixth form. But in fact they will be at a disadvantage. At a single-sex school they do better academically because they don't have to keep looking over their shoulders at boys.[7]

Kellett's claim that girls performed better in a single-sex environment prompted John Rae to challenge these schools to publish their results alongside those of coeducational schools. 'The fact is that some girls get sixth form academic stimulus in a boys' school. Boys' schools are more inclined to persuade their pupils to aim higher,' he said.[8]

As the flight to boys' schools continued, the reaction of many a headmistress became ever more indignant. Avril Burgess, headmistress of South Hampstead High School and president of the GSA in 1989, dismissed the reasons given by these schools for going coeducational as a veneer for the real motive – the need to keep up numbers. For many boarding schools it was a choice between girls or recruitment trips to Hong Kong.

Enid Castle, principal of Cheltenham Ladies' College, told the *Times Educational Supplement* in June 1991 that she had little time for schools that called themselves coeducational on the back of a minority of girls in the sixth form. 'There's plenty of evidence to show that boys are more assertive and take up more of the teacher's attention,' she asserted. 'Girls at boys' schools will also have fewer role models because none of the heads of the so-called co-ed schools are going to be women in the near future.' She added that male culture would continue to dominate in the future, stating, 'I can't believe that they will give the same predominance to the girls' netball team as the rugby First XV. Rugby is almost a religion in some schools.'[9]

These female broadsides prompted their male colleagues to return fire as coeducation suffered a temporary setback in the early 1990s following a number of unseemly incidents that attracted much bad publicity. One particular school in the firing line was Marlborough as it went fully coeducational. Roger Ellis, its ex-master, attributed criticism of this sort to the natural hostility of the headmistresses 'who sedulously spread rumours that all girls in the college were advised to be on the pill'[10]. Meanwhile David Jewell, master of Haileybury, denounced the 'unscrupulous propaganda instigated by some headmistresses and encouraged by the national press concerning sexual behaviour and mores in coeducational schools, and the increasing and now almost universal practice of the offering of financial inducements by girls' schools to girls in their fifth form to stay on'.[11]

According to Richard Barker, headmaster of coeducational Sevenoaks, girls in his experience didn't underperform in schools like his. 'We've got to think about what we are educating pupils for,' he stated. 'School is a staging post that should prepare them for adult life and nowadays that means educating girls to lead men. How on earth can you do that in a single sex environment?'[12]

Despite the genuine outrage felt by these headmistresses regarding the way that the boys' schools had treated them, not least in depriving them of their most talented pupils, they did present a fairly soft target. By the 1970s, many girls' boarding schools looked obsolete; even the reputable Downe House was struggling with empty beds and facing the possibility of closure. The expectation still held that because well-bred girls would marry well and have families, their education was a lower priority than that of their brothers. Rather than being great centres of intellectual and cultural enlightenment, these boarding schools were places of social deportment where girls could make friends with those from a similar background. As an old girl from St Mary's Calne told the *Independent on Sunday* in 1993,

For seven years you were with exactly the same type of girl from exactly the same type of background as you. We were the children of fourth or fifth generation public school parents, who placed great importance on status. An important but unspoken part of things was that your father was something in the City, and you had a house in the country and a flat in Chelsea. If he wasn't and you didn't, it wasn't quite right. I felt I wasn't in the real world.[13]

Often housed in rambling old country mansions, these schools, for all their stunning locations, lacked the means to invest in capital development and attract good all-round staff. With married women deterred by the long hours, low pay and inadequate accommodation, the majority of the common room comprised spinsters steeped in values from a bygone age. Judith McClure, later a distinguished headmistress, remembers the narrow and rigid regime at St Helen and St Katharine, Abingdon, where staff weren't encouraged to speak at all, compared to the more relaxed atmosphere at Kingswood, to which she moved in 1984.

'Girls' schools depressed us,' wrote Amanda Atha and Sarah Drummond, editors of *The Good Schools Guide*, in *The Times* in October 1986. 'We were struck, in the private sector, by a lack of direction. It is difficult to ascertain what many girls' schools are trying to achieve; great swathes, for example, claiming to be "academic" and catering for "high fliers" [by which they mean potential Oxbridge undergraduates] but are no such thing.'

Expectations were low all round, with indifferent teaching and unimaginative subject options. 'There is a lack of energy and, sometimes, a lack of interest in anything outside the gossip columns of the *Daily Mail*,' they continued. Gyms were often small, computing rooms untouched, playing fields tiny, and '[i]ndeed the overall size of girls' schools is often too small to make economic sense'.

'There is a tremendous feeling of missing out: we cannot blame pupils, who, as soon as O-levels were over, bolted to "Marlborough and freedom". Girls' schools are simply not where the action is,' they opined.[14] Exempting a number of schools such as Bolton Girls' School, JAGS and the Godolphin and Latymer School from the criticism, Atha and Drummond contended that coeducational school pupils were far more mature – and a good deal more natural – than their peers at single-sex schools: the girls were less giggly and more mature, the boys less cynical.

With limited contact with the local community and little to do at weekends, many girls were bored, but this they might have forgiven had the authorities not appeared so distant and repressive. The *Sunday Times* columnist India Knight described her time at Wycombe Abbey in the early 1980s:

> I hated everything about what I saw as my forced incarceration: the filthy food, the endless petty rules. ... Also the endless church-going; the sadistic house-mistresses; the being sent to detention for reading Macbeth [Macbeth!] after lights out; palpable pressure to conform to some fantastically misguided, antiquated notion of Ideal Womanhood [best] encapsulated as Be Good at Tennis and Marry Well. ...[15]

The journalist and writer Rosie Boycott expressed similar sentiments about her schooldays at Cheltenham Ladies' College a decade earlier:

> It was a fantastically hateful school and it did me terrible damage. You had to belong and toe the line, and if you departed from this in any way you paid for it. ... The awful thing about being at a school like that is that the school is always bigger than the child. You had to accept what was going on.[16]

These musings weren't simply those of a couple of mavericks looking to repay old scores. 'I've talked at reunions to women who attended in previous decades and many had a horrible time here,' admitted Vicky Tuck, former principal of Cheltenham Ladies' College. 'The boarding houses were quite miserable places, run by women who didn't understand children and didn't really like them. That had changed by the time I got here, but most of the former pupils wouldn't look at us for their children.'[17]

Even Isabel Berwick who enjoyed her time at the Alice Ottley School during the early 1980s recalls fighting

> futile adolescent battles against its strict rules and high Anglican ethos. Everything was strictly controlled. The then-headmistress censored all books and magazines that came into the school – our library copies of *Paris Match* looked like sewing patterns, with holes cut out where she had removed all 'unsuitable' material. We had to wear hats all year round – little blue caps in winter and blue boaters in summer. We had brown indoor sandals and black outdoor lace-up shoes, and until the age of thirteen, the girls wore blue Victorian smocks over their uniform at all times. 'Coming out' of the smock, at the start of upper fourth [year 9], caused huge excitement.[18]

Such attitudes were increasingly out of kilter with the times. Women were on the march in their quest for greater freedoms and opportunities, not least in the labour market. Clare Balding, head girl at Downe House in the late 1980s prior to her success as a BBC sports presenter, recounts in her autobiography how she challenged long-held assumptions in her family, fully shared by her mother and grandmother, that men were the dominant sex. When she objected to her father and brother being excused domestic duties, her mother told her that she would get along much better in life 'if you learn to massage a man's ego'. It was advice she found hard to accept. 'I would not back down from doing the things I wanted to do and I would not wait for a man to define my position in the world,' she said.[19]

When Gillian duCharme returned from the US after nineteen years to become headmistress of Benenden School in 1985, she was surprised by how very different parental expectations were for their sons compared to their daughters. 'They were going to spend their money on the boys because the girls would get married,' she said. 'Now there is a much greater sense of equality, as parents recognise that a first-rate education, excellent facilities and a wide range of courses are equally important for girls.'[20]

Confronted with the exodus of their sixth forms to boys' schools, girls' schools began to put their houses in order. Increasingly, spinster headmistresses and housemistresses – some of whom were very good – were replaced by younger married couples more in touch with the outside world, the finances were reformed, marketing expanded, facilities modernised, salaries increased, curriculum widened and discipline relaxed. Sixth-form girls were increasingly allocated their own accommodation, given disposition to wear their own clothes and allowed more time off the premises. More important, aspirations were raised with headmistresses encouraging girls to smash glass ceilings. 'I don't think girls should be shielded from competition,' declared Suzanne Farr, headmistress of Downe House, a school that had previously rejected it on the grounds that it was unladylike. 'We live in a competitive world. If women's claims for equality are to be successful, they have to be adaptable: in that way competition comes as a matter of course.'[21]

When Clifford Gould became headmaster of Badminton School in 1987 and conveyed to the common room his failure to understand why the academic results were so poor, they applauded him. From then on academic success would be crucial so that, when interviewing new applicants, Gould told them that every teacher must be better than him. Under his leadership the school fulfilled its academic potential and soon its results were among the best in the country.

With the advent of league tables and the leading position of many single-sex girls' schools, academic excellence became the most powerful weapon in their armoury as they made up some lost ground in the recruiting war. When the 1993 league tables showed that eight of the top ten schools at GCSE were girls' independent schools, an editorial in the *Independent* opined that not only were girls more mature than boys at sixteen, they performed better academically 'without the attention seeking behaviour of the opposite sex'. It continued, 'Observational studies have shown that, confronted with a mixed class, teachers of either sex will tend to devote 70 per cent of their attention to the boys, mainly because the latter are more demanding.'[22] Safe from the disruptive influence of boys in the classroom, it argued, girls not only could express themselves fully, they could also attain their full potential. It is an argument that the GSA has deployed time and again since.

The bitter rivalry surfaced once again in 1995 when 135 HMC coeducational schools commissioned research by Alan Smithers and Pamela Robinson at Liverpool University to see whether the mixing or the separation of the sexes for secondary education made any difference. Their report, while accepting that single-sex schools produced the best exam results, attributed their success to their ability to attract the brightest pupils.

The jousting continued as coeducation became ever more popular. One school expected to stand out from the stampede was Cranleigh because of its link under a joint charter to neighbouring St Catherine's, Bramley. Breaking this 100-year-old charter in the courts led to much acrimony. 'In fact working at Cranleigh in 1999 was a ticket to being snubbed and cold-shouldered by anyone from the independent girls' schools nearby,' recalled Andrew Cunningham a few years later. 'So poisonous was the atmosphere that when I left Cranleigh and bumped into a senior teacher from St Catherine's at a party, she promptly said: "At last I can speak to you – you're no longer at Cranleigh." She wasn't joking.'[23]

Whatever the respective merits of a single-sex education compared to a coeducational one, there was no denying the fact there was still a market for a top-flight girls' boarding education. In May 2004 the headmistresses of Benenden, Downe House, St Mary's Ascot, Cheltenham Ladies' College and Wycombe Abbey wrote to the *Daily Telegraph* to refute an article it had published suggesting that girls' schools were in decline. Reporting that they were all completely full with the longest registration lists ever, they told of the millions of pounds they had invested in facilities to meet the growing demand for places. This popularity they attributed to parental realisation that their schools could provide the best education available: a strong academic programme, a fun, caring environment, in which the girls took the lead in everything, and their subsequent success in the wider world. All five schools could indeed boast of excellent exam results, none more so than Wycombe Abbey.

With more high-achieving parents working in London or abroad than in most girls' boarding institutions, Wycombe wasn't simply a finishing school for blue-blooded young ladies. It took its work and culture seriously. 'You had a sense that you were the crème de la crème, but standards were punishing,' recalled Lucinda Matthews of her time there as a pupil in the late 1970s and early 1980s. 'Even though I was doing four science A-levels I was expected to discuss *Ulysses* with the headmistress and speak Italian.'[24]

Narrow, conformist and austere in other ways, Wycombe began to open up during the 1980s, establishing more contact with the world outside. Debates, concerts and dances with boys' schools, more visiting speakers and a growing international intake all added to the educational breadth of the school. In May 1982 the school hosted a debate with Eton and was treated to a virtuoso performance from Boris Johnson who caused much merriment with his observation that Wycombe Abbey resembled a gothic horror movie set on a golf course.

Building on the legacy of Patricia Lancaster, headmistress between 1974 and 1988, Wycombe has been fortunate in the quality of its leadership since then. Its staff, now comprising more marrieds and men, combine inspiration in the classroom with care and dedication outside, with each girl valued for herself. With a demanding entry system, supportive parents and a rigorous work ethic from which very few dissent, the pursuit of excellence, always strong, has become all-embracing. From the time when league tables were introduced, Wycombe's rankings have always been exceptional, heading the A-level table for girls' boarding schools in more than half of the years between 1997 and 2014 and topping the A-level table for private schools for six successive years. Girls regularly attain over 90 per cent of A* or A grades at A-level and 98 per cent of A*s or As at GCSE.

At its 2004 conference, the GSA persuaded journalists to publish some research it had conducted with 5,000 of its pupils that purported to show that girls were more likely to become mathematicians, scientists and engineers in a single-sex environment. In response, the HMC turned once again to Alan Smithers and Pamela Robinson, now at Buckingham University, to give a second opinion. Their report, published in June 2006, and based on a decade of research, found no difference in educational attainment between different types of school. The reason why single-sex schools dominated league tables was because they were grammar, former grammar and independent schools. They noted that while girls in single-sex schools achieved slightly better results than girls in coeducational schools, there was no difference in performance between boys in single-sex schools and those taught in coeducational ones. Research from other countries such as Australia, New Zealand and Canada had found little evidence of consistent advantages one way or the other.

Their findings were disputed by Dr Brenda Despontin, headmistress of Haberdashers' Monmouth School for Girls, who argued that the percentage of girls attaining As at A-level was 10 per cent higher in single-sex schools than coeducational ones. 'Some headmistresses make me out to be the bogeyman simply because I challenge what to them appears to be an absolute truth and something which helps their marketing because it is the main thing they can offer,' the affable Smithers told the *Daily Telegraph*.[25]

If the GSA remained unduly defensive, it is easy to see why. Despite the pedigree of many of its schools, their plight continued to worsen. Some opted to go coeducational but, while a school such as St Leonards in St Andrews has prospered, it has been the exception rather than the rule. 'For most boys the prospect of going to an all-girls school, would, to put it bluntly, be rather emasculating,' opined Andrew Halls, headmaster of KCS.[26]

In 2007 Norwich and St Benedict's announced their intention to go fully coeducational, much to the chagrin of their sister schools. That same year, prior to the merger of the Alice Ottley School with the Royal Grammar School Worcester, Isabel Berwick wrote that

> Something precious – the informality, the friendliness, the calm – is lost every time the life of a dedicated women's institution comes to an end. Perhaps the full importance of that loss, that silent void, will one day be fully recognised by the noisy, and hierarchical mixed world that rushes in to fill up the space.[27]

In April 2012, the day after official figures recorded a drop of 1,300 in the number of GSA pupils over the previous year, Lord Lucas, owner of *The Good Schools Guide*, incensed his audience at St Mary's Calne, by warning that girls' schools were undergoing a gradual decline because they were no longer providing the best preparation for the world of men, marriage and career. They should place a renewed emphasis on subjects such as science and engineering and provide positive reasons for choosing a girls' school. 'The old reason that without boys they can concentrate may be true for some girls, but most girls who grow up in a co-educational environment do pretty well and find they can manage quite happily,' he said.[28] Retorted Dr Helen Wright, headmistress of St Mary's, 'It was a fascinating day and extremely important for the girls to see that chauvinist attitudes to women and girls' schools are still there. I explained to them that there was a big generational issue here – those kinds of attitudes are dying out.'[29]

Other headmistresses waded in, accusing Lord Lucas of an outdated view of girls' schools, and pointing to their greater academic success than their counterparts in coeducational ones, but their bravado didn't impress Andrew Halls, whose own school, KCS, had the year before admitted girls into the sixth form. He thought that attacking schools that taught both sexes was the worst possible response. He found the use of vocabulary deployed by some headmistresses such as 'poaching' and 'stealing' unsettling because of what it said about their own girls. Girls' schools were rightly proud of the sense of empowerment they had given to their pupils and the ability to think for themselves. 'Why, then,' he asked, 'do some feel the moment that a girl exercises that independent mind, and makes what may for her be rather a brave or difficult choice, she has actually become a listless victim of forces she is too feeble to withstand?'[30] The best girls' schools, like the best boys' schools, would flourish for many years to come, but to suggest that the exercise of free will was, paradoxically, a form of passivity wasn't fair to the girls whose interests they otherwise espoused so formidably.

While many girls' schools, especially day ones, continue to offer an excellent education, the stark fact is that such schools are in an ever-growing minority. An ISC census in April 2014 showed that in twenty years the number of girls' schools in the independent sector had fallen from 230 to 150. 'Single-sex schooling continues its long term decline,' commented Janette Wallis, senior editor of the *The Good Schools Guide*. 'The single-sex schools that are still going strong are the ones parents choose because they are fabulous schools, not because they are single sex.'[31]

Chapter 13

NEW WINE IN
OLD BOTTLES

To supporters and detractors alike, the introduction of girls to boys' schools in the 1970s and 1980s was an historic event. Girls were novelty value and treated like celebrities wherever they went. The more gregarious senior boys revelled in the opportunity to have an active social life and girlfriends, while junior ones appreciated the softer touch that girls brought to the school. At Haileybury, Sarah Le Huray (Weldon) recalled plenty of moments when the girls were made to feel rather special, especially the tradition of tea with the Removes (Year 10s) when the boys would go to great trouble buying cakes and biscuits. Every so often they would receive tokens of affection from the younger boys which they found rather touching.

At the same time coeducation often generated opposition when boys, masters and alumni feared that their school's essential character would be lost forever, especially its sporting reputation. What particularly piqued was the conversion of boys' houses into girls' ones, given their strong sense of history and the loyalty that those houses inspired down the generations. At Fettes the decision to admit girls in 1970 attracted little comment since there were only two of them, including Amanda Mackenzie Stuart, Tony Blair's first girlfriend, though she later recalled a debate on her very first day regarding whether she should be permitted to eat in the dining hall with the boys. A gradual increase in the number of girls during the 1970s was broadly welcomed; 'They bring gaiety, grace and a great deal of brains to our society, and are never any trouble. What never? Well – hardly ever!' rhapsodised Anthony Chenevix-Trench.[1] What really sparked outrage, though, was the decision to turn Arniston House into a girls' house when the school went fully coeducational in 1982. Cameron Cochrane, then-headmaster, recalls the rumble of disapproval from those affected when he announced the decision to the school, unbecoming behaviour that so irked the senior master that he urged Cochrane to come down hard on the dissenters, something which Cochrane, fully understanding of their grievances, was loath to do. As the number of girls continued to grow it became necessary to convert School House, the bastion of masculinity at Fettes, into a second girls' house two years later, provoking further unrest, especially given the superior facilities that would now accrue.

The similar conversion of a boys' house into a girls' house at Dean Close led to the resignation of the boys' housemaster, and when Robin Pittman, headmaster of St Peter's, York, announced plans for the school to admit girls in the sixth form at the 1986 Commemoration Dinner, it prompted a walkout from one of the tables.

Even in more recent times coeducation has continued to divide opinion. At Uppingham, headmaster Stephen Winkley's decision to admit girls at thirteen in 2001 was opposed by all the housemasters and housemistresses. At Downside, in 2005, eleven pupils, including the head of school, were suspended following a nocturnal drunken rampage through the school to register their opposition to Caverel, the primary house, being converted to use for girls. 'Boys tend to be quite conservative', commented Dom Leo Maidlow Davis, headmaster, when explaining the unrest.[2]

Shrewsbury's decision to admit girls in the sixth form in 2008, badly handled by the authorities as a result of their failure to explain the rationale behind the move, led to the resignation of two governors and the immediate retirement of the registrar. More distressing, the headmaster, Jeremy Goulding, was subjected to an eighteen-month campaign of vituperation by the interested parties, an ordeal that he handled with great dignity.

Given the reclusive environment of many single-sex schools, it is perhaps not surprising that attitudes towards the opposite sex often lacked poise and maturity. Will Carling recalled school dances at Sedbergh with neighbouring Casterton as excruciatingly painful. 'The contact was so contrived, so short-lived, that it was almost impossible to behave normally and it unnerved me completely,' he said. Because of the exclusively male surroundings in which he lived, 'women remained almost alien creatures for me'.[3]

Keen to scotch any opposition to the admission of girls, schools went out of their way to reassure alumni and prospective parents that their traditions and values remained very much intact. In practice, this often meant a laddish subculture with its jostling in corridors, sexual banter and taunts of one-upmanship which made few concessions to the more sensitive girls. Subjected to rigorous scrutiny in public, their clothes, their appearance and the company they kept, the girls were the topic of endless conversation.

'It was relentless,' wrote Rebecca Willis, associate editor of *Intelligent Life*, recalling her time as one of forty girls at Charterhouse in the late 1970s:

> the sense of being watched and assessed and commented on, and this non-stop critical attention was compounded by isolation and by there being no one sympathetic to turn to ... Most of the boys didn't know how to behave towards girls, and the school didn't give them any clues, so they treated girls as they would a weak member of their own sex ...[4]

Eleanor Mills, editorial director of the *Sunday Times*, was a pupil at Westminster between 1987 and 1989. She recalled that every girl there was given a score out of ten for their looks as they walked into supper:

> Crudity permeated the place. It was the result of an ingrained kind of hostile fascination for these strange females who were parachuted in long after the boys had set up their pecking orders. Our presence undoubtedly caused confusion for the boys too. Many had awaited our arrival only to find they were ignored.[5]

A similar experience befell *The Times* columnist Alice Thomson at Marlborough during the same period: 'You can't be precious or a perfectionist when you're on a cross-country run and a boy yanks your games skirt off for a dare. You just keep running.'[6]

'The boys did treat the girls in, frankly, quite an unpleasant way,' remembered David Cope, the master of Marlborough between 1986 and 1993. He continued:

> The Marlborough expression was: 'Getting grief'. You 'got grief' if you were a girl and you 'gave grief' if you were a boy.

It was basically male territory. The school only selected the kind of girls who would be robust enough not only to keep up the academic pace but to withstand the male culture. Shrinking violets were not accepted on the whole. Even so, there was the odd casualty who left in her first year because she found the atmosphere daunting.[7]

Charterhouse's equivalent to 'giving grief' was called 'beating up', which put a premium on girls not being too sensitive. Cathy Newman, the Channel 4 presenter, recalls that when starting there in 1989 the boys in her house 'treated girls as interlopers from outer space'. For ten days the boys wouldn't communicate.

Other schools were no better. The travel writer and broadcaster Alexandra Tolstoy recounted that Wellington was 'very macho and sports-oriented' during her time there in the early 1990s. 'The ethos of the school had become overtaken by a reverence for rugby. There were about fifty girls and hundreds of boys. It was very difficult being a girl,' she said,[8] a view amply borne out there a few years later when several demeaning incidents, including a girl being photographed having sex with her boyfriend by two other boys, exposed the school to some dreadful publicity. In light of this, and because of the success of coeducation at his previous school, Brighton, it's not surprising that Anthony Seldon's first act on being appointed master of Wellington in 2006 was to introduce full coeducation and appoint Lucy Pearson, head of sixth form at Solihull School, as his deputy. It proved an inspired choice as Pearson, a former England women's cricketer, accomplished much at Wellington before her appointment as head of Cheadle Hulme School in 2010.

In class, a girl's minority status could count in her favour as the more gallant masters sought out her opinion and displayed a leniency out of character when she came up short. Peter Wilmshurst, a longstanding teacher of modern languages at Edinburgh Academy, remembers the disaffection among the boys in his class when he granted a girl an extension to an essay, something he would never have previously tolerated, they said. Conversely, in those classes where sarcastic asides and acerbic wit prevailed, girls could be cowed into silence. At Repton, John Billington recalled sixth-form girls being distracted from their work in the library. When the headmaster, David Jewell, decided to ban the girls from the library, Billington wrote him a stiff note saying that girls had as much right to use the study as the boys and pointing out the damage to the school's reputation should the ban become public knowledge. Within hours the ban had been rescinded.

Dress was another cause of contention. While some boys railed against the laxer regulations concerning girls' uniform – sixth-form girls in those early days often wore their own uniform – bachelor masters in particular took exception to transparent shirts and short skirts, often voicing their objections in politically incorrect language. Even the introduction of a girls' uniform didn't end the arguments. If it wasn't the tied-back hair or the wearing of jewellery, it was the question of make-up. One staff meeting at Fettes agonised *ad infinitum* over whether senior girls could wear make-up before coming up with the bizarre compromise that they could, provided it was invisible.

Perhaps it was on the games field that girls felt most discriminated against. Too few of them at first to constitute a team, they were left to their own devices or consigned to the sports hall for a game of badminton or squash. As their numbers grew and organised practices and matches became the norm, the girls laboured under the disadvantage of inferior coaches, facilities and pitches – at Aldenham they had to borrow netball posts from a neighbouring school. Whereas girls would loyally turn out to watch the First XV, few boys returned the compliment by watching the First XI hockey or First XII lacrosse. A win for the boys would be greeted with acclaim, a win for the girls would be treated with indifference, a boys' First XI or XV would be recognised on the school honours board, while such a privilege would rarely be extended to the girls.

An insight into the troubled origins of coeducation can be gleaned by looking at Rugby where girls were first admitted in 1975. By 1979 there were seventy of them in the sixth form accommodated in two boarding houses. The author Isabel Wolff, one of the first girl boarders, recalled the neighbouring boys' house yelling and whistling at them every morning as they made their way to classes. Many of them were given unflattering nicknames by the boys, who either competed to talk to them or simply ignored them. An investigative article by Stephanie Richards, the assistant editor of the *Meteor*, the school magazine, described the resentment felt by the boys over the superior quality of female accommodation and their greater choice in dress, conveniently ignoring the fact that the girls had grievances of their own: no studies, a lack of privacy, no sixth-form privileges, little sport and no representation among the prefects. In order for a coeducational sixth form to work with one sex being in the minority, it was imperative for the minority to take an extremely active part in the pursuits of the majority. According to Richards:

> Our greatest contribution so far has been to naturalise the Public School Sixth Form … but this has taken no more effort than our mere presence. There are many areas such as the less constructive traditions which our influence could diminish and relax the barriers of the ferociously hierarchical system. The expected greater numbers will contribute to our cause.[9]

That cause appeared on the brink of a major breakthrough with the appointment of Richard Bull, an Old Rugbeian, as headmaster in 1985. A genuine pioneer of coeducation, Bull had introduced it at Oakham in 1972 and was approached to do something similar at Rugby at a time when school rolls were falling. Coeducation would alter the character of the school, Bull admitted, but he thought it important that boys should get used to the idea that women were equals and even their superiors. 'We can't go on for ever with the notion that men rule the roost,' he said.[10] No school should ever think about taking girls unless it was going to take them on absolutely equal terms. They shouldn't be there just to benefit the boys.

In June 1986 Bull prepared a report and feasibility study outlining the advantages and disadvantages of coeducation. Academic standards would be raised by a more stringent entry requirement, but the majority of the common room worried that the costs of the alterations needed to accommodate the girls would be prohibitive. Confronted by opposition from his colleagues and from Old Rugbeians, Bull backed down. Before his departure in 1990, he felt that the school's masculine aggression had softened but admitted he 'would like to see Rugby a gentler place'.[11] He handed over the torch to Michael Mavor, the charismatic principal of Gordonstoun where he had introduced full coeducation at thirteen, and now, with the full support of the Rugby governing body, he was intent on doing something similar there.

In an interview with the *Meteor*, Mavor justified coeducation on the grounds of needing to make boys and girls at Rugby feel normal again. Girls at present were treated as a special group, which wasn't good for them and their relations with the boys or for the boys and their attitudes towards the girls. He hoped to see an even ratio of boys and girls but accepted that that might not be possible given the constraints of accommodation. Asked about the prospect of turning boys' houses into girls' ones, he appealed to the character and common sense of Rugbeians and, later, when he conveyed the bad news to the boys affected, he recalled: 'There was grief but they were big enough to see there was life after death ...'.[12] The fact that the boys' accommodation was to be modernised to the same standard as the girls' helped temper any sense of resentment.

With a more supportive common room and the first of the younger girls arriving in 1993, Rugby seemed to be moving with the times only then to take a temporary step backwards following the appointment of Louise Woolcock as joint head of school, in June 1995. It wasn't that a girl had been appointed to the top position – traditionally the head of school was a boy – that upset the boys so much as the fact that Louise had only been in the school for one year. The rebels accused Mavor of pandering to political correctness and erected posters all around the school proclaiming 'We are not sexists, we are traditionalists', and 'Girls don't play rugby, boys don't play netball – don't mix us up'.

Two hundred boys also boycotted a chapel commemorating the two-hundredth anniversary of the birth of Thomas Arnold, Rugby's most famous headmaster. (The boys from Louise's boyfriend's house largely turned up.) In his sermon, the chaplain, referring to Arnold's reputation as a radical reformer, thought it ironic that the people demonstrating weren't responding to change at this particular time. The rebellion generated extensive press coverage, with Bee Wilson, the food writer and Old Rugbeian, unsurprised by the attitude of the boys. 'Each time you walk down a street it is like running the gauntlet. Every gaggle of boys you pass will greet you with insults, whether they know you by name or not. Then there is a whole range of guttural noises they make at girls to express contempt,' she said.[13] The taunts were indiscriminate and girls were subjected to such pressure that eating disorders were rife.

With Mavor sounding the essence of moderation while not giving ground and with Louise Woolcock's deft handling of the media and subsequent competence in office, the storm soon subsided. By the time the next joint head of school was appointed the reaction was entirely muted as genuine coeducation became a reality.

By no means were all girls scarred by the experience. Not only did the majority find the atmosphere of a boys' school more liberating than girls' ones, a number positively relished being the centre of attention and the opportunity to shine in plays, concerts and choirs where a female presence was much appreciated. Karren Brady, the well-known businesswoman and star of BBC television's *The Apprentice*, greatly appreciated the opportunity to join the sixth form at Aldenham after enduring loneliness and boredom at an all-girls convent. When not writing letters to the headmaster with ideas about how the school could make money, she was enjoying an active sporting and social life, learning how to mix with boys, an experience that equipped her well for the world of business.

Early pioneers of full coeducation in the 1970s such as Oakham, Gresham's and Bryanston, all liberal institutions, found their enterprise rewarded with the smoothest of transitions, the first intake of thirteen-year-old girls at Bryanston winning over the sceptics with their gaiety and charm.

When Clifton agreed to admit girls from September 1987, the decision to take them at every level from the prep school upwards was met with near-universal approval. The ramifications of such a move were examined very carefully and every effort was made to cater for the needs of both girls and boys. Starting from scratch had its advantages, as Fiona Hallworth, housemistress in the girls' house, told her prefects since they would make the rules, an imaginative initiative that helped create the right atmosphere. With an enlarged curriculum, a more healthy diet, a greater choice of games and new activities such as dance, Clifton was moving with the times. 'The girls had a great sense of fairness, and would not tolerate the boys enjoying any privileges not available to them,' recalled Hallworth.[14] When the girls' First XI played their first ever hockey match, they found the First XV there to support them, a gesture that told them that their sport would be treated on an equal footing with that of the boys. Within a very short time, coeducation seemed the natural order of things at Clifton and even the more hidebound bachelor masters were converted, won over by the girls' diligence, vivacity and calming effect on the more rowdy boys. By 2004 a further girls' house, a mixture of day and boarding, was opened as the number of girls comprised some 40 per cent of the intake, a figure that many coeducational schools now adhere to.

As schools such as Eastbourne, Epsom, St Edward's, Oxford, Bloxham, Glenalmond and Chigwell moved effortlessly towards full coeducation in the late 1990s, the greater value society now placed on equal opportunities was reflected by more women in school hierarchies, giving the girls a greater voice. Girls also benefitted from the appointment of more female staff, better pastoral care and greater public accountability, all of which made schools less intimidating places. An expansion of the arts gave girls a higher profile and even their sport was looking up now that they had more access to professional coaches, national tournaments and the opportunity to go on overseas tours.

Another hurdle overcome was the appointment of the first female head of school, or joint head of school. Rugby had registered its dismay at Louise Woolcock's appointment in 1995; in contrast, four years later, when the headmaster of Loretto, Keith Budge, announced that Marie Clare Drummond was to become the first female head of school, the hall erupted in cheers. More girls have risen to prominence in the prefect hierarchy, societies and the CCF and, while some have found dealing with recalcitrant boys problematic, leadership has helped boost their confidence and convince them that it is their school as much as the boys'.

Although coeducation originated primarily for economic reasons and took some time to evolve to the point that girls felt fully integrated, the benefits have been numerous. To start with, a number of schools wouldn't have survived and, although some continue to struggle, the majority have gone on and prospered following the decision to go coeducational. Greater emphasis has been placed on schools' physical appearance and the standard of accommodation for both sexes. The journalist Will Heaven, on visiting his old school Downside several years after the girls had arrived, remarked that its Gothic gloom had disappeared and the school had become smarter and livelier.

Although less proactive than the boys in class — not surprisingly since they have often been a minority — girls have compensated with their industry and attention to detail in written assignments, thereby excelling in coursework. Given their maturity they have opened up a lead over the boys at GCSE. At A-level and IB, the gap has narrowed as the boys' willingness to express themselves has stood them in good stead, but with girls lacking nothing in ability or drive, their results have rarely disappointed, helping to lift the overall academic reputation of coeducational schools.

At a time when schools' cultural life was breaching new frontiers, the introduction of girls has added to the richness and variety of art, music and drama. When John Arkell, later headmaster of Wrekin and Gresham's, staged an acclaimed production of *Guys and Dolls* at Fettes in 1982, the critics were suitably impressed.

> The choosing by Mr Arkell, a tireless proponent of a coeducational Fettes, of a swansong by this title smacks of proselytizing. In fact, it is proof, not preaching. The ability to stage this production to such remarkable standards is admirable demonstration of one virtue of the existence of Fettesian dolls. The show was a triumph.[15]

Most telling of all has been the change in atmosphere in schools as the old boorishness of the boys and their patronising attitude towards the girls has given way to a more equal relationship based on mutual respect. As Claire Bisseker wrote in the *Financial Times* in October 2001,

> Following the admission of girls in 1993 and a sustained and dramatic improvement in academic performance, Rugby School has at last emerged from the shadow of the novel 'Tom Brown's Schooldays', which defined it as a place of bullying and cruelty. Fagging has long been banned and girls have smoothed the school's rough edges.[16]

Of course, coeducation runs the risk of intimate relationships getting out of control, the most extreme example of which was the elopement of two sixteen year olds from Stonyhurst to the Dominican Republic in January 2014. History has shown that stringent school regulations prohibiting sexual misconduct on pain of expulsion have been no deterrent to illicit activity, but with schools more closely supervised than in times past and better able to foment a culture of mutual respect between the sexes, there are fewer displays of unbridled passion. 'I think they learn to see each other less as sex objects and more like human beings, and it fosters respectful and loving relationships,' opined Anthony Seldon.[17]

According to Richard Cairns, who had never taught in a coeducational school before becoming headmaster of Brighton, boys are much gentler there. They learned that they didn't have to be in the First XV to impress. Girls could be just as impressed by cultural achievement.

The last word I leave to Jim Bellis, former housemaster of a girls' house at Giggleswick. He believes that coeducation takes time to evolve and depends on a proactive SMT to ensure that girls are allowed to integrate fully:

Coeducation can only be a good thing overall, though I think the model formula has yet to show itself. The general consensus is that the boys give the girls spine, endeavour, ambition and challenge, and the girls bring a degree of conciliation, a tempering of the macho spirit and a greater sense of compassion. They also bring a great deal of academic competition and ambition. I tend to subscribe to this with amendments. There has been much said about the benefits of single sex education to girls and that for both boys and girls coeducation is distracting. This is surely dependent upon the management and organisation of the pastoral system in the school. A well led boarding house where the senior house staff inculcate strong leadership as a counter to 'girlyness' can be a more than adequate single sex environment, where the negative effect of boys can be ameliorated.

Girls typically work quite a lot harder than teenage boys and with the right stewardship enjoy greater success than the boys academically. Boys will actually improve their game on the sports field with the presence of girls and whilst there may be some temptation not to train as hard because of social distractions they also find themselves academically driven to keep up with the girls rather than accept the status quo. Again it is not about the influence of the cohort of one gender but is far more about the approach to the pastoral system. Girls at Giggleswick take part in the Royal Marines section and compete in the Pringle Trophy [the national competition for school CCF Marine sections]. We have had female head cadets and female heads of school – on merit. Boys on the other hand happily take art, drama and home economics whilst the same boys will be driven on to extremes of performance in the tug of war competition. At the same time as all of this is happening, these prototype adults are learning by experience a healthy understanding and respect for each other in good time for adulthood.

And the bottom line – don't blame the gender, blame the system.[18]

Chapter 14

EXORCISING FLASHMAN

'It has been hard to convince people that *Tom Brown's Schooldays* really are dead,' lamented Peter Hobson,[1] when headmaster of Giggleswick in 1992, as he surveyed the declining popularity of boarding. His frustration in one sense was understandable because the boarding sector had gone a long way to laying its draconian past to rest, only for the ghosts of yesteryear to come back to haunt them with a series of lurid child abuse scandals.

In 1995 Fr Bernard Green, a housemaster at Ampleforth, received two years' probation for molesting a boy, and in 2002 another housemaster from the same school, Fr Christian Shore, was dismissed after a complaint from a former pupil about his inappropriate behaviour. Several other incidents then came to light when the abbey hired a psychologist to conduct risk assessments on staff. These led to the imprisonment of Fr Gregory Carroll in 2005 for four years after pleading guilty to abusing ten boys between 1979 and 1987, and his colleague, Fr Piers Grant-Ferris, for two years after admitting twenty indecent assaults on fifteen boys at Gilling Castle, Ampleforth's prep school, between 1966 and 1975. Three other monks would have been charged had they still been alive.

Other Catholic schools were implicated in child abuse. In 2004 a Benedictine monk who had taught at Downside was jailed for eighteen months for taking indecent images of schoolboys and possessing child pornography; later, in 2012, Fr Richard White was jailed for five years for gross indecency against two pupils in the late 1980s and two other Downside monks, also teachers at the school, received police cautions during the trial. St Benedict's School suffered unwelcome publicity when Fr David Pearce, a former headmaster of its junior school and a monk at Ealing Abbey, was jailed in 2009 for eight years, subsequently reduced to five, for sexual offences committed over a period of thirty-five years. With Stonyhurst also tainted by scandal, it seemed that the country's leading Catholic schools were merely echoing the wider problems of the Roman Catholic Church regarding child abuse. However, not only Catholic schools were at fault.

In 2012 an assistant housemaster at Wellington College, Bruce Roth, was jailed for eleven years for abusing five young boys over a twenty-year period, and KESB and Haberdashers' Aske's Boys' are among the other schools that have been tarnished by child abuse. Above all, the world-renowned Cheetham's School of Music became mired in scandal, the difference here being that all the assaults were directed against girls. In February 2013 Michael Brewer, its former director of music, was imprisoned for six years for indecently assaulting his pupil, Frances Andrade, between 1978 and 1982, and his wife was given twenty-one months for the same offence. The victim killed herself at her home after giving evidence during the trial.

At the trial it was claimed that sexual activity between teachers and pupils at Cheetham's wasn't uncommon during the 1980s, and in the ensuing publicity an investigation began into allegations against others associated with the school in the past. That May, Greater Manchester Police revealed that more than thirty women had reported incidents of abuse and, during the next year, five more teachers at Cheetham's or its neighbouring school, the Royal Northern College of Music, were arrested and bailed. Meanwhile, after two damning reports by Manchester Children's Service and the ISI accusing Cheetham's of failing to meet child protection guidelines, the school worked with the former and the Department of Education to institute more robust policies, something which it has successfully accomplished.

If all these crimes weren't bad enough, what particularly shocked was the unwillingness of the authorities in these various institutions to take the appropriate action when confronted with clear evidence of paedophilia.

In 2005 the police investigating the abuses at Ampleforth discovered that the abbot, Basil Hume, later Cardinal-Archbishop of Westminster, had failed to alert them or the social services to Grant-Ferris' offence when the initial incident came to light, moving him instead to a parish in Cumbria. Had he done so, the police believe it could have avoided some of the later abuse committed at the school.[2]

At Downside, the authorities, in light of Fr White's first attack, sought legal advice as to whether they were obliged to report it. Informed that they weren't, they chose not to report the matter to the police nor a second attack in their junior school, after which White was sent away to monastic communities across the country for twenty years. It was only when police investigated another Downside teacher for child pornography that they came across a file in the school detailing White's various offences. It is not surprising, then, that in its 2010 report on Downside the ISI criticised the school for its lack of urgency in improving its child protection measures, a judgement it later revised in 2013 when it called its arrangements for safeguarding and pastoral care excellent.

At St Benedict's, allegations about Fr Pearce were made to the new abbot, Fr Martin Shipperlee, by one of his victims in 2000. The abbot informed the police, but in 2007 he readmitted Pearce to the abbey, a decision he subsequently regretted in the wake of Pearce committing a second assault, against two teenagers.[3]

After revelations about Pearce came to light in *The Times*, allegations were made against other priests at St Benedict's, including Fr Laurence Soper, abbot of Ealing Abbey during the 1990s. In 2010 Soper was arrested at a monastery in Rome where he was living, but vanished when he was due to return to London to answer bail in March 2011. In the face of a 2010 report by the ISI highlighting shortcomings in the school's child protection policy, Shipperlee commissioned an inquiry by the Liberal-Democrat QC, Lord Carlile of Berriew. His report, published in October 2011, linked twenty-one separate cases of child abuse by five masters from 1970. Aside from strongly criticising the cover-up of sexual abuse at the school, he called its governance outdated, lacking elements of independence, transparency and diversity. The fact that St Benedict's was under the total control of the monks was a significant cause of the school's failure to stop child abuse. In order to remove any conflict of interest, religious orders should no longer run faith schools and control should pass to independent educational trusts, recommendations that St Benedict's immediately implemented.

In truth, the autonomous nature of independent schools and the lack of accountability of those working there made them prone to paedophiles. In January 2014 *The Times* reported that fifty HMC schools had been linked to child abuse over the decades. Over the past twenty years, one or more teachers at sixty-four independent schools, including prep schools, have been convicted of abusing children, eighteen since 2012.[4] This article prompted a surge of allegations against teachers at forty-one schools, twenty-six of them not on the original list. After further investigations, *The Times* published revelations that six former members of staff at St Paul's and its junior division, Colet Court, were implicated in numerous alleged assaults against pupils between the 1960s and the late 1980s.

With many other victims from St Paul's and Colet Court now coming forward, a criminal investigation set up by the Metropolitan Police in April 2014 recorded complaints of sexual misconduct against a further twelve former masters at these two schools, a number of whom are no longer alive. In addition to the original sixty-four schools mentioned by *The Times*, male staff members at another thirty schools have been sentenced for possessing indecent images and the reputations of a further thirty-six have been tainted by ongoing investigations. In 2014 the journalist Alex Renton, who suffered abuse at his prep school during the 1970s, asked readers of the *Observer Magazine* to tell him of their experiences. Hundreds obliged, revealing some of the desperate hurt and bitterness they endured. According to Nick Duffell from Boarding School Survivors, 'the prevalence of institutionalised abuse is finally emerging to public scrutiny, but the effects of normalised parental neglect are more widespread and much less obvious'.[5]

What originally brought the question of child abuse to the public's attention was its exposure at Crookham Court School, near Newbury, by Esther Rantzen on BBC television's *That's Life* during the 1980s, an exposure that led to the owner and two other masters being jailed for sexual offences against pupils. The result was the Children Act 1989, which compelled local authority social service departments to implement annual checks on pupils' welfare in private schools and laid down appropriate standards of accommodation, privacy, discipline and complaints procedures.

It wasn't a moment too soon. A helpline set up in boarding schools by trained counsellors in January 1991 for an experimental six-month period took 10,000 calls (many rang off), the majority complaining about bullying and loneliness at a time when pastoral care was often inadequate.

Although understandably apprehensive about scrutiny from outside, the first welfare reports left many schools agreeably surprised. Philip Evans, headmaster of Bedford, took it as an opportunity for a complete overhaul of the school's pastoral system and instituted a comprehensive network of support and counselling that compared favourably with many of his colleagues. 'I do think that public schools generally have been failing to provide pastoral care. … Yet boarders spend more time at school than at home throughout their most formative years, so some structure of support is absolutely essential,' he opined.[6]

The Care Standards Act 2000 removed from local and health authorities the powers of registration and inspection and gave them to a new public authority, the National Care Standards Commission (NCSC), which oversaw far stricter standards in boarding schools, not least in terms of pupil privacy and access to facilities such as a telephone. Every school now had to ensure that suitable child protection policies and procedures were in place for dealing with allegations of abuse; anyone dismissed or who resigned because of doubts about their suitability to work with children would be reported to the Department of Education for investigation. According to Leo Chamberlain, the HMC's representative on the National Boarding Standards Committee, the committee was skewed towards the search for evil rather than the identification of good. Ten years of growing trust with the social services had been disrupted.

He need not have worried. The first major study into boarding life by the Commission for Social Care Inspection (the successor to the NCSC) in 2004 concluded that standards of care were good or outstanding and that bullying was barely mentioned. In the opinion of Roger Morgan, England's first director of children's rights, boarding schools:

> come out very well from this survey. Neither boarders nor their parents identified any single major changes that needed to be made. Boarding schools are seen as offering a positive social life, with plenty of friends and activities, often across cultures, and with strong benefits of learning social skills and independence.[7]

With the ISI and the Care Inspectorate in Scotland carrying out frequent and thorough checks of boarding schools, and with schools having to provide a lengthy document of self-evaluation every year, pastoral care is now of the utmost importance. The school child protection officer is responsible for ensuring that all staff are acquainted with developments in child protection policy and that an effective complaints procedure is in place. Staff are trained how to identify problems and, as well as making themselves available to pupils for consultation, they are expected to pass on any concerns they have to the appropriate people. Individual pupils are increasingly a source of discussion at staff meetings and between staff and parents, and most schools provide access to counsellors and child psychiatrists where appropriate. 'Schools have now adapted to the idea of looking after the individual and helping those in trouble,' commented Marco Longmore, rector of Edinburgh Academy. He recalls that, when deputy at Alleyn's School, a former member of staff approached him and said, 'Marco, I've been meaning to speak to you. It's not the school it used to be. It's much better.'[8]

The murder of Victoria Climbié in 2000 and the public inquiry by Lord Laming led to further changes in child protection, while the killing of two young girls at Soham in 2002 by the caretaker at their local school exposed the inadequacy of the existing List 99 – people barred from teaching in state schools – and other checks. Following the recommendations of the Bichard Inquiry, the Safeguarding Vulnerable Groups Act 2006 paved the way for the Vetting and Barring Scheme in the hope that it would reduce the risk of paedophiles being allowed access to children. Those coming into contact with children would undergo Criminal Record Bureau checks run by the Independent Safeguarding Authority (ISA) whose remit included parents and occasional volunteers working in schools.

The Vetting and Barring Scheme caused an outcry in the media and among Conservative MPs as foreign trips had to be cancelled, community service was reduced and guest speakers thought twice about visiting schools. The National Society for the Prevention of Cruelty to Children criticised the regulations, which, it said, threatened perfectly safe and normal activity; and headmasters from both sectors protested in a letter to the Children's Minister, Ed Balls, in November 2009 that not only was the legislation excessive and disproportionate, but it also placed a number of school activities in jeopardy. A review by Sir Roger Singleton, chairman of the ISA, proposed a series of exemptions from the rules, which the government accepted.

Although public accountability has been critical to improved pastoral care, voluntary internal reform has also played its part. The change began in the late 1960s when prefects in a gesture of solidarity with the times voluntarily abrogated much of their authority. At Eton the introduction of patrols by Pop, the self-electing body of senior pupils responsible for school discipline, to detect delinquents drinking in Windsor pubs proved counter-productive as Pops were more inclined to join them for a drink than turn them in.

Fagging and beating faded away during the 1970s, relations between the years began to relax, the treatment of juniors improved, more tolerance was shown to those of an eccentric disposition and use of Christian names became more common. A closer relationship also began to develop between staff and pupils now that the martinets of the past gave way to those of a more emollient disposition raised in a more permissive age and committed to the welfare of the individual.

And yet, for all the seeds of reform, the green shoots of this Prague Spring did not sprout in every school and house. David Elleray has recollections of becoming a house tutor at Harrow in 1977 and witnessing the dying embers of a more repressive age. When he became a housemaster there in 1991, he received a delegation from the head of house and his deputy complaining that he was on the boys' side too often and that he should leave them to run the house. Elleray replied that he would go round the house whenever he wanted as he was ultimately responsible for its running.

Spurred on by the new regulatory regime of the 1990s, houses became more closely supervised by housemasters and housemistresses or their various deputies. With house staff increasingly appointed on grounds of merit rather than seniority, a younger, more approachable type became the norm. They and their spouses have made themselves more available to their charges, inviting them in for informal meals and acting as trusted confidants whenever necessary. Kept fully briefed by colleagues and house prefects about their charges, house staff have become better acquainted with their problems and now liaise frequently with their parents in their attempts to solve them.

Matrons often play a vital maternal role in looking after pupils' health and welfare and give houses a family atmosphere. One successful innovation has been the establishment of a tutorial system whereby each pupil is assigned a tutor, normally attached to their house, who is responsible for their academic and pastoral development. Although such a system had long flourished in schools such as Eton, Shrewsbury and Tonbridge, in others it depended very much on the individual whim of the various tutors. Now the expectations are much greater and so is the commitment.

Although the kudos of being a school prefect still means something, their disciplinary powers and privileges are now very limited. Training runs and other humiliating rituals have been outlawed and replaced by standard punishments under staff supervision. Encouraged to be receptive to all types, most prefects live up to the ideal, either dealing with bullying themselves – something that David Cameron did to good effect when head of his house at Eton – or reporting it to adults and promoting a healthy house spirit in which everyone can freely participate. In contrast to his own unhappy time as a boarder at Tonbridge, Anthony Seldon believes that today's generation are much better cared for. 'Fear, formality and regulations are far less dominant in their young lives,' he wrote. 'Partly as a result, they are less angry, and far more openly loyal, supportive of each other and even affectionate.'[9]

The fact that house competitions now extend much further than sport, giving greater opportunities for all types to make their mark, is one positive development. Another is the staging of house outings, charity runs and informal concerts, which not only add colour to the routine of school life but also accentuate communal spirit.

Yet while the last vestiges of serious physical bullying may have been more or less eradicated – seven boys were expelled from Uppingham in May 2010 as a result of this offence, a decision that prompted a mass boycott of class by hundreds of boys in support of the seven before order was restored – it lives on in other forms. This was highlighted in April 2011 when the Duke and Duchess of Cambridge requested that guests to their wedding should send donations to Beatbullying, the country's anti-bullying charity, instead of a present, unleashing a flurry of speculation that the duchess had been picked on at Downe House, the school she briefly attended in 1995–96 before moving to Marlborough.

Old girls of the school contacted by the *Sunday Times* recalled a culture of snobbery and strict hierarchy at the time, in which some of the quieter, less-fashionable girls were ostracised, and Susan Cameron, then-headmistress, while denying that the duchess had been subjected to any serious bullying, acknowledged she hadn't been particularly happy there. She stated:

Yes, there would be teasing. It's all part of the normal competition of growing up, of establishing a pecking order. Girls are cliquey by nature and they can be rather cruel. If you're attractive too, that can be seen as rather a threat. They can sense those who are slightly weaker, or who haven't shown their strengths yet, and it's those girls who are likely to end up being picked on or teased.[10]

Girls were different from boys. They could be more insidious and catty. 'They know where it hurts,' she continued. 'I've seen my fair share of that. Any school that says they don't have any bullying at all is probably lying. It depends how you define it.'[11] Joanne Harris, the best-selling author who taught for twelve years at Leeds Grammar School, offered a similar perspective on boys. She recalled a macho-posturing atmosphere there where the more studious and non-sporting boys were singled out for mild discrimination by their peers. It wasn't just these types who suffered. The former England rugby captain Lewis Moody recounted in his autobiography how he had been verbally bullied at Oakham, especially during his younger years.

Whatever schools do to try to alleviate tension between individuals they cannot force pupils to befriend each other and those who don't conform to type, while less exposed than in times past, can remain on the periphery alone and unloved. Even worse is the treatment meted out to those who have fallen foul of their peers on social media – highlighted in December 2010 by the website Little Gossip on which privately educated teenagers were spreading malicious slander about their fellow pupils. According to Andrew Halls, the rise of networking sites has put children at greater risk of bullying than ever before. 'We know that social networking sites require every 21st century teenager to live his or her life under the eye of an electronic adjudicator far more cruel and censorious than any examiner, schoolteacher or parent,' he says. 'No wonder that every teenager can feel like the hopelessly inadequate star of his own second-rate biopic.'[12] How many within the independent sector have been victims of cyber-bullying is unknown but Beatbullying estimates that one-third of all young people have been affected.

Paradoxically, one of the problems of a more caring, regulated environment is that pupils are less able to withstand the vagaries of fortune. According to Gordon Woods, warden of Glenalmond, the modern tendency to involve parents in every conceivable setback reflects an inability of the pupil body to take responsibility and make decisions. 'I do fear we are producing pupils so wrapped up in cotton wool that they can't stand on their own two feet when they have to,' he opined.[13] His view was endorsed by Louise Robinson, headmistress of Merchant Taylors' Girls' School, Crosby: 'So many parents nowadays treat their offspring as friends, so children do not know how to react when they fail or when someone says "no".'[14]

As the pace of life has quickened and the global economy become ever more competitive, so the pressure on teenagers has grown.

Following Princess Diana's revelation of her bulimia during her famous *Panorama* interview in November 1995, an illness which was previously something of a taboo was given a much greater airing. Although it particularly affected girls, high-achievers with an urgent desire to please were particularly at risk. Eleanor Mills attended St Paul's Girls' School in the mid-1980s and found it to be a 'hothouse of horror':

> Beautiful, intelligent, fabulous girls were broken by the expectation that it wasn't enough to be brilliant intellectually, you also had to be trendy, designer-clad, have a cool boyfriend, be grade 8 on the cello, lacrosse captain and in the top set for everything.
>
> The result for many was a deep-rooted insecurity, a sense that they were no good that lingered for years despite them being the crème de la crème; eating disorders and perfectionist neurosis abounded. I left at 16 for sixth form elsewhere.[15]

As girls began to outperform boys academically from the late 1980s onwards, there was a corresponding rise in their levels of anxiety. In July 1997 reports surfaced of the growing number of privately educated girls suffering from eating disorders. Penelope Penney, headmistress of Haberdashers' Aske's School for Girls, perceived it to be a greater threat to young girls than drugs; South Hampstead School employed a counsellor to help cope with those afflicted by anorexia and Dr Dee Dawson, one of the country's leading anorexia experts, was called in by the GSA to advise it on eating disorders. She told its annual conference that society should stop making girls feel guilty about food.

The pressure to both excel academically and look perfect according to the dictates of the fashion industry has led not only to a continued growth in anorexia but also in self-harm and depression. Although the problem extends well beyond the independent sector – a 2007 UNICEF study rated Britain the worst out of twenty-one developed nations in terms of childhood well-being – it has been particularly affected. In 2012 Professor Carrie Paechter at

Goldsmiths, University of London, told the GSA that too many independent school pupils led stressful lives in the desire to live up to expectations, and the following year Tanya Byron, an eminent British psychologist, declared that she was treating more privately educated pupils than at any time in her twenty-year career.

In February 2014 *The Times* reported that, according to Beat, the eating disorder charity, anorexia among girls from aspirational families at independent schools was increasing at an alarming rate. Investigations revealed that a number of schools lacked a mental health care professional on site. That omission, the newspaper contended, should change as a matter of urgency and Andrew Halls berated those schools that had been reluctant to discuss mental illness openly, let alone offer the professional help their pupils needed. He stated:

> High-achieving schools are walking a tightrope, in a sense that we are telling children to do their very best, and be their very best, but in doing so, some of those children will end up not feeling good enough.
>
> There is a risk that academic success comes at a cost. It's not professional or humane for schools to ignore the growing problem of mental health issues among their pupils.[16]

The risk of mental illness was highlighted by Jayne Triffitt, headmistress of Woldingham, in her end-of-year speech to parents in 2014. She directed her ire towards the universities for 'demanding ridiculously high grades' as the admission process became ever more competitive. Because of their anxiety to please their teachers and parents, girls were particularly susceptible to exam pressure. 'Some just become very tired, with their physical health suffering along with their ability to sleep well,' she said. 'Some start to think that exercise is more important than food and seek to regain control of their world by strictly controlling the amount of food they eat. Others sadly find relief in self-harming.'[17]

It isn't just girls that are under duress. Boys are also struggling to cope with the demands of the exam system, the ubiquity of social networking sites and the pressure to have a perfect body that has led to a worrying compulsion to work out in the gym. With this in mind, KCS has been researching ways of developing emotional resilience in its pupils by working with Nihara

Krause, a consultant clinical psychologist, to develop its mental health programme. Its initiative follows those of Anthony Seldon at Wellington. In 2005 he met Professor Nick Baylis, head of Cambridge University's Wellbeing Institute and leading proponent of the science of positive thinking, which aims to understand what happens in the human mind when things go right.

Inspired by his work, Seldon introduced well-being classes to Wellington in 2006, to some derision, but nine years later, and in the wake of much-improved exam results, he has been vindicated by his decision. More important, other schools have trodden a similar path in teaching pupils positive thinking and how to bring the best out of themselves by staying healthy, forming harmonious relationships and coping with negative emotions.

With Seldon now championing the value of mindfulness, the Eastern tradition of meditation that can help people cope with depression and enhance performance under pressure, he is once again setting a trend in the sector.

In a more tolerant age in which relations between pupils and school hierarchies have much improved, discipline has relaxed. Punitive sanctions for pettifogging offences have disappeared and even for more serious ones such as smoking, drinking and drugs the authorities are prepared to show greater clemency than hitherto, not that there is any evidence to suggest that these offences are on the wane.

According to John Rae, the use of illegal drugs wasn't only the most serious disciplinary problem to confront heads, it was the most difficult to deal with because of the subterranean nature of an activity that only came to light when a parent or prefect brought it to the attention of the school authorities. Even when the evidence seemed fairly compelling, securing confessions from suspects wasn't easy and heads often had to resort to heavy-handed tactics to break their resistance.

Because of their greater access to suppliers on the street and in clubs and bars, city schools were particularly vulnerable to drugs, but provincial and country ones were by no means exempt. John Thorn recalled that the last of many drugs incidents that he had to deal with as a headmaster occurred on the day of the Eton–Winchester cricket match during his final term in June 1985:

> There were interviews late in the night. There were lies and confessions and parental tears. There were expulsions and suspensions and problems over

examinations. It was all very familiar, the kind of thing which is probably the worst part of twentieth-century headmastering in independent schools.[18]

They were sentiments shared by Jonty Driver, master of Wellington between 1989 and 2000. He later recounted that, when David Newsome, his predecessor, was warned by various housemasters that the school had a drug problem, he replied, 'The Wellingtonian doesn't take drugs.' According to Driver, 'The problem was lots of Wellingtonians were taking illegal drugs; and because they thought the staff knew and didn't care, went on taking them.' Despite Driver's repeated warnings to the school that those who took drugs faced expulsion, his words went unheeded. 'After two miserable years, almost all pupils seemed to realize I meant what I said; and I knew that what I was doing had the support of most [perhaps even all] the staff and the parents ...'[19] When one of the boys told Driver that the main reason he had refused drugs at a party was the knowledge that expulsion beckoned if he were caught, Driver knew that he had won a victory of sorts.

Despite the greater emphasis that independent schools placed on educating their pupils about drug misuse – the most effective tended to be talks by reformed drug addicts – the problem showed no sign of abating. In 1990 seven boys at Marlborough between the ages of fifteen and eighteen were expelled when found smoking cannabis and four more left in May 1991 after police were called there twice in three weeks. The following month Canford expelled nine for drugs and in 1993 the headmaster of Whitgift, Christopher Barnett, accused some of his parents of using illegal drugs after incurring their disapproval for expelling ten and suspending a further fifteen.[20]

In 1994 Ardingly expelled eight for drugs and Ampleforth expelled four and suspended six, then in the summer of 1995 there were major drugs incidents at Eton, Wellington, Uppingham, Pangbourne, Westminster, Millfield and Sevenoaks. Yet while the majority of boarding schools continued to adhere to the logic of James Flecker, headmaster of Ardingly, that drug offenders would be less deterred by heads showing leniency, others were prepared to show mercy. David Jewell described his approach at Haileybury as a 'New Testament' policy of hating the sin and loving the sinner.[21] Even those who supplied drugs weren't automatically expelled. This more enlightened approach reflected a change in wider society. Release, the national legal and drugs advisory service, reported increased concern in the private sector about drug testing, a practice that humiliated children, an opinion shared by the Medical Officers of Schools Association which was opposed to testing.

Following the results of research conducted with 50,000 teenagers by Exeter University's Health Education Unit demonstrating that one-third of all fifteen and sixteen year olds smoked cannabis, three times the number taking it since 1989, and after a summer of drug expulsions the sector began to change tack in 1995. An HMC committee under Keith Dawson, headmaster of Haberdashers' Aske's Boys', ruled out random drug testing as eroding trust and, in line with government advice, proposed a more flexible approach to pupils involved in taking drugs. Expulsion should only be used as a last resort since it prevented heads from making allowances for differing degrees of guilt and encouraged the closing of ranks among drug-users. Instead, those who proved positive would have to submit to regular testing as a condition of continued attendance at the school and automatic expulsion would follow reoffending.

Such an approach had been pioneered at Sevenoaks the previous June when one pupil had been expelled and nine suspended. Other HMC schools began to follow suit so that by 1998 more than half of them had stopped expelling for a first offence, a move that was given official backing by Estelle Morris, Schools Standards Minister, when she spoke at the GSA conference that year. She understood parents' desire for zero tolerance and the need to protect the wider community but it was often better to give a second chance to lessen the risk of children sliding into repeated usage.

In 1998 the HMC commissioned a study by the Exeter Health Unit based on a private questionnaire sent to 2,400 fifteen to seventeen year olds in twenty independent schools. It found that 43 per cent of sixth formers and 30 per cent of fourteen and fifteen year olds had experimented with drugs, with 12 per cent of the former and 10 per cent of the latter using them regularly.

Acknowledging that the situation was even worse than it had thought, and with many pupils unconvinced of the danger, the HMC resolved as an association to renew its determination to tackle the problem as effectively as possible. In January 1999 it reiterated its opposition to the legalisation of drugs, convinced that the decriminalisation lobby was 'very confusing to young people', but advocated efforts to raise self-esteem and more support for those in distress. The day after urging heads to adopt a more tolerant approach towards drugs, Patrick Tobin, previous chairman of the HMC, and principal of Stewart's Melville, was compelled to deal with a major incident at his school. On this occasion Tobin felt he had no option but to expel four boys for drug dealing and suspend six for drug taking: 'If schools do find out there has been provision of drugs by pupils to other pupils, that is where the zero option comes in. That is what happened here. The boys were the essential link between the outside drug world and the inner school community. That cannot be tolerated.'[22]

Although some schools still adopted an uncompromising position in relation to drugs – Glenalmond expelled four pupils in 2001 for manufacturing and consuming an ecstasy-like drug – the spirit of the age was moving in the opposite direction. When David Blunkett, Home Secretary, announced the reclassification of cannabis in July 2002, Michael Spens, headmaster of Fettes, complained that the government's relaxed stance had undermined his traditional approach of zero tolerance.[23] Others sympathised with his view but Mark Pyper, principal of Gordonstoun, declared that heads had to face up to the fact that, if they applied the ultimate sanction on pupils trying cannabis, they faced the prospect of losing substantial numbers.[24]

By 2005 drug-related incidents were so commonplace that the number of schools that expelled pupils with a drug habit had halved during the previous five years, with fewer than one in thirty adopting such a policy. Increasingly schools were following the example of Eton and Malvern in creating rehabilitation and counselling schemes, but major drugs incidents at Gordonstoun in 2008, Fettes in 2009 and Latymer Upper School and Stewart's Melville in 2010 showed that the epidemic has yet to be controlled.

Chapter 15

HOLDING THE LINE

Amid the culture wars of the 1960s and 1970s few institutions endured more flak than the school chapel as pupils objected to what they saw as religious indoctrination and the reinforcement of social control. While displays of protest such as refusing to sing weren't unknown, sometimes in solidarity with recalcitrant pupils who had fallen foul of the school authorities, their disillusion was often more clearly manifested by indifference. Norman Drummond, then a charismatic young chaplain to the Parachute Regiment and Black Watch, recalls preaching at Charterhouse in the late 1970s and observing boys reading comics as he spoke.

According to Patrick Tobin, there was a yawning contrast at Tonbridge between the evident integrity of the chaplain and the apathy of the pupils for whom the school was essentially the route to worldly status, while a 1982 report by the Bloxham Project, set up to investigate the way boarding schools communicated Christian ideas, acknowledged its failure to turn vision into reality. Chapel would only have meaning if there were a vibrant community spirit in which every individual felt valued. In the narrow conformist culture of that era, that wasn't the case. For while there were some outstanding chaplains such as Willie Booth at Westminster, Laurence Gunner at Bloxham and Stuart Taylor at Clifton, too often they failed to provide the necessary inspiration and leadership. With many young Anglican priests now opting for parish work rather than the privileged independent sector, schools tended to be left with the residue and, conscientious though many of them were, they often came across as remote figures, uncomfortable with the hurly burly of school life.

When Eric Anderson arrived at Shrewsbury in 1975, he found chapel services dreary and the chaplain out of sync with the boys. After one sermon he asked his deputy, Michael Charlesworth, if he could find any meaning in what they had heard. Gloomily they couldn't and so Anderson resolved to find a new chaplain who could engage more effectively with adolescents.

In response to dissenting voices, many schools began to cut back on the number of weekly services and reduce compulsory attendance at others. Winchester introduced optional services for senior boys and an informal Eucharist which very few attended. More popular were those services where the whole school participated in lusty renditions of well-known Anglican hymns that fostered a real sense of communal well-being; however, 'very few schoolboys now seem able to relate those services to an idea of God, or even to find in them a means of seeking Him', wrote the school's historian James Sabben-Clare.[1]

At Eton, it was a similar story. More questioning attitudes to religion, shared by Justin Welby, current Archbishop of Canterbury, when a boy there in the 1970s, had led to less obligatory attendance but not to any revival in religious fervour. Despite the ambience of its magnificent gothic chapel and the superb music and choir, the services lacked variety, few masters attended and the boys looked bored even when singing. According to Tim Card, the school's historian, Eton had 'clearly not escaped the malaise affecting the Church of England as a whole, and possibly the loss of confidence of those in authority was to blame in both cases'.[2]

It wasn't just the Church of England that was swimming against the powerful secular current. In 1983 Fr Christopher Jenkins, Roman Catholic chaplain at Cambridge University, in a confidential report to his superiors, lamented the number of lapsed Catholic freshmen, noting that out of seventeen students who had arrived at Cambridge from Ampleforth, Belmont, Douai, Downside, St Benedict's and Worth, only one was still a practising Catholic. It made nonsense of the public school claim to be forming Christian gentlemen who would be future leaders. While these students were immensely amiable and very good company, they were impervious to the Gospel. Over the previous three years privately educated Catholics had taken little part in Catholic worship and action in the town.

Despite the decline in spiritual commitment, not least from members of staff, it would be wrong to suggest that all schools descended into agnosticism. One-hundred-and-fifty Radleians went to voluntary candle-light communion on a regular basis in the mid-1980s, the Christian Union at Dean Close, an evangelical foundation, was the largest single voluntary activity there, and the Christian Union flourished at Kingston Grammar School because of its support from the headmaster, the prefects and leading members of the cricket XI. What's more, the tide was beginning to turn throughout the decade. When David Jewell reintroduced compulsory chapel at Repton he caused a near riot and had to endure a hissing campaign by the pupils, but the unrest soon subsided and chapel resumed its central place in the life of the school, as it did at Wellington.

At Haberdashers' Aske's Boys', chaplain Donald Lindsay found that the general contempt he had encountered for religion at the beginning of the 1980s among the older boys had all but disappeared by the end of the decade, so that even among atheists there was at least a general recognition that it was interesting and deserving of support.

Throughout all these spiritual upheavals, few schools, least of all the boarding ones, were prepared to make chapel entirely voluntary. Even John Rae, a religious sceptic, gave no ground to the secular advance by insisting that every pupil at Westminster attend Abbey services, although his arguments contained a stronger utilitarian motive than those of most of his colleagues. Aside from the gesture towards the school's sixteenth-century foundation, he believed that morning attendance at a Christian service gave the pupils a knowledge of a particular faith that had fashioned European civilisation for two thousand years. He also thought Christianity helped support moral awareness and curb the less attractive side of human nature. 'When parents choose a school with a religious tradition their instincts are sound,' he opined. 'They may not be Christians themselves but they suspect that regular religious observance will help to moderate the natural excesses of youth.'[3]

Although the quality of chaplains still varies, there has been a significant shift in the value placed on their role, especially in their pastoral work. Eric Anderson always believed in the concept of the chaplain-schoolmaster who related to all levels of school life and could act as a trusted confidant to one and all. Traditionally this had been the domain of the housemasters and that was the way they wanted to keep it. When Philip Goff arrived as chaplain at Aldenham in 1979, he sought to offer pastoral care to the many whom he felt were lost in the system. He faced resistance from the housemasters but with the support of the headmaster, Michael Higginbottom, Goff eventually had his way. In time his new role became accepted as chaplains have since looked to extend their ministry beyond the chapel by visiting boarding houses, befriending individuals and making themselves available for consultation. Another new dimension to the chaplain's role concerns the amount of time they spend with parents and attending to their pastoral needs now that many of them no longer have attachments to an institutional church.

All of this has helped chaplains relate more easily to their congregation in the more formal confines of chapel, although even here the style is more informal.

Aware that old-style public school Christianity had often come across as unimaginative, chaplains have adopted a more positive approach, discarding a prescriptive faith that imposed rigid standards of behaviour to a more personal one that stresses God's love for each individual. Aware too that congregations are more agnostic than in times past, they have begun to tackle some of the doubts that have preoccupied theologians in the post-*Honest to God* era, discussing how these doubts could be resolved.

As schools have become more multicultural in their composition they have opened up dialogue with other denominations. Eton now employs an imam to provide spiritual guidance for its Muslims, as well as a Roman Catholic chaplain, and multi-faith schools have provided alternative forms of worship for those requesting it both during the week and on Sundays. At the same time many non-Anglicans choose to attend chapel where matters of faith, morality and culture are explored in a way that tries to appeal to all-comers. 'There is no room for sectarianism or easy fundamentalist certainties,' opined Kim Taplin, chaplain of Clifton. 'The approach is inclusive and not judgmental. Open hearts and inquisitive minds are encouraged. The truth is out there to be explored and discovered.'[4]

At Rugby the giving of a talk is still the central chapel activity. 'The life, teaching and example of Jesus Christ are the heart but not the whole of our learning,' wrote chaplain Richard Horner. 'Chaplains, members of staff and pupils take turns to address the School. ... The choir sings, the Bible is read, prayers are offered. The sum is an act of worship which allows anyone to move easily between the roles of observer and participant.'[5]

One of the more successful innovations has been the greater variety of services. Most schools now encourage active lay participation, with services often led by staff or pupils, many of the latter communicating their message through drama, poetry or music.

At Fettes Brian McDowell, chaplain between 1999 and 2007, found that participation by the pupils gave them a much greater sense of school chapel being 'their chapel' and they went about their responsibilities with a real sense of purpose. Compared to the chaplain and the headmaster, their contributions tended to be more subjective, dealing with contemporary issues that affected their own generation: minority rights, the inequalities of the wider world and the belief in community work. While the quality varied, the best were excellent and even those of lesser distinction still managed to generate intense discussion within the peer group.

Keen to alter the perception that chapel was an opportunity for the school hierarchy to be prescriptive in a way that left little room for the pupils' own reflection, McDowell asked the latter for their guidance regarding the topics to be addressed and he tried to present them in a contemporary and biblical manner. His success could be measured by the fact that the inspection before he left specifically commented on the fact that all the pupils spoken to had been positive in their evaluation of morning chapel as a helpful and valuable part of the school day.

A further concession to modernity is evident in the changing nature of religious studies and its current emphasis on a comparative approach to world religions and the consideration of ethics and philosophy. 'I'm an agnostic myself,' declared Leo Winkley when he was head of religious studies at Cheltenham Ladies' College back in 2002:

> The days when religious studies meant a cup of tea with the chaplain and a chat about the Bible have long gone. The school does not have a faith agenda and although one or two girls study RS for devotional reasons, most of them approach the subject with an open mind. Our priority is teaching them how to think for themselves and then to express themselves in argument. It is not what they believe: it is how they justify what they believe.[6]

Sunday services tend to be more orthodox, with traditional hymns and readings and a visiting preacher, although these preachers tend to be drawn from a wider spectrum than hitherto, partly because the Church of England establishment feels less inclined to be associated with such institutions.

John Bell, radical theologian and sometime leader of the Iona Community, proved a popular draw at Merchiston and Richard Holloway, former maverick Bishop of Edinburgh, at Fettes, but a number struggle to engage with a teenage audience. Aldenham congregations disliked preachers who lacked authenticity, while Norman Drummond noted that the most effective speakers at Loretto were those who spoke from the heart about the fluctuating fortunes of their lives. Dr Ronald Selby Wright, former radio padre, was one such person, with his ability to illustrate a timeless truth through anecdote and personal experience, laced with innocent humour.

In addition to chapel most schools host regular meetings of the Christian Union, which often attract a surprisingly large turnout, lured partly by the opportunity to discuss the great issues of the day in relaxed surroundings and partly by the quality of the cakes on parade. Leading the way in many a Christian Union are often those of an evangelical persuasion who have often been reared in devout Christian households and are members of well-known evangelical churches. Invariably among the school's intellectual elite, they have impressed by their reliability and integrity. Most relish the opportunity to take chapel to proclaim their biblical faith and provide a more uncompromising interpretation of that faith than is now the norm.

Yet, highly principled though many evangelicals are in both their faith and lifestyle, their commitment to absolute truth doesn't sit easy with those of a more sceptical bent. Good works and loving one's neighbour pass for an acceptable form of Christianity but challenges to their relationship with God does not. John Rae thought that a small group of religious enthusiasts in a school could be a curse to that community because of the friction they aroused. 'They criticize the chaplain for his lack of enthusiasm [the headmaster is, of course, beyond redemption], they mark down for conversion the most insecure of their contemporaries, they close their minds under the pretence of opening their hearts, in short they give Christianity a bad name,' he opined.[7] More recently, John Richardson, headmaster of Cheltenham between 2004 and 2010, has expressed concern about the surfeit of aggression displayed by evangelicals, counter to the spirit of a pluralist society that promotes tolerance of views, provided none are pushed too strenuously. When the evangelical 'Christians in Sport' visited Aldenham a few years ago, their conventional Christian morality raised hackles among their audience because it was deemed to be too judgemental. With religious fervour sometimes giving way to intolerance, chaplains have been forced to make tactful interventions to protect religious enthusiasts from the disdain of their peers.

The evangelical critique of contemporary Christianity in the independent sector has been echoed by Roman Catholic schools, which have to some degree rediscovered their sense of mission and conviction. Fr Dominic Milroy, headmaster of Ampleforth between 1980 and 1992, worked very hard to get to know the boys and to understand what was happening in the adolescent world, looking for a new language in which to speak to the young. He became much more explicit in conversation and teaching about what it meant to be a Benedictine school and the implications of belonging to a living community. 'By being lovingly obedient to God and one's neighbour, one becomes free to be fully human, a counter culture to the culture of individual success,' he stated.[8] Milroy's successor, Leo Chamberlain, claimed that religious ideals were vanishing from many Anglican schools just as an increasing number of Catholics were attending them. 'In many non-Catholic schools, day or boarding, religion is a marginal event,' he said. 'Rare is the Anglican school which has all its pupils in Chapel on a Sunday.'[9]

In contrast, Ampleforth's Catholic ethos had in no way been diluted. Fr Leo denied that schools like his indoctrinated. Rather, he said, they evangelised, empowering the individual to choose:

> There is no comparison at Eton with what we offer. Prayers here are prayers, not an announcement of notices. There is Mass in the houses during the week and in the Abbey on Sunday. Everyone in the school studies Christian theology up to GCSE. They travel to Lourdes to help the sick, they go on retreats and, if they wish, boys can spend a night in monastic accommodation. That is always over-subscribed. And we have eight or nine teachers who are monks.[10]

Chamberlain's critique was repeated in 2014 when Dr James Whitehead, headmaster of Downside, accused Anglican schools of dropping any reference to Christianity on the advice of marketing officers. They risked becoming ideologically bland because they didn't want to alienate anyone, an interesting perspective because the majority of these schools still like to pride themselves on their Christian heritage. Following the conscious decision of Peter Green, headmaster of Ardingly between 2007 and 2014, to make his school (a Woodard foundation) more explicitly Christian, the number of parents attracted by its ethos rose substantially.

That said, even if one accepts that weekly boarding has forced a number of schools to hold their traditional Sunday service on a Friday evening, there can be no denying the fact that in those schools where the headmaster and staff haven't provided strong Christian leadership the religious life has suffered. Some schools that are non-denominational or multi-faith – mainly day schools – make no secret of their permissive approach to worship; others talk about Christian values in matters of community living and charitable giving, but, admirable though these values are, they aren't necessarily the monopoly of the Christian faith.

More committed are those schools such as Radley, Rugby and Glenalmond, which hold daily chapel, although that in itself doesn't guarantee religious commitment. 'Really, of course, only a minority of the School are Christians in anything but a nominal or cultural sense,' opined Richard Horner. 'Rugbeians, like teenagers everywhere, are open-minded, but on the whole undecided about matters of faith. Chapel is there to offer them all the opportunity to listen for, hear, and respond to the voice of God.'[11] This appears to be the prevailing sentiment among school chaplains, but, paradoxically, in a more secular age chapel has played a more meaningful role in the lives of the pupils than in earlier times when Christian belief was more the norm. To begin with, it is very probably the one occasion in the day when the school meets together as a community and can be challenged, encouraged and comforted, especially on occasions of international tragedy such as 9/11 or causes of great sadness closer to home. According to Charlie Kerr, chaplain of St Edward's, Oxford, the chapel acts as 'a vehicle for holding, containing and uniting teenagers in a stage that seems to involve ever and increasing levels of stress and anxiety . . . it is a place of belonging to each other and to God.'[12]

Aside from the opportunity to listen to sublime music, reflect on great moral dilemmas and learn more about other faiths, chapel does help provide a clear sense of civic responsibility and good living. And because of its potential to sow the seeds of a future faith even among the uncommitted, most independent heads will continue to view Christian worship as central to the kind of education they offer.

Chapter 16

THE GREAT DIVIDE

When Tony Little was an Eton exhibitioner during the late 1960s and early 1970s, he travelled every day to the school from his home in west London by bus in full school uniform. 'It was fine if it was a 457 but the 457A stopped outside a secondary modern in Slough and then things could get a bit rough,' he recalled.[1]

The experience of the future headmaster of Eton is one that many in the independent sector would recognise. In February 2008 Highgate pupils were advised by the police to remove their jackets and ties before going home to avoid being mugged and abused by locals, and a privately educated Cambridge student told Fiona Millar the following year that the rift between his school and a neighbouring comprehensive was so great that the students were instructed to use separate stations for their daily journey. A number of independent schools took to locking their gates when the neighbouring state school finished each afternoon so as to avoid unseemly confrontation, and when schools from the independent and state sectors came into contact on the rugby pitch, matches often descended into a fracas.

John Rae noted the uneasy contact between state and independent pupils when groups of the former visited Westminster, and while a party from a Hounslow comprehensive enjoyed their week's stay at Harrow during the 1980s, they were bemused by the Harrovians' assumption that their school resembled Grange Hill, the fictional tough north London comprehensive featured in the long-standing BBC series.

A 1997 BBC documentary *A Class Apart* featuring Gillian duCharme, headmistress of Benenden, on a week's teaching assignment to a south London comprehensive did nothing to alter perceptions. Subjected to near chaos in the classroom and her accent taunted, duCharme confessed that she had felt terrified by the experience, leaving her deeply depressed about the state system. (It should be said that when the school's headmaster and his deputy visited Benenden they made a very favourable impression on the staff.)

Aside from raw class antagonism, political and philosophical differences added to the gulf between the two systems. John Thorn recalled that, when Winchester joined the assisted places scheme in 1981, a decision he never regretted, he received a letter from the headmaster of a comprehensive on the Isle of Wight, a man he much admired, telling him that by accepting it he was sipping the 'poisoned chalice'. Transferring bright pupils to the independent sector, he said, would make ailing state schools struggle even more. His attitude reflected the disillusion of the entire state sector, especially when its schools were facing severe financial restraint, a point acknowledged by David Jewell when chairman of the HMC in 1990. He berated his colleagues for denuding the state sector of its brightest pupils and told them that they should admit more problematic children on the assisted places scheme.

With the fate of many independent schools dependent to some extent on the performance of their state counterparts, the former weren't slow to blow their own trumpets when comparing themselves to the latter. According to John Wilson, a philosophy tutor at Oxford University's Department of Educational Studies, writing in the *Times Educational Supplement* in January 1986, both sides regarded each other with some bitterness. The independent schools had failed to show how their values were desirable for all children and not merely those from a particular social background, let alone offered much practical guidance in helping others to institute them. 'Hence, unsurprisingly, they are often still regarded with a mixture of envy and hostility and seen as largely unconcerned with the fate of the vast majority of children,' Wilson wrote. The state sector in turn had to realise that the motives of the independent sector weren't just a matter of snobbery or a desire for power. He continued:

> They genuinely believe [rightly or wrongly] that education in the maintained sector is badly astray, both ideologically and in its practice. ... They think schools should have more autonomy and less bureaucracy; more power and less politics; more structure and less disorder; more solid values and less moral

uncertainty. Adherents of the maintained sector do not always takes these points seriously.

These images, and the passions that underlie them, have so far prevented anything like serious rational debate about what each side has, educationally, to offer the other.[2]

And yet for all the frostiness that still existed between the two sectors, signs of a gradual thaw could be detected by the 1990s, with the influx of state-educated teachers entering independent schools and many a common room becoming more socially diverse. What's more, the introduction of the national curriculum, national testing and league tables brought the two systems closer together. Teachers of all stripes disliked government interference in education and the independent sector wasn't slow to support the boycott of national tests by the teaching unions in 1993.

Another encouraging trend was the growing acknowledgement by the independent sector that it should rediscover some of its charitable purpose after a decade in which making money had become the guiding ambition of so many of its pupils. Although such worldly success didn't sit easily with their Christian foundations, these schools, according to John Rae, put their private misgivings to one side and endorsed the priorities of the age; 'every man for himself in the competition for good A-levels, a good university, a well-paid job and a red Porsche to roar up the school drive, scattering your former teachers like nature's rejects in the race of life,' he opined.[3]

The writer and broadcaster Jeremy Paxman, on a visit to Rugby in 1988, found in conversation with the sixth formers that they were obsessed with A-level results and whether they would be accepted by Oxbridge. 'By comparison with the vision of nineteenth century idealists, there was a frankly selfish streak to their view of the world. The question "Does the idea of service mean anything to you?" drew only bewilderment,' he said.[4] Increasingly, Paxman concluded, the ideal of self-denial catering for the needs of others survived only in the platitudes of headmasters.

As one of the few headmasters in the independent sector to have worked in a state school, David Jewell thought that schools like his should be doing more to justify their charitable status. In his chairman's speech to the HMC, he alluded to a recent survey that suggested that the 1990s generation of teenagers would be greedy, affluent and concerned for little other than their own pleasure. 'It is the function of schools like ours to instil in young people a sense of service to the community, a desire to repay by service some of the privileges they have been given by their parents,' he opined.[5] Calling the underfunding of state schools a national scandal, he insisted that boarding schools should be valued government allies in combating any form of discrimination in education. He urged his colleagues to encourage the communal use of their facilities, and make themselves indispensable to the national educational system.

Stung by charges of insularity from the Labour Party, ISIS organised a survey of 1,000 of its schools in 1992, which revealed that two-thirds of them loaned out their facilities to community groups and one-quarter to state schools, but only 10 per cent were involved in joint ventures with the latter, such as sharing classes and teachers. Early pioneers of such partnerships included Bloxham, Tudor Hall School and Sibford Ferris, a Quaker school, which joined a comprehensive consortium in Banbury back in the 1970s. They were followed by Malvern and Dauntsey's School, both of which had a good rapport with local state schools, during the 1980s. Thereafter Dulwich and JAGS hosted literary classes for primary children on Saturday mornings, and JAGS also set up its extremely popular School for Performing Arts for local pupils to act, sing and dance; Leeds Girls' High School students helped young Asian children with their reading and Manchester Grammar School sixth formers taught science to five and six year olds in local primaries. In 1995 Frank Gerstenberg, principal of George Watson's, instigated plans to work closely with three neighbouring secondary schools, only to be thwarted by Elizabeth Maginnis, the Labour convener of Lothian education committee. Claiming that Watson's only wanted cooperation with the best of the state sector, she forbade the three schools to take part.

Although something of a faltering start, this concept of partnership was given an additional boost by the rise of New Labour and Tony Blair's olive branch to the independent sector. While his initiative might have had something to do with political calculation, it showed a willingness to work with former opponents to break down barriers and raise educational standards. Thus, in return for Labour's pledge to maintain charitable status, he wanted independent schools to justify their tax concessions by sharing their facilities and teachers with one and all.

It was in this spirit of partnership that Blair met Martin Stephen, high master of Manchester Grammar School, early in 1997 to discuss how schools like his could provide specialist teaching, as well as host summer schools to prepare state-educated pupils for Oxbridge. That November, following Labour's coming to power, Stephen Byers, Schools Standards Minister, addressing the GSA, reached out to his audience. He praised the independent sector for its excellence but declared that excellence should be more widely disseminated. He invited the sector to join a new partnership with state schools to work together on projects that would raise standards in education. An advisory group was duly set up under Chris Parker, headmaster of Nottingham High School, to recommend ways in which cooperation could be advanced, and in January 1998 all schools were invited to apply for £600,000 worth of funding towards joint community projects by submitting a detailed description of their proposed plan.

As hopes rose of a major breakthrough in relations between the two sectors, John Witheridge, headmaster of Charterhouse, writing in *The Times*, tried to dampen expectations. Although supportive of greater cooperation in principle, he foresaw problems with this partnership. Would all parents paying expensive fees be reconciled to the idea that children at state schools could benefit and would state schools in any case want hand-outs from the independent sector? They had their pride, and it is true that a number of them, along with local Labour authorities, stayed clear of a scheme they deemed to be patronising.

Many independent schools also refrained from participating, chiefly because of its bureaucratic complexities, but among those that did Downside formed a close link with Writhlington School in Bath, and Eastbourne College derived fulfilment from working with several local primaries. Eastbourne's neighbour, Brighton, was another school to benefit from its association with a neighbouring comprehensive, Falmer High School, in maths classes, sailing and team-building exercises. Falmer, situated in a deprived part of Brighton, was a failing school scheduled for closure until the arrival of a charismatic young headmaster, Antony Edkins, who worked all hours to improve discipline and raise standards. Overcoming an initial wariness, the pupils at both schools were soon at ease in each other's company and, according to Edkins, within a couple of days 'you couldn't tell the difference between them'.[6] He thought his pupils had learned a lot in terms of self-esteem and the ability to relate to people from a different background, and he was grateful to Anthony Seldon, headmaster of Brighton, and Patricia

Metham, headmistress of Roedean, for their advice on budgeting and staffing matters.

When Ofsted removed Falmer from its list of failing schools in 2001, it attributed much of its improvement to its links with Brighton and Roedean. 'This is the first intelligent attempt by any government since the second world war to bridge the huge divide between state and private schools,' concluded Seldon in the *Financial Times*. 'It deserves every support from the independent sector.'[7] Reflecting on the success of his cooperation with Seldon, Edkins, soon to leave Falmer, echoed his views. He thought that partnership was the way to alleviate tension between the two sectors but was under no illusion about the mistrust that still existed on both sides. 'Look at the e-mails we received after our recent booklet ['Partnership not Paternalism'] was published. The basic perception is that independent schools shouldn't be playing around with oiks like us,' he asserted.[8]

Adhering to this theme, Seldon shocked MPs on the joint parliamentary committee scrutinising the Charities Bill in 2004 when he blamed a small minority of elite schools for giving the independent sector a bad name. Parents sent their children to these schools for socially exclusive reasons, he said. 'They don't want their children to mix with "spiky" children.' These schools paid lip-service to public benefit but failed to give anything back to the wider community.[9] Prior to this, at an HMC conference in Brighton in May 2004, Charles Clarke, Education Secretary, an alumnus of Highgate like Anthony Crosland, told of his desire to move the independent–state school partnership to a new level. Some private schools fostered social exclusiveness and did little to educate their pupils about contemporary society. Others had a strong guiding ethos and shared their facilities with local schools. Announcing that government funding, up to then a meagre £4 million, was available to help state pupils take classics in independent schools, he assured the latter that they had an important role to play in widening choice.

This was certainly the view of Ofsted. After visiting twenty-nine of the forty-five partnerships set up in 2003–04, it opined that the independent–state partnership had been breaking down negative perceptions of one another. 'By working together, instead of in isolation,' commented David Bell, chief inspector, 'independent and state schools are sharing ideas, resources and the expertise of their teachers, and pupils are benefiting from these new structured relationships.'[10] This may well have been true but an earlier independent assessment by Leeds University's Department of Education, while noting the success of some partnerships, pointed to the lack of sustainability. Partnerships were fragile and prone to fall into abeyance if an influential teacher left, a project had run its course or funds had dried up. The latter point was the crux of the matter. Andrew Boggis, warden of Forest School and chairman of the HMC in 2006, criticised the lack of government funding and accused ministers of trying to 'hijack' the brand of independent schools on the cheap. Fee-paying parents shouldn't be expected to subsidise these partnerships.

Paradoxically, attempts to bring the two sectors together in some ways merely underlined the differences between them, especially when the gap was widening academically. In 2006 Eric Anderson told the HMC that Britain would slip behind its international competitors if it didn't reintroduce selection in its secondary schools. 'With our forty-year-old weapon of a comprehensive system we are not winning the battle to educate our best brains. … We have replaced selection by ability with selection by neighbourhood,' he stated.[11] A comparison of state and independent schools in thirty-one nations put English independent schools in top place. 'Given that we have some of the most successful schools in the world, it might be worth adopting universally the characteristics vital to success,' he concluded.

In January 2010 Barnaby Lenon, addressing a conference of leading state and independent school heads, accused state schools of cramming their pupils with worthless qualifications that failed to provide them with necessary skills for later life. Grade inflation and a shift to vocational qualifications was masking a failure to teach enough pupils to a successful standard. He concluded, 'If we want the brightest children from our poorest homes to fulfil their potential we must not deceive them with high grades in soft subjects or allow them to believe that going to any old uni to read any subject is going to be the path to prosperity, because it is not.'[12]

The most notorious attack on state education was issued by Chris Parry, newly appointed secretary of the ISC in June 2008. A former rear admiral who was mentioned in dispatches during the Falklands War, Parry employed some belligerent metaphors when addressing a committee of MPs during an inquiry into links between the two sectors. State schools were so poor in his area, he claimed, that parents were being forced to pay. The Charity Commission's proposal that independent schools should justify their public benefit had heightened tension and could cause some smaller schools to go bust. Parry declared that the proposal 'looks like a missile from the maintained sector into the independent sector'. There was a sectarian divide between the two sectors, he added. 'During the Cold War, you had misconceptions of what's going on on the other side.'[13]

Despite the furore that his comments unleashed, Parry wasn't yet finished. In an interview with the *Guardian*, he reiterated many of his views about the inadequacies of state education in provocative language. Under fire from all sides, his resignation was inevitable and Bernard Trafford, that year's chairman of the HMC, tried to repair the damage with an emollient column in the *Guardian*. Divisions between the two sides were exaggerated and few recognised the epithet of apartheid used by Anthony Seldon to describe this division:

> The independent sector isn't just Eton and Harrow. ... There is an extraordinary breadth. Yet the toff myth continues. We work our socks off to fund bursaries for far-from-affluent children. ... We work hard to be good neighbours – just because it's right to. We admire what our neighbours in maintained schools achieve.[14]

Trafford's words and his assurance there was no cold war cut no ice with Tony Mitchell of the Campaign for State Education, who wrote that,

> no amount of goodwill can alter the fact that private schools in Britain, whatever their individual merits, collectively undermine public provision. There may be variety within the independent sector but this cannot obscure the social role of most private schools, which is to act as the gated communities of British education, keeping out hoi polloi and those thought to be too difficult to educate.[15]

That some schools sought good community relations was greatly to their credit, 'but,' continued Mitchell, 'I would struggle to demonstrate this was typical of the sector'.

As social mobility became an ever-greater priority, so the independent sector continued to play its part, although, to its critics, this was too little, too late. From the nineteenth-century scholarships to the public schools were increasingly awarded to pupils from affluent backgrounds, a sharp divergence from the intention of many of the founders of these schools. During John Rae's time at Westminster only one out of 180 Queen's Scholars was awarded to a state pupil and that was because he had received private tuition.

From 1991, thanks to the efforts of David Jewell and Martin Marriott, headmaster of Canford, the HMC agreed that scholarships should not exceed 50 per cent of fees, unless parental need dictated, to enable the provision of a greater number of bursaries, then worth less than 2 per cent of fee income, to be given to children from low-income backgrounds. Such a move would not only help schools live up to their reputation as charitable institutions, but also boost their credibility at a time when a revitalised Labour Party was threatening a review of charitable status.

Ultimately, Labour chose to drop any reference to charitable status during the 1992 election, but its abolition of the assisted places scheme in 1997 galvanised many a school affected to establish its own funds. The Girls' Day School Trust launched a £70 million bursary scheme to maintain support for 20 per cent of its girls at its twenty-six schools; the two Monmouth schools sold property left to them in 1614 to fund £42 million worth of new bursaries; and Latymer Upper School, Manchester Grammar School, City of London School, City of London School for Girls, Newcastle RGS, NLCS and the King Edward's Foundation were among the larger day schools that raised millions to fund free places. Many of those places at KESB have gone to Asian pupils, helping to make the school, with its 60 per cent Asian intake, the most ethnically diverse in the independent sector, and one of the most socially diverse. 'When we have our Eid party, and there are 200 Muslim boys and old boys praying with an Imam, I'm really moved by seeing my school – this is Enoch Powell's old school – being one that's successful at being multi-ethnic,' commented chief master John Claughton.[16]

At first the boarding schools were less munificent. In January 2003 Graham Able, master of Dulwich and chairman of the HMC, proposed a switch from a 50–50 to a 40–60 scholarship-bursary. St Paul's and KCS went further by reducing their scholarships to a third, but some schools were loath to follow because they used generous scholarships to attract bright pupils to help boost their position in the league tables. At the HMC's annual gathering that year, the philanthropist Peter Lampl denounced the independent sector for providing meagre resources to pupils who really needed it, despite its efforts to appear philanthropic. Of the 3 per cent of income that was spent on bursaries, the majority went to those in the middle class who had fallen on hard times and the children of teachers employed by these schools. The following year Fiona Mactaggart, Home Office Minister, told the independent sector to give more bursaries or lose charitable status, and with the Charity Commission maintaining the pressure, the schools resolved to act.

In 2007 Eton instigated a £50 million foundation to subsidise fees for one-third of its pupils, Eric Anderson, now the provost, expressing hope that the school would be open to all within a decade, and Harrow established one for £40 million. The following year Winchester imposed a levy of £1,400 on each parent to help fund its bursaries, its headmaster Ralph Townsend warning that a continual narrowing of access threatened the independent sector. In 2008 the funds for bursaries exceeded those for scholarships for the first time and by 2014 the amount for bursaries reached £320 million – compared to £145 million for scholarships – as many schools reduced the latter to next to nothing. Some 41,000 pupils – one in twelve – now receive a means-tested bursary, but nearly 60 per cent of these recipients pay at least half fees and only 5,391 receive an entirely free education, a statistic that has concerned the Scottish charity regulator.

While some of the smaller schools disliked asking financially stretched parents to pay for someone else's child, especially if those recipients then under-performed, Peter Lampl favoured a different approach that benefit-ted a greater number of pupils. Lampl was an Oxford-educated investment banker who rose from humble origins in Yorkshire to make his fortune in the US. Returning from there in the late 1980s, he was horrified to learn that his old school, Reigate Grammar School, a former direct grant school, was charging £6,000 a year and how limited educational opportunities were compared to earlier decades. Concerned in particular that the percentage of state-educated pupils gaining places at Oxbridge had dropped quite con-siderably, he formed the Sutton Trust in 1997 to give bright children from underprivileged backgrounds a better chance of getting into university. Aside from university summer courses, he resolved to establish a network of inde-pendent schools accessible to those on low incomes.

In 2000 the Sutton Trust instituted a pilot open-access scheme at the Belvedere School, a high-achieving girls' school in Liverpool, with the Girls' Day School Trust, its owners, allocating places on merit and parents paying on a sliding scale according to their means. To ensure wider recruitment, Lampl appointed an outreach officer to visit local primaries. One hundred out of 120 in the city participated and applications throughout remained buoyant. According to research by Alan Smithers and Pamela Robinson, the scheme was a great success not only in raising academic standards but also in promoting a wider social mix. Encouraged by this endorsement, Lampl wanted the Belvedere scheme, backed by government subsidy, extended nationally, but the Labour government wouldn't wear it, given its emphasis on academic selection.

Undeterred by this setback, the Sutton Trust, with the support of eighty leading independent day schools, proposed in 2012 that 30,000 of the nation's underprivileged children be selected by academic merit to receive £180 million in means-tested bursaries. Speaking to the HMC that September, Lampl argued that it cost less to subsidise the places than providing those children with a state education, but to Martin Stephen, ex-high master of St Paul's, the scheme ignored the major failing of the educational system – that struggling state schools had persistently low expectations and that removing the brightest children from them would merely impoverish these schools further. As for the Coalition government, not even the Conservatives were prepared to risk political controversy by supporting a scheme that backed selection.

In December 2013 Matthew Parris, former Conservative MP turned columnist, caused a flurry in *The Times* by advocating something more radical than Lampl. Aligning himself with former Prime Minister John Major's recent critique of the British establishment as a privately educated elite, Parris proposed that all schools, day and boarding, enjoying charitable status should be forced to accept 25 per cent of their intake as scholarship pupils funded by the state on a means-tested basis. His proposal won support from Anthony Seldon, his one caveat being that the 25 per cent should be from the disadvantaged. However, with all the major parties now attached to the academy programme, it is unlikely to come to pass.

At the heart of the programme has been the belief that independent schools and their foundations could act as their sponsors, taking complete responsibility for their governance and leadership. Such involvement, according to Andrew Adonis, architect behind the academies, would help raise standards, strengthen communities and bring the independent sector in from the cold. While the independent sector hedged its bets, the Blair government published its Five-Year Plan in July 2004 committing itself to creating 200 academies by 2010, and with Conservative support overcame opposition from Labour backbenchers in Parliament in 2006. The Labour target was duly achieved and the momentum accelerated once the Coalition government came to power. The new Education Secretary, Michael Gove, was an enthusiastic advocate of academies and his 2010 Academies Act, pushed through Parliament at breakneck speed, enabled all schools to apply for academy status and permitted the creation of free schools.

Despite this growing consensus that independent schools could play a vital role in facilitating social mobility, the sector remained unmoved by overtures to its expertise. Only a few obliged, such as Canford and Dulwich, the latter pioneering an academy on the Isle of Sheppey in Kent, as did a number of City Livery Companies such as the Haberdashers and Mercers. Most spectacular of all was Wellington College's takeover of a failing school near Tidworth, an army garrison town on Salisbury Plain, and the construction of a new £32 million state-of-the art building. Opened in 2009, the new Wellington Academy, catering largely for military families, was soon attracting much media interest as all parties commended the virtues of partnership. A joint production of *Oliver Twist*, which won a standing ovation at both schools, proved an exhilarating experience, while reciprocal visits helped break down barriers. 'They go to Wellington College and they like it,' declared Andy Schofield, principal of Wellington Academy. 'You can see them thinking, "Those posh people are just the same as us. There's so much more we could do if we had that confidence."'[17]

Following Winchester's sponsorship of the Rother Academy in the West Sussex town of Midhurst in 2008, Benenden, Eton and Westminster have since come on board, but the indifference of the sector as a whole increasingly disillusioned Adonis and Seldon, who admitted that it had been the most frustrating challenge of his career. Was this indifference simply down to traditional insularity or was there method in its madness? The independent sector has always prided itself on its autonomy above everything else and the suspicion that the Labour government was using the threat to end charitable status to browbeat it into sponsoring academies accounted for some of the early coolness. Adonis attempted to flatter the HMC by comparing academies to the successful DNA of a private school in 2007, but Bernard Trafford, the HMC's chairman, countered by noting that academies weren't fully independent. They had no freedom over admissions, were compelled to teach core elements of the national curriculum and were subject to Ofsted inspection.

The previous September Keith Wilkinson, headmaster of King's, Canterbury, a school that had helped found an academy in Folkestone, told the HMC that dealing with the Department of Education had been very time-consuming and frustrating. Although King's hadn't directly financed the academy, the cost of staff given over to the project over two years was estimated to have been £500,000.

According to Martin Stephen, the Labour minister had ignored two fundamental realities. First, the reputation of independent schools was based on their profound work ethic and commitment to the individual. If they diverted staff and resources to a secondary school, they ran the risk of destroying the success that had made them attractive in the first place. Second, not all parents and pupils in the state sector had high academic aspirations. 'To think that an independent school can waltz in and solve the type of problem that creates is akin to asking a historian to design the next version of the space shuttle,' Stephen opined.[18] Similar misgivings, albeit from a different perspective, were expressed by Dame Joan McVittie, headmistress of Woodside High School, a comprehensive in north London:

Many academies operate in very challenging circumstances. They will be dealing with young people from backgrounds they are not familiar with; there will be challenges they are not familiar with. ... I don't think being a headteacher at an independent school will give you the skills and experience to deal with an inner-city school.[19]

Although Adonis and Seldon made light of such reservations, they were borne out by setbacks that confronted Dulwich and Wellington in the autumn of 2013. The former pulled out of its sponsorship of the troubled Isle of Sheppey Academy, admitting that its staff weren't equipped to help the pupils, while a dramatic decline in Wellington Academy's GCSE results led to the immediate departure of the principal, Andy Schofield. Seldon took over as executive principal and was soon in the wars when a display of teenage insolence in a school assembly roused him to fury. Looking back a few months later, Seldon admitted that he had been naive in thinking it would be sufficient to sponsor an academy and to do it in a hands-off way. In January 2014 he took a term's sabbatical from Wellington College and was able to spend more time at Wellington Academy, learning more about the running of state schools. While there was a considerable overlap, he found that,

> There are a whole bundle of things … about the monitoring of performance and about behaviour and attendance, about special needs, about the quality of teaching and learning and performance management as well as appraisal of staff, that probably feature far less heavily in the life of an independent head.[20]

The question of cost was a particular concern to those schools run on tight budgets. 'Why should our parents – most of whom struggle hard to pay the fees to educate their children – prop up the state system and so effectively pay twice?' declared Helen Wright, president of the GSA, at its 2011 conference.[21]

For years people such as John Rae had warned that the greatest challenge facing the independent sector wasn't hostility from the Labour Party so much as an improved state system. Many comprehensives had made great progress over the previous decades and discerning a further threat in the shape of the generously subsidised academy movement, a number of independent schools had no wish to sign their own death warrant by helping potential usurpers.

At the GSA conference in 2012 Chris Wormald, permanent secretary at the Department of Education, incurred displeasure with his suggestion that the independent sector should be doing more to help academies. When he compared its reluctance with universities and business that had also been asked to sponsor academies, one headmistress shouted out: 'We're in direct competition with state schools and universities are not.'[22]

The failure of the independent sector to dance to Adonis's tune frustrated Sir Michael Wilshaw, chief inspector of schools and previously an inspirational headmaster of the much-improved Mossbourne Academy in Hackney. At an educational conference at Wellington in June 2013, he warned the sector that isolation was a thing of the past. Heads should be helping struggling comprehensives before opening schools in other countries. He asked why Repton had opened a boarding school in Dubai when parents living twenty minutes away in Derby had only a 50 per cent chance of finding a good primary school for their children. It was the first time that Wilshaw had criticised the independent sector during his eighteen months as chief inspector. Three months later, at the HMC's annual gathering, he delivered an even more stinging attack. Only 3 per cent of members were sponsoring or co-sponsoring academies, and 5 per cent loaning staff. Many schools offered little more than the odd master-class for A-level students or the use of playing fields. Welcome though these were, the effort expended couldn't be compared to sponsoring an academy. 'It's thin stuff,' he said. 'These are crumbs off your table, leading more to famine than feast.'[23]

Not enough schools were willing to go the extra mile. They had to help the nation's state schools and dispel the perception that they didn't care about the educational world beyond their cloisters and gates. If the independent sector treated the state sector as a rival, it shouldn't be surprised if it returned the compliment. It would be a moral retreat and tactical mistake to confuse independence with isolation. He warned that haughty detachment would only provide ammunition for those who would like even stricter quotas to be applied to university admissions.

Wilshaw's words didn't endear him to his audience. Barnaby Lenon thought it offensive to the many heads who worked with state schools; Martin Reader, headmaster of Wellington School, said that local comprehensives had spurned his offers of help because they politically objected to independent education; and Adam Petitt, head of Highgate, complained that Wilshaw wasn't in control of his facts. His school was involved with three academies and a free school, was joint host of a free summer programme for local children and was committed to outreach teaching in maths and science to able GCSE candidates. A year later, when Tristram Hunt, Labour's Shadow Education Secretary, berated the independent sector for failing to fulfil its charitable obligations, a number of schools in Camden placed on record their indebtedness to Highgate for its help and support.

Many others in the independent sector now do similar outreach work, few more than Hunt's old school, UCS. City of London School seconds teachers to inner-city primaries to help with the development of English and maths, and pupils run a homework club for children from a nearby housing estate; Cheadle Hulme School offers specialist A-level teaching in minority subjects to local sixth formers and KCS established the Wimbledon partnership with seven local state schools to share good practices in a training programme for middle management. In addition, it provided revision classes for over 200 GCSE pupils and arranged for 300 of its pupils to work in local schools.

Other independent schools have formed local links with their state counterparts, such as the Southwark Schools Learning Partnership and the City of York Independent–State School Partnership to learn from each other through curriculum development, joint concerts and school trips. A particularly constructive partnership was formed between two Edinburgh schools, St George's and Tynecastle High School, with the head teacher of the latter, Alex Wood, a committed socialist, very appreciative of the support he received from his opposite number, Judith McClure, in introducing an early education child-centred course. 'Serious professional leadership regards active engagement with whatever is good and admirable, wherever it may be found,' he wrote in the *Times Educational Supplement*.[24]

Inspired by his own life-enhancing experience of a free education, Patrick Derham wanted to widen access when he went to Rugby in 2001. With the support of his governors, he established the Arnold Foundation to provide fully funded places, subject to means-testing, to a small but significant number of young people from difficult backgrounds. In order to make his vision a reality, Derham appointed a dynamic director of development to tap into the generosity of parents, former pupils and friends of the school – the sum now stands at £16 million. Next, Rugby forged a partnership with two educational charities in inner London, Into University and Eastside Young Leaders' Academy, and schools in the state sector, to identify suitable candidates who would gain from a boarding experience. To help the scholars acclimatise to Rugby, older peers act as mentors, specially designated tutors oversee their needs and a dedicated parent liaison support officer helps their families on a regular basis.

Eleven years on, the Arnold Foundation has been a resounding success. Eighty-six pupils, forty-two currently at Rugby, have participated fully in the life of the school and have seen their expectations raised and confidence bolstered. Eight are graduates and pursuing professional careers, seventeen are attending Russell Group universities and together they work hard to support the current generation of Arnold scholars. Aside from the benefits that have accrued to Rugby as a result of making it a more diverse community, the National Foundation for Educational Research has praised the Arnold Foundation for liberating the scholars from a culture of low expectation and helping others in their communities to raise their sights.

Out of the success of the Arnold Foundation has emerged the

Springboard Bursary Foundation, a national charity that works with partner organisations to fund disadvantaged children with the potential to inspire aspiration within their communities. Launched in September 2012, the charity has the support of sixty state and independent boarding schools and aims to provide 2,000 bursary places over the next decade. With its emphasis on top quality care, its chief executive, Ian Davenport, ex-headmaster of Blundell's and a former bursary pupil himself, visits each school to assess its standard of provision and, once he is satisfied, he brings the various parties together. So far forty pupils have been placed in ten accredited schools and another fifty schools are working towards accreditation.

One other great experiment in social mobility has been the London Academy of Excellence, which arose out of an encounter between Richard Cairns, headmaster of Brighton, and Joan Deslandes, head teacher of Kingsford Community School in east London, on a visit to China for schools that teach Mandarin. From this encounter the two heads instituted links between their schools, running joint drama productions and CCF exercises. The contrast between the two schools couldn't have been greater because Kingsford is situated in one of the most deprived parts of London where violence and drugs are rife. In 2007 two of its pupils were stabbed to death in the street and a policeman patrols its premises during school hours to help deter trouble. Yet for all the tension and heartache, the teachers at Kingsford are enthusiastic and conscientious and many of the pupils keen to get on.

It was with this in mind that Brighton introduced a sixth-form scholarship (Kingsford doesn't have a sixth form) for three of its pupils each year. One of the earliest applications was Tocsin Toriba. She astonished the panel by describing how she had recently addressed a memorial service for Stephen Boachie, one of the pupils stabbed to death, and had called for a general stand against knife crime. Helped by the hospitable welcome they have received at Brighton, the scholars have adapted well to their new environment. Cairns and Deslandes cemented the partnership not only by joining each other's board of governors, but also by establishing the London Academy of Excellence, a selective sixth-form college in the state sector, with the aim of getting as many people in to top universities as possible.

Gaining approval from the Department of Education in November 2011, Brighton, the lead sponsor, sought help from seven other independent schools – Eton, Forest, KCS, Caterham, Highgate, City of London School and Roedean – each of whom took responsibility for one subject and shared their academic expertise. The academy wasn't without controversy, with local colleges unhappy that successful students would be enticed away, but none of this concerned the large number who applied. Entry is dependent on five As at GCSE and interview, and half of the entrants must come from Newham, the local borough. The school opened in September 2012 for 250 pupils, housed in a revamped office block in Stratford. Students wear uniform, work a nine-to-five day and are attached to houses, all of which are named after one of the sponsor schools. Introduced to a more Socratic style of teaching by passionate young teachers, the work ethic paid off in August 2014 when more than one-third of the first intake won places at top universities, four of them to Oxbridge. One of the four was Onkar Singh, the son of a builder, who sat by the window for three hours waiting for the postman to arrive. When he proudly told his mother that he had won a place at Cambridge to read Modern Languages, she began to cry.

So, after nearly two decades of closer links between the two sectors, how much progress has been made? More optimism is expressed by the independent than the state sector, the latter citing the great barriers that remain for those at the bottom of the ladder. According to Andrew Adonis, the relationship is very varied, with many state heads still of the view that independent schools are socially divisive and possess a limited understanding of mixed communities.

Anthony Seldon believes that some independent schools have established excellent partnerships with their state counterparts, but concedes that the two sectors remain far apart with little meaningful contact when actually there is a great deal they could learn from each other. (Many independent heads think that staff appraisal and in-service training are more advanced in the state sector.)

With Labour committed to the withdrawal of rate relief unless the independent sector does more to help state education, the dynamics necessary for further cooperation remain. Yet while political pressure can play its part in breaching the divide, one senses that a real breakthrough will only come about when there is a genuine willingness by both sides to engage fully with each other, and that might prove to be a step too far.

CONCLUSION

On retiring as headmaster of Oundle in 1984, Barry Trapnell, looking back on his time in education, expressed regret that the independent sector was too isolated and inward-looking. 'The world is too complex, too professional for individual schools and burdened Headmasters to cope by themselves, for us to hope that creativity in our movement will emerge out of thin air,' he said. 'One might perhaps argue that, if the independent system is brought down, it will be because of its own failure to respond dynamically to the changing demands of the society in which we live.'[1]

It is true that, for all the reforms of the 1970s, many schools remained self-contained communities divorced from the world around them. However, as the old loyalties began to fade in a more consumer-driven market, they were obliged to promote themselves much more aggressively as centres of academic excellence. As ancient buildings gave way to renovation and new facilities sprang up, independent schools flourished during the 1980s, helped by an influx of first-generation parents made good.

Yet this expansion couldn't disguise the steady decline in boarding, undermined by rising fees and changing cultural trends. Confronted with empty beds, the boarding sector was compelled to adapt in order to survive. Weekly boarding was one option, coeducation was another and, following the recession of the early 1990s, heads went in search of overseas custom, first to Hong Kong and China, then to Germany, Russia and Spain. By 2014 the number of non-British boarders was in excess of 24,000, which comprises over one-third of the overall boarding roll, helping to keep a number of schools in business.

With governing bodies, bursarial departments and development offices raising significant funds, the larger schools have been successful in developing their assets, not least the expansion of franchise schools in the Middle East and Far East.

Buoyed by the surging economy of London and the South-east and the international esteem in which British independent education is held, demand for places in those areas has never been greater. While the large city day schools have been the greatest beneficiaries, so have boarding schools such as Charterhouse, Haileybury and Marlborough.

Yet the flight to quality has come at a cost. Capital development, better-remunerated staff – leading headmasters now command salaries of £200,000 and more – and higher regulation costs have caused fees to quadruple in real terms since the 1990s.

Set against this fact and a background of depressed regional economies and declining incomes, the plight of many independent schools in the Midlands and the North, many of them ex-direct grant schools no longer cushioned by the assisted places scheme, isn't surprising. A number have merged or joined the state sector as free schools or academies, with others set to follow.

In contrast to times past when parents were kept at arm's length, they now attend school events at will and take a close interest in their children's development. Some parents, especially those from a business-managerial background, take their concern to excess, but their high expectations have helped drive up standards.

In a more meritocratic age when academic attainment has become critical to getting on in the world outside, schools now give much greater priority to how they perform in exams. Teachers are appointed for their pedagogic expertise rather than their sporting prowess and are kept under constant scrutiny by head of departments, who in turn are held accountable for their results. With a greater work ethic, better mentoring for all pupils and the spur of league tables, results have soared. While selective schools such as Westminster and St Paul's have maintained their prominence, others such as Brighton, St Peter's, York and Norwich have improved dramatically.

Whatever the political ramifications of the disproportionate number of privately educated students at elite universities, it is proof of a job well done. What's more, these schools have carried the torch for less-fashionable subjects such as maths, the sciences and modern languages, and for academic depth and breadth at a time when exam boards appear to have had different priorities.

As the academic and cultural life of schools has blossomed, sport has lost some of its mystique, with cricket in particular losing out to the plethora of exams. With team sports ceding some ground to individual ones and the greater access of specialist coaches, the opportunity for all-comers has grown accordingly. Even girls' sport, so long the bridesmaid to boys' sport, has made real progress, not only in hockey and netball but also in football and rowing.

Taking their lead from on high, a greater professionalism now permeates independent school sport with its specialist coaches, intensive training, overseas tours, elite programmes, participation in national competitions and introduction of sports scholarships. Not everything about this professionalism elicits admiration, but it has helped these schools nurture much of the nation's sporting talent, not only in traditional team sports but also in individual events such as fencing and shooting, as evidenced by recent Olympic triumphs.

Although prefects had begun to forfeit their authority to stand alongside their peers back in the 1970s, and fagging had all but disappeared from the scene, the laddish culture remained, offering little succour to those deemed to be vulnerable. Many a girl was subjected to humiliating treatment until full coeducation, better staff supervision and a greater inclusiveness, reflecting the spirit of the age, ushered in a more tolerant atmosphere.

With the introduction of coeducation, not only did girls come fully into their own, contributing greatly to all facets of school life, but boys also shed much of their boorishness and learned to mix more naturally with the opposite sex.

Public accountability has also played its part for, aside from improvements in food, warmth, comfort and safety, it has made the treatment of pupils an overriding priority. Although schools still like to stress communal responsibilities, the narrow conformity of the past has given way to a more rounded education that places individual opportunity as a top priority. Consequently, levels of happiness, for all the tribulations of modern life, have risen accordingly and this, in turn, has boosted all-round achievement.

Despite this achievement, schools are less arrogant and inward-looking than hitherto. With greater access to the outside world and its problems, many schools have rediscovered their charitable purpose. Communal service is at an all-time high and the leaders of the future are likely to be more socially aware than their predecessors in the 1980s.

Scarred by its long period in the political wilderness during the Thatcher decade, the Labour Party abandoned its outright hostility to private education (although parts of it remain unreconciled) and embraced partnership with the independent sector when it returned to government in 1997. In 2001 Tony Blair commended the best of private education to teachers in the state sector; the following year Andrew Adonis appealed to the HMC to donate its DNA to the new academies; and in 2006 Alan Johnson, Home Secretary, declared that state schools could learn from their socially adept counterparts in the independent sector by virtue of the skills they had gleaned from extra-curricular activities.

Sir Michael Wilshaw, chief inspector of schools, delivered a similar message when analysing the great disparity at Oxbridge between privately and state-educated entrants. The independent sector had been very good at inculcating in its pupils a sense of self-estimation. Comprehensives had to learn lessons from independent schools on how to realise the early promise of the most able children.

Yet for all the accolades heaped upon these schools, their very success has highlighted the divisions of a nation in which social mobility has stalled. Research conducted by the Social Mobility and Child Poverty Commission in 2014 showed that 71 per cent of senior judges were privately educated, as were 62 per cent of senior armed forces officers, 55 per cent of Whitehall permanent secretaries, 53 per cent of senior diplomats, 43 per cent of newspaper columnists and 33 per cent of MPs. According to the commission's chairman, Alan Milburn, the situation wasn't only unfair but also unacceptable because neglecting a diversity of talents made British institutions less informed, less representative and less credible. Milburn's verdict corresponded with that of historian David Kynaston. Writing in the *New Statesman* in February 2014, he argued that unless drastic action was taken to redress this stranglehold of the privately educated in the top jobs, the current political consensus on the need to improve social mobility was meaningless.

It was a theme taken up by Baroness Morgan of Huyton, former Labour minister and outgoing chairman of Ofsted, when addressing the HMC in

September 2014. Urging it to do more to share its expertise, she said while some schools had tried to make their pupils more socially aware,

> the fact is that privilege is politically and socially toxic now in a way it hasn't been for many years. It is not only the poor that feel excluded; so do many of the middle class. You cannot afford to be seen as complicit in that exclusion. You have to be seen as part of the wider educational community.[2]

Confronted with the familiar charge that they are bastions of privilege, independent schools retort that they are agents of social change, pointing to the fact that nearly half of their intake are first generation, they provide an unprecedented number of means-tested bursaries and they are more ethnically diverse in England than schools in the state sector (28.7 per cent compared to 26.6 per cent, according to ISC figures in 2014). All of this is true but, while it may add up to more than mere crumbs from the table, it falls way short of jam for all tomorrow.

For years many on the right have argued that, aside from enabling more pupils to attend independent schools, the best way to promote greater social mobility is to restore the grammar schools. No government has felt disposed to do so, coming up with academies and free schools instead. The fact that only 3 per cent of the ISC have accepted the invitation to sponsor or co-sponsor these academies has disillusioned both Andrew Adonis and Anthony Seldon, who lamented the loss of a historic opportunity to heal social divisions.

With few schools having the resources of Wellington, they have deemed sponsorship to be too fraught an undertaking and have instead established their own partnerships with neighbouring state schools. Many of these partnerships have been positive and of lasting mutual benefit but do they go far enough in helping to repair a polarised society? Most critics of private education would argue that they merely touched the surface; however, short of proposing abolition, now an unrealistic prospect, or ending charitable status, a move that would affect the smaller, more socially diverse schools rather than larger ones such as Eton, they have added little to the debate.

It is to Seldon's credit that he has continued to look for solutions. In February 2014 his proposal to the cross-party Social Market Foundation that the affluent middle class should pay for the privilege of attending top state schools was laughed out of court — although it could well yet find its time given the growing demands on the welfare state — but a second proposal, that the independent sector should educate the bottom 25 per cent of society, attracted much less comment. For all the potential pitfalls that bear some resemblance to the ill-fated Newsom Report, it is an imaginative idea that builds on the success of the Arnold Foundation at Rugby, and merits serious consideration if the country genuinely desires greater integration.

The independent sector has achieved much since 1979 and can be rightly proud of its contribution to national life, but while glaring social inequalities remain it cannot afford to rest on its laurels. Helping the less fortunate was always central to the historic mission of these schools and, for all the good work of the last two decades, much still needs to be done. The next decade or so will determine whether they can rise to that challenge.

ACKNOWLEDGEMENTS

During my year's teacher training at Durham University in 1981–82 I wrote a short dissertation on British Independent Schools, leaning greatly on John Rae's *The Public School Revolution*.

It is a pleasure to be able to update that book and I'm grateful to the following who shared their recollections of the post-1979 independent school with me: The Rt Hon Lord Adonis, Sir Eric Anderson, Dr Vivian Anthony, Mark Appleson, Jean Arkell, John Arkell, Alastair Armstrong, Tony Beadles, Dr Margaret Beckett, Ross Beckett, Ian Beer, Jim Bellis, Ian Black, Geoff Blair, Steve Benson, Hugh Bradby, Sylvia Brett, Chris Brown, Ann Butler, Dr John Byrom, Richard Cairns, Judy Campbell, Chris Carruthers, Jonathan Carthew, Paul Cheetham, Neville Clark, Cameron Cochrane, Douglas Collins, James Croft, Ian Davenport, Gregg Davies, Dick Davison, Patrick Derham, Father Giles Dove, Fi Drinkall, Rev Professor Norman Drummond, Nicola Dudley, John Edward, Adam Edwards, Roger Ellis, Martin Evans, John Fern, Sarah Fletcher, Frances Fowle, Alasdair Fox, Jamie Frost, Neil Gemmell, Frank Gerstenberg, Jonathan Gillespie, Edward Gould, Gary Griffin, Sam Griffiths, Chris Hall, Susan Hamlyn, Tim Hands, George Harris, Carolyn Harrison, Helen Harrison, Neil Henderson, Alison Hogan, Pam Houston, Gavin Humphries, Richard Jefferson, Stephen Jones, Alasdair Kennedy, James King, Jean Leaf, John Leaf, Barnaby Lenon, Tony Little, Barrie Lloyd, Jeremy Lloyd-Jones, Marco Longmore, Elizabeth McClelland, Dr Judith McClure, Rev Brian McDowell, Alex McGrath, Emma McKendrick, David McMurray, Rona MacVicar, Simon Mair, Michael Meredith, Fr Dominic Milroy, Jeremy Morris, Cllr Andrew Morrison, Andrew Murray, Colin Niven, Claire Oulton, Lucy Pearson, Jane Pendry, Jonathan Perry, George Preston, Robert Proctor,

Daphne Rae, Sarah Randell, Tony Reeves, Dr Harry Reid, David Rhodes, Richard Rhodes, William Richardson, Liz Robertson, Stephen Robertson, Charles Robinson, Fiona Robinson, Sally Rosser, Bruce Russell, Bill Sayer, Andrew Shackleton, Sir Anthony Seldon, Kirsty Shanahan, Dennis Silk, Jonathan Smith, David Spawforth, Michael Spens, Martin Stephen, Peter Sutton, Charles Swan, Ben Thomas, Betty Thomson, D. R. Thorpe, Malcolm Thyne, Jeremy Tomlinson, Malcolm Tozer, Bernard Trafford, Dale Vargas, Dr Ian Walker, David Ward, Andrew Widdowson, Darryl Wideman, Fiona Wideman, Bob Williams, Rev Gavin Williams, The Rt Hon Baroness Williams of Crosby, David Willington, Peter Wilmshurst, Heather Wilson, David Woodhead, Jim Woodhouse, Gordon Woods, Dr Helen Wright, John Wright, Cameron Wyllie.

I am greatly indebted to Nigel Richardson who besides offering many a shrewd insight was generous in answering my many queries.

I'd also like to record my gratitude to the staff of the National Library of Scotland for all their efforts on my behalf and to the staff of Third Millennium Publishing for permitting me to use their facilities during my research.

Simon Jacot and Jessica Fellowes were good enough to read the book and offered much invaluable advice. I owe them much, as I do my agent Andrew Lownie and the team at Elliott and Thompson; Lorne Forsyth, the chairman, Jennie Condell and Pippa Crane, who coped with my foibles with great tolerance and efficiency.

BIBLIOGRAPHY

Adonis, Andrew, *Education, Education, Education: Reforming England's Schools* (London: Biteback, 2012)

Adonis, Andrew and Pollard, Stephen, *A Class Act: The Myth of Britain's Classless Society* (London: Hamish Hamilton, 1997)

Anthony, Vivian, *'Good Wit and Capacity': The History of Colfe's School 1972–2002*, (Stamford: Spiegel Press, 2012)

Anthony, Vivian and Pittman, Robin, *Head to Head: How to Run a School* (Woodbridge: John Catt Educational Ltd, 1992)

Avery, Gillian, *The Best Type of Girl: A History of Girls' Independent Schools* (London: Andre Deutsch, 1991)

Balding, Clare, *My Animals and Other Family* (London: Viking, 2012)

Beer, Ian, *But Headmaster!*, (Wells: Greenbank Books, 2001)

Benn, Melissa, *School Wars: The Battle for Britain's Education* (London: Verso, 1991)

Bennett, Anthony (ed), *Charterhouse: A 400th Anniversary Portrait* (London: Third Millennium Publishing, 2010)

Blair, Tony, *A Journey* (London: Arrow, 2011)

Botten, Simon, *A Shining Light: 150 Years of Bloxham School* (London: James and James, 2010)

Bowers, Chris, *Nick Clegg: The Biography* (London: Biteback, 2011)

Brady, Karren, *Strong Woman: Ambition, Grit and a Great Pair of Heels* (London: Collins, 2012)

Callaghan, Daniel, *Conservative Party Education Policies, 1976–1997*, (Eastbourne: Sussex Academic Press, 2006)

Cannadine, David, *Class in Britain*, (New Haven: Yale University Press, 1998)

Card, Tim, *Eton Renewed* (London: John Murray Ltd, 1994)

Carling, Will, *Will Carling: My Autobiography* (London: Hodder & Stoughton, 1998)

Carman, Dominic, *Heads Up: The Challenge Facing England's Leading Head Teachers* (London: Thistle Press, 2013)

Charlesworth, Michael, *Behind the Headlines: An Autobiography* (Wells: Greenbank Press, 1994)

Cook, Jonathan and Richardson, Nigel (eds), *Work of the Bursar: A Jack of all Trades* (Woodbridge: John Catt Educational Ltd, 2011)

Dallaglio, Lawrence, *It's in the Blood: My Life*, (London: Headline, 2007)

Despontin, Brenda and Richardson, Nigel (eds), *Heads: Essays in Leadership for Changing Times* (Woodbridge: John Catt Educational Ltd, 2007)

Despontin, Brenda and Richardson, Nigel, *Senior Management Teams* (Woodbridge: John Catt Educational Ltd, 2008)

Drysdale, Richard (ed), *Over Ancient Ways: A Portrait of St Peter's School* (London: Third Millennium Publishing, 2007)

Duffell, Nick, *The Making of Them: The British Attitude to Children and the Boarding School System* (London: Lone Arrow Press, 2000)

Farage, Nigel, *Flying Free* (London: Biteback, 2011)

Fraser, Nick, *The Importance of Being Eton* (London: Short Books, 2006)

Ganesh, Janan, *George Osborne: The Austerity Chancellor* (London: Biteback, 2012)

Gay, Brenda M., *The Church of England and the Independent Schools* (a Culham monograph), (Culham College Institute for Church Related Education, 1985)

Gimson, Andrew, *Boris: The Rise of Boris Johnson* (London: Simon & Schuster, 2006)

Hibbert, Christopher, *No Ordinary Place: Radley College and the Public School System, 1847–1997* (London: John Murray, 1997)

Hinde, Thomas, *Paths of Progress: A History of Marlborough College* (London: James & James, 1992)

Holdsworth, Angela (ed), *Bryanston Reflections: Et Nova et Vetera* (London: Third Millennium Publishing, 2005)

Horsler, Val and Davies, Robin (eds), *Eastbourne College: A Celebration* (London: Third Millennium Publishing, 2007)

Horsler, Val and Kingsland, Jennifer (eds), *Downe House: 'A Mystery and a Miracle'* (London: Third Millennium Publishing, 2006)

Hunter, Nicola, *St Edward's 150 Years* (London: Third Millennium Publishing, 2013)

Hutton, Will, *The State We're In* (London: Vintage, 1996)

Jones, Martin D.W., *Brighton College*, (Stroud: Phillimore and Co, 1995)

MacLaurin, Ian, *Tiger by the Tail* (London: Pan Books, 1999)

McGrath, Alex, *Lifting Our Heads: The Challenge Facing Our Schools*, (Woodbridge: John Catt Educational Ltd, 2013)

Meredith, Michael, *Five Hundred Years of Eton Theatre* (Windsor: Eton College, 2001)

Merrett-Crosby, Anthony, *A School of the Lord's Service: A History of Ampleforth*, (London: James & James, 2002)

Mileham, Patrick, *Wellington College: The First 150 Years* (London: Third Millennium Publishing, 2008)

Monaco, Mario di, *Cradles of Success: Britain's Premier Public Schools* (Buckingham: University of Buckingham Press, 2012)

Moody, Lewis, *Mad Dog – An Englishman: My Life in Rugby* (London: Hodder & Stoughton, 2011)

Muir, Thomas, *Stonyhurst College, 1583–1993* (London: James & James, 1992)

Payne, Roger, *Heirs and Rebels: Aldenham School, 1973–1998* (Roger Payne, 2004)

Peel, Mark, *The Land of Lost Content: The Biography of Anthony Chenevix-Trench*, (Edinburgh: Pentland Press, 1996)

Philp, Robert, *A Keen Wind Blows: The Story of Fettes College* (London: James & James, 1998)

Piggott, Jan, *Dulwich College: A History, 1612–2008* (Dulwich: Dulwich College, 2008)

Plowright John (ed), *Repton to the End* (London: Third Millennium Publishing, 2008)

Purnell, Sonia, *Just Boris* (London: Aurum, 2011)

Rae, John, *The Public School Revolution: Britain's Independent Schools, 1964–1979* (London: Faber and Faber, 1981)

Rae, John, *Letters from School* (London: Harper Collins, 1987)

Rae, John, *Letters to Parents* (London: Harper Collins, 1989)

Rae, John, *Delusions of Grandeur* (London: Harper Collins, 1993)

Richardson, Nigel (ed), *Public Relations, Marketing and Development* (Woodbridge: John Catt Educational Ltd, 2010)

Sabben-Clare, James, *Winchester College after 600 Years, 1882–1982*, (Southampton: Paul Cave Publications, 1981)

Salter, Brian and Tapper, Ted, *Power and Policy in Education: The Case for Independent Schooling* (Abingdon: Routledge Falmer, 1985)

Sampson, Anthony, *Anatomy of Britain* (London: Hodder & Stoughton, 1962)

Sampson, Anthony, *The New Anatomy of Britain* (London: Hodder & Stoughton, 1971)

Sampson, Anthony, *The Changing Anatomy of Britain* (London: Hodder & Stoughton, 1982)

Seldon, Anthony, *Blair's Britain, 1997–2007*, (Cambridge: Cambridge University Press, 2007)

Seldon, Anthony and Kavanagh, Dennis (eds), *The Blair Effect 2001–5*, (Cambridge: Cambridge University Press, 2005)

Smith, Ed, *Luck: What It Means and Why It Matters* (London: Bloomsbury, 2012)

Smith, Jonathan, *The Learning Game* (London: Abacus, 2001)

Smith, Jonathan, *The Following Game* (Woodbridge: Peridot Press, 2011)

Stevens, Robert, *University to Uni: The Politics of Higher Education in England since 1944*, (London: Politicos, 2004)

Tapper, Ted, *Fee Paying Schools and Educational Change in Britain* (Ilford: Woburn Press, 1997)

Thorn, John, *The Road to Winchester*, (London: Weidenfeld & Nicolson, 1989)

Tobin, Patrick, *Portrait of a Putney Pud* (Co. Durham: Spennymoor Memoir Club, 2004)

Tozer, Malcolm (ed), *Physical Education and Sport in Independent Schools* (Woodbridge: John Catt Educational Ltd, 2012)

Trafford, Cheryl (ed), *'The Best School of All': 150 Years of Clifton College*, (London: Third Millennium Publishing, 2009)

Turner, David, *The Old Boys: The Decline and Rise of the Public School*, (New Haven: Yale University Press, 2015)

Tyerman, Christopher, *A History of Harrow School, 1324–1991* (Oxford: Oxford University Press, 2000)

Walden, George, *We Should Know Better: Solving the Education Crisis* (London: Fourth Estate, 1996)

Walford, Geoffrey, *Life in Public Schools* (London: Methuen, 1986)

Walford, Geoffrey (ed), *British Private Schools: Research on Policy and Practice* (Ilford: Woburn Press, 2003)

Walston, Catherine (ed), *With a Fine Disregard: A Portrait of Rugby School* (London: Third Millennium Publishing, 2006)

Watson, Nigel, *And Their Works Follow Them: The Story of North London Collegiate School 1850–2000* (London: James & James, 2000)

Watson, Nigel (ed), *Badminton School: The First 150 Years* (London: James & James, 2008)

Westlake, Martin, *Kinnock: The Biography* (London: Little, Brown, 2001)

Whitney, C.E., *At Close Quarters: Dean Close School, 1884–2009* (Almeley: Logaston Press, 2009)

Willington, David, *Alumni Montium: Sixty Years of Glenalmond and Its People* (London: Elliott & Thompson, 2008)

Winterbottom, Derek, *The Tide Flows On: A History of Rossall School*, (Fleetwood: Corporation of Rossall School, 2006)

Woodburn, Roger, Parker, Toby and Walston, Catherine (eds), *Haileybury: A 150th Anniversary Portrait* (London: Third Millennium Publishing, 2012)

Journals and Periodicals Used

Ampleforth College News	*Fettesian*	*Rugby World*
The Australian	*Financial Times*	*Salopian*
Attain	*Guardian*	*School Sport*
Bath Chronicle	*Harrovian*	*Scotsman*
Brighton Argus	*Herald*	*Spectator*
Bristol Evening Post	*Independent*	*Sun*
Catholic Herald	*Independent on Sunday*	*Sunday Telegraph*
Church Times	*Mail on Sunday*	*Sunday Times*
Conference and Common Room	*Meteor*	*Sunday Times Magazine*
Cricketer	*New Statesman*	*Tablet*
Daily Mail	*Northern Echo*	*Times Educational Supplement*
Daily Telegraph	*Observer*	*The Times*
Evening Standard	*Press Association*	*Yorkshire Post*

NOTES

Introduction

1. *Posh and Posher: Why the Public School Elite still Rule Britain*, BBC2, 26 January 2011
2. Moore, Charles, 'Never Have Our Politicians Been Posher, or More Prolier-than-thou', *Daily Telegraph*, 29 January 2011
3. Davis, Anna, 'Ofsted Chief Urges Private Heads to Help State Schools', *Evening Standard*, 21 June 2013

Chapter 1: The curse is lifted

1. Adonis, Andrew and Pollard, Stephen, *A Class Act: The Myth of Britain's Classless Society* (London: Hamish Hamilton Ltd, 1997), p. 39
2. Thorn, John, *The Road to Winchester* (London: Weidenfeld & Nicolson, 1989), p. 93
3. Paxman, Jeremy, *Friends in High Places* (London: Penguin Books, 1991), p. 163
4. *Times Educational Supplement*, 11 January 1980
5. Westlake, Martin, *Kinnock: The Biography* (London: Little, Brown, 2000), p. 154
6. *Meteor*, 1983, p. 15
7. Rae, John, 'New Life to the Old School Tie/Revival Of Independent Education', *The Times*, 14 December 1985
8. Broom, Douglas, 'Parent Power Could Push Independent Schools Into the Hands of The Receivers', *The Times*, 28 March 1990
9. *The Times*, 22 February 1993
10. Hutton, Will, *The State We're In* (London: Vintage, 1996), p. 214
11. Walden, George, 'Major's Moonshine Preserves Our Educational Apartheid', *Sunday Times*, 17 September 1995
12. Blair, Tony, *A Journey* (London: Arrow, 2011), p. 579
13. Macwhirter Iain, 'In Knots Over School Ties', *Observer*, 28 January 1996
14. Hennessy, Patrick, 'Angry Brown Hits Out At Oxford's "Old Boy Network"', *Evening Standard*, 25 May 2000
15. Wilby, Peter, 'Debate: Oxbridge's Admissions Policy' *Observer*, 28 May 2000
16. Clare, John, 'Morris Attacks Class Divide At University', *Daily Telegraph*, 23 October 2001
17. Pyke, Nicholas, 'Universities Try US Tests', *Sunday Times*, 8 December 2002
18. Clare, John, 'Seven Universities Accused of Bias Against Private Pupils', *Daily Telegraph*, 1 October 2002
19. Heffer, Simon, 'There's a Class War to be Fought Over the Future of Private Schools', *Daily Telegraph*, 15 July 2009
20. 'Minister Wants Eton to Open Inner-City Campuses', *The Australian*, 19 October 2002

21. Sandbrook, Dominic, 'Nick, Dave and the Death of Social Mobility', *Daily Mail*, 15 May 2010

22. Garner, Richard, 'Michael Gove: "My first priority is to improve state schools"', *Independent*, 18 February 2010

23. Shepherd, Jessica, 'David Cameron Warned to Stop Interfering By Headteachers', *Guardian*, 8 October 2010

24. Clark, Laura, 'We Shouldn't Have to Open Our Facilities For State Pupils, Insists Private Schools Chief', *Daily Mail*, 20 November 2012

25. Henry, Julie, 'Politicians Are Demonising Independent Schools, Says Top Head', *Daily Telegraph*, 17 November 2011

26. Jowitt, Juliet, 'Nick Clegg Using "Old-Style Communist" Tactics, Says Public School Head', *Guardian*, 23 May 2012

27. Adams, Richard, 'Love Has Disappeared From State Education, Says Private School Leader', *Guardian*, 1 October 2013

28. ibid.

29. Berliner, Wendy, 'Are the Tories Turning on Independent Schools?', *Guardian*, 4 October 2013

Chapter 2: A question of affordability

1. Dixon, Michael, 'School Fees: Practical Approach in Jeopardy', *Financial Times*, 19 June 1982

2. Langdale, Simon, 'The Survival Of Boarding', *Conference and Common Room*, Spring 1995, p. 22

3. ibid.

4. Rae, John, 'Many Public Schools Like "Refugee Camps"', *The Times*, 30 September 1989

5. Rae, John, *Delusions of Grandeur* (London: Harper Collins, 1993), p. 198

6. Adonis, Andrew, 'Lessons In Economics For Private Schools', *Financial Times*, 27 April 1991

7. Rae, John, *Letters to Parents* (London: Harper Collins, 1989), p. 7

8. Turner, Graham, 'Faith in the Future', *Daily Telegraph*, 25 January 2003

9. Whitworth, Damian, 'Why British Schools Are a Chinese Mecca', *The Times*, 27 May 2013

10. Hattersley, Giles, 'Here Come the Girls', *Sunday Times*, 23 October 2011

11. Garner, Richard, 'Recession-hit Private School Rescued by Overseas Pupils', *Independent*, 29 April 2010

12. Hamlyn, Susan, 'What Does it Take to be a Superhead?', *Daily Telegraph*, 20 June 2014

13. Woodburn, Roger, Parker, Toby and Walston, Catherine [eds], *Haileybury: A 150th Anniversary Portrait* (London: Third Millennium Publishing, 2012), p. 151

14. 'Public Schools Behaved Badly – As Did Labour', *Daily Telegraph*, 25 February 2006

15. 'Parents Pass Judgement On Blair's Schools Policy By Opting Out In Record Numbers', *The Times*, 4 May 2007

16. Carman, Dominic, *Heads Up: The Challenge Facing England's Leading Head Teachers* (London: Thistle Press, 2013), p. 72

17. Berwick, Isabel, 'Mixed Blessings', *Financial Times*, 21 July 2007

18. Paton, Graeme, 'Private Schools "More Exclusive" As Fees Rise, *Daily Telegraph*, 29 September 2008

19. Stephen, Martin, 'State and Independent Schools Must Learn to Jaw-jaw', *Daily Telegraph*, 4 October 2013

20. Robinson, Stephen, 'Private Grief', *Spectator*, 19 May 2012

21. McGrath, Alex, *Lifting Our Heads: The Challenge Facing Our Schools* (Woodbridge: John Catt Educational Ltd, 2013), p. 89

22. ibid., p. 111

23. Middleton, Christopher, 'When the Going Gets Tough, the Toffs Move Along', *Daily Telegraph*, 19 January 2008

24. Wallis, Janette, 'A Series of Damaging Admissions', *Sunday Telegraph*, 16 February 2014

Chapter 3: The uneasy partnership

1. Alasdair Fox, interview with the author, 5 December 2012

2. Smith, Jonathan, *The Learning Game* (London: Abacus, 2001), p. 221

3. ibid., p224

4. Ann Butler to the author, 29 March 2014

5. Rae, *Delusions of Grandeur*, p. 152

6. Gurney-Read, Josie, 'Schools Tackle "Perfectionism" In Pupils', *Daily Telegraph*, 1 August 2014

7. Griffiths, Sian, 'Head Slams Hothouse Parents', *Sunday Times*, 3 March 2013

8. Hugh Woodcock obituary, *Daily Telegraph*, 26 April 2011

9. Tozer, Malcolm [ed], *Physical Education and Sport in Independent Schools* (Woodbridge: John Catt Educational Ltd, 2012), p. 226

10. Harris, Sarah, 'Too Pushy Parents Are Banned From Sports Day', *Daily Mail*, 23 June 2005

11. Anthony, Vivian, 'Discipline The Parents First', *The Times*, 14 February 1994

12. O'Leary, John, 'Divorce "Bigger Than Drugs Or Alcohol" To Children', *The Times*, 6 October 1998

13. Clare, John, 'Head Blasts Divorce as Selfishness', *Daily Telegraph*, 7 October 2003

14. Ward, Lucy, 'Private School Head Rounds on Parents Who Lie', *Guardian*, 3 November 2003

15. Paton, Graeme, 'Schools "Harassed" by Pushy Parents, Says Eton Head', *Daily Telegraph*, 5 May 2010

16. Carman, *Heads Up*, p. 136

17. Judith McClure, interview with the author, 21 January 2013

18. Carman, *Heads Up*, p. 136

19. Cameron Wyllie, interview with the author, 15 January 2013

Chapter 4: *Primus inter pares?*

1. Rae, John, *Letters from School* (London: Harper Collins, 1987), p. 208

2. Sampson, Anthony, *Anatomy of Britain* (London: Hodder & Stoughton, 1962), p. 205

3. Horsler, Val and Kingsland, Jennifer [eds], *Downe House: 'A Mystery and a Miracle'* (London: Third Millennium Publishing, 2006), p. 118

4. Rae, *Delusions of Grandeur*, p. 109

5. Purnell, Sonia, *Just Boris* (London: Aurum Press Ltd, 2011), p. 57

6. Features, *Meteor*, 1991, pp. 1–2

7. Macleod, Donald, 'Head Teacher Bitter at GCSE Resignation', *Independent*, 18 August 1992

8. 'The Lessons of St Pauls', *Independent*, 19 August 1992

9. Grove, Valerie, 'Interview With David Cope, The Master Of Marlborough', *The Times*, 25 September 1992

10. 'The Unhappiest Days – Running Public Schools', Editorial, *The Times*, 21 September 1992

11. Cohen, Julie and Hymas, Charlie, 'School Heads Replaced if Rankings Fall', *Sunday Times*, 2 October 1994

12. O'Leary, John, 'Nowhere to Hide the Skeletons', *The Times*, 2 October 1992

13. Sir Eric Anderson, interview with the author, 3 December 2012

14. Mavor, Michael, 'Lessons for the Headmaster', *The Times*, 18 September 1989

15. Rev Professor Norman Drummond, interview with the author, 10 January 2013

16. Petre, Jonathan, 'Downside Head Quits After Attack on Government', *Daily Telegraph*, 8 October 2002

17. 'Kingswood Says a Fond Farewell to Headteacher', *Bath Chronicle*, 10 July 2008

18. Rae, John, *Letters from School*, p. 123

19. Hibbert, Christopher, *No Ordinary Place: Radley College and the Public School System 1847–1997* (London: John Murray, 1997), p. 324

20. Tony Little, interview with the author, 28 February 2013

21. Green, Miranda, 'Lessons In Opportunity', *Financial Times*, 31 August 2007

22. Derham, Patrick, 'The Lesson John Prescott Failed To Learn', *The Times*, 3 November 2008

Chapter 5: Mr Chips as history

1. Charlesworth, Michael, *Behind the Headlines: An Autobiography* (Wells: Greenbank Press, 1994), p. 256

2. Peel, Mark, *The Land of Lost Content: The Biography of Anthony Chenevix-Trench* (Edinburgh: The Pentland Press, 1996), p. 152

3. Woodburn, Parker and Walston [eds], *Haileybury*, p. 94

4. Tobin, Patrick, *Portrait of a Putney Pud* (Spennymoor Memoir Club, 2004), p. 106

5. Winterbottom, Derek, *The Tide Flows On: A History of Rossall School* (Fleetwood: The Corporation of Rossall School, 2006), p. 319

6. Smith, *The Learning Game*, p. 95

7. Farage, Nigel, *Flying Free* (London: Biteback, 2011), p. 24

8. Mount, Harry, 'Trust Me: TJP Would Gain Nothing From Taking a PGCE', *Daily Telegraph*, 12 October 2004

9. D. R. Thorpe to the author, 24 September 2012

10. ibid.

11. Sarah Fletcher, interview with the author, 15 November 2012

12. John Byrom, interview with the author, 11 September 2012

13. McGrath, *Lifting Our Heads*, p. 49

14. ibid., p. 90

Chapter 6: Top of the table

1. Wilby, Peter, 'A Parent's Guide To Private Education', *Sunday Times, Magazine*, 22 November 1981, p. 31

2. *The Harrovian*, Vol. CIV, No. 27, 15 June 1991, p. 71

3. Wilkinson, Max, 'Back To School: Rugby Bows To The Gentler Sex', *Financial Times*, 19 May 1990

4. Turner, David, *The Old Boys: The Decline and Rise of the Public School* (New Haven: Yale University Press, 2015), p. 217

5. Letters To The Editor, *Daily Telegraph*, 29 August 1991

6. Bates, Stephen, 'Results Tables Upset Private Heads', *Guardian*, 29 August 1992

7. Tytler, David, 'Right On The Competitive Edge', *The Times*, 15 November 1993

8. Rae, John, 'Battle of the A-levels', *The Times*, 23 August 1996

9. Carvel, John, 'Super Exam to Challenge Brightest Sixth-formers', *Guardian*, 20 March 1999

10. Leigh, Jonathan, 'It's All Work And No Play', *Daily Telegraph*, 30 May 2001

11. Hackett, Geraldine, 'Architect Of AS-Level Doubts Own Exam', *Sunday Times*, 10 June 2001

12. 'A Step-By-Step Approach To A-level Reform', *Daily Telegraph*, 13 June 2001

13. 'Clare, John, A-level Cheats: The Exam Board and Their "Watchdog"', *Daily Telegraph*, 18 September 2002

14. Halpin, Tony, and Charter, David, 'Head Teachers Join Forces to Condemn A-level "Fix"', *The Times*, 19 September 2002

15. 'A Step-By-Step Approach To A-level Reform', *The Times*, 28 September 2002

16. 'Stick With A-levels', Letters To The Editor, *The Times*, 1 October 2010

17. ibid.

18. ibid.

19. 'GCSE Is Trivial And An Insult To Bright Pupils, Head Says', *The Times*, 10 July 1989

20. Halpin, Tony, 'Schools Free To Drop "Too Easy" GCSEs', *The Times*, 11 August 2003

21. Green, Miranda, 'GCSEs Are Too Easy, Say Private Schools', *Financial Times*, 3 September 2005

22. Kershaw, Alison, 'Top Head Hails Benefits Of GCSEs', Press Association, 3 September 2011

Chapter 7: The great leap forward

1. Lightfoot, Liz, 'The Pros And Cons Of A Private Education', *Independent*, 3 February 2011

2. Halpin, Tony, 'The Independent Sector Seeks to Find All the Ways a Child Can Succeed', *The Times*, 12 October 2004

3. Smith, *The Learning Game*, p. 162

4. Sugden, Joanna, 'The Perfect Excuse To Get Out Of The Classroom: All Work And No Play Makes Jack A Dumb Boy', *The Times*, 3 June 2009

5. Figes, Kate, 'Teach A Child To Learn Self-Esteem', *The Times*, 21 September 2000

6. Griffiths, Sian, 'Old-School Principles Come Out On Top', *The Times*, 3 June 2009

7. Woods, Richard, 'Teaching an Old School New Tricks', *The Times*, 13 June 2007

8. Wark, Penny, 'I Don't Believe In League Tables; Interview With Pat Langham', *Sunday Times*, 13 November 2011

9. Leonard, Sue, 'Star Quality Shows as Brighton College Rocks', *Independent*, 27 September 2012

10. Pozniak, Helena, 'Time to Study the Private Options?', *Daily Telegraph*, 10 March 2007

11. Cunningham, Andrew, 'How To Spot The Best Schools', *Daily Telegraph*, 10 March 2007

12. ibid.

13. Smith, *The Learning Game*, p. 202

14. Stephen, Martin, 'We Can Free Ourselves from the Tyranny of League Tables', *Daily Telegraph*, 29 April 2008

15. Rae, *Letters to Parents*, p. 49

16. Carman, *Heads Up*, p. 160

17. Richardson, Nigel, 'Publish Or Be Damned?', *Conference And Common Room*, Summer 2002, p. 5

18. Ian Walker, interview with the author, 21 April 2013

19. Bowers, Chris, *Nick Clegg: The Biography* (London: Biteback, 2011), p. 50

20. MacKinnon, Rod, 'We Thrive Because We Do Not Have to Respond to the Latest Educational Whim', *Independent*, 3 February 2011

21. Birbalsingh, Katharine, 'What Makes A Good Teacher?', *Sunday Times*, 21 November 1999

22. ibid.

23. ibid.

24. Adonis, Andrew, *Education, Education, Education: Reforming England's Schools* (London: Biteback, 2012), p. 157

25. 'Head Who Puts Girls On Top. Profile: Bernice McCabe', *Sunday Times*, 21 November 1999

26.   Judd, Judith, 'Bright Pupils Are "Betrayed" By Society', *Independent*, 29 April 1999

27.   Garner, Richard, 'Schools Are Failing Brightest Pupils', Independent Online, 13 June 2013

Chapter 8: A class apart

1.   Sampson, *The Changing Anatomy of Britain* (London: Hodder & Stoughton, 1982), p. 144

2.   Charter, David, 'Top Private Schools Fear "Oxbridge Chaos" Will Hit Students', *The Times*, 7 October 1996

3.   Prescott, Michael and O'Reilly, Judith, 'Turning Back to Class Warfare', *Sunday Times*, 28 May 2000

4.   Bentham, Martin, 'Oxbridge Interviews "Rude and Aggressive"', *Sunday Telegraph*, 2 December 2001

5.   Hands, Tim, 'Screaming Spires: Pressure In The University Scene', *Conference And Common Room*, Spring 2005, p. 12

6.   Collins, Nick, 'Bias Against Public Schools is "Hatred That Dare Not Speak Its Name"', *Daily Telegraph*, 26 January 2013

7.   Carman, *Heads Up*, p. 76

8.   Woolcock, Nicola, 'Ivy League Generosity Is Luring Brightest Away From Oxbridge', *The Times*, 24 December 2007

9.   ibid.

10.   Jagger, Suzy and Woolcock, Nicola, '"Obama Effect" Is Attracting British Students To US', *The Times*, 20 November 2009

11.   Paton, Graeme, 'Private School Students Looking to Foreign Universities', *Daily Telegraph*, 5 April 2011

Chapter 9: The cultural awakening

1.   Thorn, *The Road to Winchester*, p. 149

2.   Morrison, Richard, 'Class With Nobs On', Viewpoint, *The Times*, 12 June 2001

3.   Dubuis, Anna, 'I Still Call My Drama Teacher for Help, Says Eddie Redmayne', *Evening Standard*, 2 April 2014

4.   *The Harrovian*, vols CIV, No. 27, 15 June 1991, p. 71

5.   Lockyer, Daphne, 'My Best Teacher: Laurence Fox', *Times Educational Supplement*, 29 July 2011

6.   Mitchison, Amanda, 'Will The Next Must-Watch Thriller Make Chiwetel Ejiofor A Household Name?', *The Times*, 23 April 2011

7.   Fanshawe, Simon, 'An Irresistible Force', interview with Chiwetel Ejiofor, *Sunday Times*, 24 November 2002

8.   Smith, Jonathan, *The Following Game* (Woodbridge: Peridot Press, 2011), p. 162

9.   Stevens, Dan, 'My Best Teacher', *Times Educational Supplement*, 23 September 2011

10.   Stirling, Rachael, 'Early Stages', *Spectator*, 2 September 2011

11.   Singh, Anita, 'Carey Mulligan: Her Journey From School Stage to Bafta's Red Carpet', *Daily Telegraph*, 20 February 2010

12.   Boarding School Beak, 'Pleasure and Perils of the School Play', *Daily Telegraph*, 15 February 2014

13.   ibid.

Chapter 10: Play up, play up and win the game

1.   Rae, *Letters to Parents*, p .174

2.   Carling, Will, *Will Carling: My Autobiography* (London: Hodder and Stoughton, 1998), p. 15

3. Quoted in Watson, Nigel, *And Their Works Do Follow Them: The Story Of North London Collegiate School 1850–2000* (London: James And James, 2000), p. 122

4. Tozer (ed.), *Physical Education and Sport in Independent Schools*, p. 102

5. ibid., p. 271

6. Rae, *Delusions of Grandeur*, p. 113

7. Aylwin, Michael, 'Cranleigh React Fiercely In The Throes Of Defeat', *The Times*, 8 December 1997

8. Ian Walker, 'Support Brief', *Conference And Common Room*, Summer 1998, p. 13

9. Tozer, *Physical Education and Sport in Independent Schools*, p. 268

10. Longmore, Andrew, 'The End Of Chivalry', in Engel, Matthew (ed.), *Wisden Cricketers' Almanack 1998* (London: John Wisden & Co Ltd, 1998), p. 34

11. Wood, Nicholas, 'Purge on the Playing Fields of England', *The Times*, 2 August, 1997

12. ibid.

13. Henderson, Douglas, 'Schools Cricket', in Booth, Lawrence (ed.), *Wisden Cricketers' Almanack 1998*, (London: Wisden, 2013), p. 771

Chapter 11: Sporting prodigies

1. Dallaglio, Lawrence, *It's In The Blood: My Life* (London: Headline Publishing, 2007), p. 43

2. Hands, David, 'A Leader Mature Beyond His Years', *The Times*, 4 November 1988

3. Tozer, (ed.), *Physical Education And Sport In Independent Schools*, p. 268

4. Harrison, David, '"Absurd, Old-fashioned and Patronising"', *Daily Telegraph*, 2 October 2005

5. Henderson, Douglas, 'Schools Cricket', in Engel, Mathew (ed.), *Wisden Cricketers' Almanack, 2006* (London: Wisden, 2006), p. 969

6. Griffiths, Sian And Jones, Sally, 'Maiden Victory For Schoolgirl Cricketers', *Sunday Times*, 28 June 2008

7. Woodburn, Parker and Walston [eds], *Haileybury*, p. 58

Chapter 12: The battle of the sexes

1. Hodges, Lucy, 'Girls Strengthen Public Schools', *The Times*, 29 March 1984

2. Thomas, David, 'Boys Benefit When Girls Join Their Schools', *Financial Times*, 14 December 1989

3. Cunningham, Andrew, 'Crossing the Great Divide', *Daily Telegraph*, 30 March 2006

4. Bunting, Madeleine and O'Kane, Maggie, 'Smells, Bells And Scandals', *Guardian*, 9 March 1996

5. Benfield, Chris, 'Ampleforth Opens Doors To Girls – But Not From 13 to 16', *Yorkshire Post*, 13 May 2000

6. Targett, Simon, 'Girl Power Gives Macho Culture A Run For Its Money', *Financial Times*, 30 January 1999

7. Lister, David, 'Crisis Call: Steady St Trinians', *Sunday Times*, 4 November 1984

8. ibid.

9. Gardiner, Josephine, 'Boarding Institutions Face Two Threats To Their Future', *Times Educational Supplement*, 21 June 1991

10. Hinde, Thomas, *Paths of Progress: A History of Marlborough College* (London: James & James, 1992), p. 226

11. O'Leary, John, 'Head's Pleas – Send Us Your Daughters', *The Times*, 6 December 1993

12. Drummond, Maggie, 'The Right Course For Top Girls', *The Times*, 19 May 1986

13. Berridge, Kate, 'From Smart Young Gel To Power-Pupil', *Independent on Sunday*, 6 September 1992

14. Atha, Amanda, and Drummond, Sarah, 'Lock Up Your Daughters To Learn', *The Times*, 8 October 1986

15. Knight, India, 'Enough To Drive Anyone To Drugs', *Sunday Times*, 24 January 1999

16. Hughes-Onslow, James, 'Boarding Schools Can Be Hell On Earth', *Evening Standard*, 4 October 1991

17. Wilby, Peter, 'Cheltenham Ladies' College: "This isn't a Pink, Frilly School', *Guardian*, 2 August 2011

18. Berwick, Isabel, 'Mixed Blessings', *The Financial Times*, 21 July 2007

19. Balding, Clare, *My Animals and Other Family* (London: Viking, 2012), p. 196

20. Berridge, 'From Smart Young Gel To Power-Pupil'

21. Horsler and Kingsland [eds], *Downe House*, p. 94

22. 'The Wiser Lesson Of Single-Sex Success', *Independent*, 8 September 1993

23. Cunningham, Andrew, 'Watch Out Chaps, The Girls Are On Their Way', *Daily Telegraph*, 11 March 2006

24. Berridge, 'From Smart Young Gel To Power-Pupil', *Independent on Sunday*, 6 September 1992

25. Lightfoot, Liz, 'Single Sex Or Co-Ed: Teachers And Heads Disagree Over Where Children Thrive Best', *Daily Telegraph*, 16 September 2006

26. Middleton, Christopher, 'Co-ed education: A Lesson in Growing Up Together', *Daily Telegraph*, 21 January 2012

27. Berwick, Isabel, 'Mixed Blessings', *Financial Times*, 21 July 2007

28. Paton, Graeme, 'Girls' Schools "Going Out of Fashion", Expert Warns', *Daily Telegraph*, 28 April 2012

29. Woolcock, Nicola, 'Pull Your Socks Up Or You'll Die Out, Peer Tells Girls' Schools', *The Times*, 28 April 2012

30. Halls, Andrew, 'Why Are Fewer Girls Attending All-Girls Schools?', *Sunday Times*, 12 May 2012

31. Paton, Graeme, 'Number of Single-sex Private Schools "Halved in 20 Years"', *Daily Telegraph*, 24 April 2014

Chapter 13: New wine in old bottles

1. Peel, *The Land of Lost Content*, p. 205

2. Hartley, Clodagh, 'Public School Toffs Rampage Over Girls', *Sun*, 15 March 2005

3. Carling, *Will Carling: My Autobiography*, p. 18

4. Willis, Rebecca, 'Private Hell in a Boys' Public School', *Daily Telegraph*, 25 November 2009

5. Mills, Eleanor, 'One Hell Of A Schooling In The Real Facts Of Life', *Sunday Times*, 28 September 2003

6. Thomson, Alice, 'You Know What They Say About Marlborough Girls', *The Times*, 20 November 2010

7. Grove, Valerie, 'A Sad End To The Terms Of Trial', *The Times*, 25 September 1990

8. Woods, Richard, 'Teaching An Old Girl New Tricks', *Sunday Times*, 13 December 2009

9. Richards, Stephanie, 'Girl's Eye View', *Meteor*, 1979

10. Drummond, Maggie, 'The Right Course For Top Girls', *The Times*, 19 May 1986

11. Wilkinson, Max, 'Back to School: Rugby Bows to Gentler Sex', *Financial Times*, 19 May 1990

12. Mavor, Michael, 'Rugby Plans A Revolution', *Independent on Sunday*, 6 September 1992

13. Wilson, Bee, 'A Girl's Life Is Hell At Rugby', *Evening Standard*, 15 June 1995

14. Turney, Lesley, 'Historic Day Beckons For Clifton College', *Bristol Evening Post*, 29 March 2005

15. Ridley, A.N., *The Fettesian*, June 1983, p. 25

16. Bisseker, Claire, 'Farewell To Tom Brown: Rugby's Traditions Still Exert A Powerful Influence', *Financial Times*, 6 October 2001

17. Griffiths, Sian and Angelini, Francesca, 'Bed And Boarders', *Sunday Times*, 24 July 2011
18. Jim Bellis to the author, 9 May 2014

Chapter 14: Exorcising Flashman

1. O'Leary, John, 'Schools Halt Fall in Numbers of Boarders', *The Times*, 23 September 1992
2. Cobain, Ian, 'Silence and Secrecy at School Where Child Sex Abuse Went on for Decades', *Guardian*, 18 November 2005
3. Booth, Robert, 'Paedophile Monk Allowed to Strike Again at Abbey School', *Guardian*, 28 December 2009
4. Norfolk, Andrew, '130 Private Schools in Child Abuse Scandal', *The Times*, 20 January 2014
5. Duffell, Nick, 'Why Boarding Schools Make Bad Leaders, *Guardian*, 10 June 2004
6. O'Leary, John, 'Why Boarding Schools Should Always Be Caring Schools', *The Times*, 25 January 1993
7. Clare, John, 'Bullying Image of Boarding School Is False, Finds Survey', *Daily Telegraph*, 30 October 2004
8. Marco Longmore, interview with the author, 8 November 2013
9. Seldon, Anthony, 'Boarding School Is Fun Now But It Took Me A Lifetime To Get Over It', *The Times*, 19 December 2006
10. Macfarlane, Jo and Trump, Simon, 'No Hockey, No Boys and a Hotbed of Oestrogen', *Mail on Sunday*, 3 April 2011
11. ibid.
12. Paton, Graeme, 'Pupils Need to Develop "True Grit"', *Daily Telegraph*, 19 March 2014
13. Gordon Woods, interview with the author, 3 January 2013
14. Hodges, Lucy, 'Pupils Embued With True Grit Are Ready to Take on the World', *The Times*, 9 April 2014
15. Mills, Eleanor, 'Happy Or Hot Housed', *Sunday Times*, 29 September 2013
16. Gibbons, Kate, 'Stressed Private School Pupils Get "Disaster" Training', *The Times*, 25 February 2014
17. Hurst, Greg, 'Girls Requesting Healthy Diet May Be Concealing Anorexia', *The Times*, 9 July 2014
18. Thorn, *The Road to Winchester*, p. 186
19. Driver, Jonty, 'Why Me?', *Conference and Common Room*, Summer 2013, p. 13
20. Preston, Ben, 'Parents Angered by Drug Expulsions', *The Times*, 1 February 1994
21. Judd, Judith, 'Education: Hard Decisions About Soft Drugs', *Independent*, 16 June 1994
22. Roberts, Lesley, 'Drug Scandal As Top Private School Expels Four Boys', *Daily Mail*, 22 January 1999
23. Grant, Graham and Clark, Laura, 'Head of Blair's School Attacks Softly Softly Drugs Policy', *Daily Mail*, 16 October 2002
24. Cowie, Eleanor, 'Gordonstoun Goes Soft on Cannabis', *Sunday Times*, 20 October 2002

Chapter 15: Holding the line

1. Sabben-Clare, James, *Winchester College after 600 Years, 1382–1982*, (Southampton: Paul Cave Publications, 1981), p. 89
2. Card, Tim, *Eton Renewed* (London: John Murray Ltd, 1994), p. 275
3. Rae, *Letters from School*, p. 137
4. Trafford, Cheryl (ed) *'The Best School of All': 150 Years of Clifton College* (London: Third Millennium Publishing, 2009), p. 117

5. Walston, Catherine (ed), *With a Fine Disregard: A Portrait of Rugby School* (London: Third Millennium Publishing, 2006), p. 178

6. Davidson, Max, 'Modern Converts to the Course', *Daily Telegraph*, 2 November 2002

7. Rae, *Letters from School*, p. 137

8. Fr Dominic Milroy, interview with the author, 16 October 2012

9. Bunting, Madeleine, 'Life At Ampleforth', *Guardian*, 15 October 1998

10. Turner, Graham, 'Faith in the Future', *Daily Telegraph*, 25 January 2003

11. Walston, (ed), *With a Fine Disregard,* p. 180

12. Caperon, John, 'Faith Is At The Heart Of Independent Schools', *Church Times*, 18 September 2009

Chapter 16: The great divide

1. Clare, John, 'Opening Up Eton is the Right Thing to Do', *Daily Telegraph*, 4 September 2002

2. Wilson, John, 'The Cold War', *Times Educational Supplement*, 3 January 1986

3. Rae, John, 'Tom Brown's Porsche Days', *The Times*, 31 July 1987

4. Paxman, *Friends in High Places*, p. 168

5. Tytler, David, 'Head Tells Public Schools To Instil Decency In Greedy Generation', *The Times*, 19 September 1990

6. Cavendish, Camilla, 'What Happens When Posh Meets Comp', *The Times*, 5 March 2003

7. Frean, Alexandra, 'Head Attacks "Snobby Elite"', *Financial Times*, 8 June 2002

8. Antony Edkins in interview with Anthony Seldon, *Conference and Common Room*, Spring 2003

9. Cunningham, Andrew, 'Projects Bridge A Class Divide', *The Times*, 1 July 2004

10. Curtis, Polly, 'School Project "Breaking Down Stereotypes"', *Guardian*, 15 March 2005

11. Eric Anderson, 'The Select Way To Raise Standards', *Sunday Times*, 8 October 2006

12. Hurst, Greg, 'Worthless Qualifications Deceiving Pupils: Harrow Headmaster Criticises Soft Subjects', *The Times*, 23 January 2010

13. Curtis, Polly, '"Cold War" Between State and Private Schools', *Guardian*, 8 May 2008

14. Trafford, Bernard, 'We're Not All Toffs', *Guardian*, 19 June 2008

15. Mitchell, Tony, 'Independent Schools Will Always Prioritise the Rich and Powerful', *Guardian*, 25 June 2008

16. Carman, *Heads Up*, p. 134

17. Exley, Stephen, 'Academy Finds Change Is Game Of Two Halves', *Times Educational Supplement*, 31 August 2012

18. Stephen, Martin, 'The Truth That Hath No Name', *Daily Telegraph*, 28 November 2011

19. Vaughan, Richard, 'Unnatural Pairings', *Times Educational Supplement*, 7 October 2011

20. Garner, Richard, 'Making the Grade: Wellington Academy Is One of the First Academies to be Sponsored by a Leading Independent School', *Independent*, 20 February 2014

21. Vasagar, Jeevan, 'Why Won't Private Schools Back Academies?', *Guardian*, 22 November 2011

22. Woolcock, Nicola, 'Girls' School Head Gives Gove's Aide A Hostile Reception', *The Times*, 22 November 2012

23. Levy, Andrew, 'Independent Schools "Must Do More For State Pupils"', *Daily Mail*, 3 March 2013

24. Wood, Alex, 'A Woman To Be Reckoned With', *Times Educational Supplement*, 5 June 2009

Conclusion

1. Trapnell, Barry, 'Onwards, Upwards And Outwards', *Conference and Common Room*, Autumn 1984, p. 14

2. Hirst, Greg, 'Privilege Is Toxic', *The Times*, 30 September 2014

INDEX